How Writers
Journey to Comfort
and Fluency

How Writers Journey to Comfort and Fluency

A Psychological Adventure

Robert Boice

Foreword by Donald M. Murray

PRAEGER

Westport, Connecticut
London

Library of Congress Cataloging-in-Publication Data

Boice, Robert.
 How writers journey to comfort and fluency : a psychological
adventure / Robert Boice.
  p. cm.
 Includes bibliographical references and index.
 ISBN 0–275–94907–9 (alk. paper)
 1. Authorship. I. Title.
PN151.B647 1994
808′.02—dc20   94–2984

British Library Cataloguing in Publication Data is available.

Library of Congress Catalog Card Number: 94–2984
ISBN: 0–275–94907–9

First published in 1994

Praeger Publishers, 88 Post Road West, Westport, CT 06881
An imprint of Greenwood Publishing Group, Inc.

Printed in the United States of America

The paper used in this book complies with the
Permanent Paper Standard issued by the National
Information Standards Organization (Z39.48–1984).

10 9 8 7 6 5 4 3 2 1

Dedicated to those writers who, unbeknownst to them, inspired me to find as much pleasure in my own writing as I experience in theirs: Peter Elbow, Joanna Field, Linda Flower, Donald Murray, David Perkins, Martin Seligman, and Paul Theroux.

Contents

Foreword

I began making notes on how writers write by reading writers' biographies and autobiographies, notebooks and letters in 1938. I was fourteen and in the ninth grade. That was fifty-six years ago, and I just bought an electronic scanner to keep up with the new material I am still collecting, studying, ordering into books on writing and teaching writing. The process of writing is as fascinating to me in my seventieth year as it was in my fourteenth.

I was excited to discover what writers said about their craft back then because I hungered to be a writer, to make unexpected meanings with words, to see the confusion of my life in narratives that had meaning, to create stories that I could share and escape my loneliness, yet the books on writing--before I read writers on writing--did not help me.

Most books emphasized style, looking first at the finished product of writing for instruction. I wanted to be a writer because I was fascinated by good writing, but good writing itself didn't tell me how to start on the road toward being a writer. I could admire Babe Ruth and Lefty Grove, but intense, frequent admiration at Boston's Fenway Park didn't help me to hit a home run or throw a curve.

Other books were filled with explicit rules for writing practice, but many of those rules contradicted what I had to do on the page to see meaning arise from the draft and to get my first newspaper stories published. In the books I was told to "know what you want to say before you say it." But it was the not knowing what I was going to say--the unexpected learning--that attracted me to writing and was beginning to get me published.

Now *How Writers Journey to Comfort and Fluency* combines what writers say about writing with what researchers and scholars say in a way that helps both experienced and inexperienced writers at the writing desk. It was one of the books I have been seeking for more than half a century.

The longer I write and study the writing act, the more I realize that attitude predicts practice. The psychological controls the cognitive, yet most books that study writing deal only with what comes after the psychological. Robert Boice explores the attitudes and feelings that make it possible for some writers to be fluent while others are not.

Robert Boice takes the testimony of writers and the research in the discipline of both composition theory and psychology and tests what he has learned in his own clinical practice with people who want or need to write, yet have difficulty becoming fluent writers. Although this book will help potential as well as productive writers such as myself, it is not a self-help book with easy, glib answers to complex problems. Boice works within all the complexities of human nature to show how people who want or need to write can become productive.

This is important for two very different reasons. The new technologies of our age have increased the demand for writing. More and more of us are part of vast global systems--corporate, academic, governmental--and we need to communicate effectively with each other to perform our jobs in an Information age.

And we also need to write to discover ourselves, to produce the evolving narratives of our lives that reveal the significance of the events and people who influenced us. Writing is both the most disciplined form of thinking and essential therapy for this writer, and Robert Boice has helped me see how I can better write for others as well as write for myself.

How Writers Journey to Comfort and Fluency is a fascinating, helpful, and significant book. Robert Boice combines his own research, the literature of the disciplines of composition theory and psychology, with the practical lessons of clinical practice in a work that extends the horizons of the academic discipline of composition study and also helps individuals become fluent writers.

Donald M. Murray
Durham, New Hampshire

Preface

Most books about finding writing fluency aim for specialized audiences. So, when my friends and colleagues glanced at early versions of this material, they assumed it was not intended for them. They thought it must either be a text for composition classes where students are learning to write, or else a self-help book for hopelessly blocked writers.

I expect that *How Writers Journey to Comfort and Fluency* will be read by writers in both these categories, but I think it will find another broad audience with writers already writing. They, in my experience, profit as much as anyone from new ideas and practices about comfort and fluency in writing.

Writers of all stripes have read these pages and tell me they are unusually helpful ("Simply seeing how other writers change is fascinating, more so when I try out the ideas on myself"). I have long letters from novelists who found more enjoyable and efficient ways to write. I have even longer letters from graduate students whose dissertations had languished until they found confidence and discipline as writers. My most cherished testimonials come from people who had been unable to write ("The pain and doubts and fears are mostly gone now; I'm feeling like a writer again").

A premise of this book is that all writers can learn more efficient, less painful ways to work. Another is that writers are curious about how other writers work and learn.

So where does this leave you, the reader? Feeling patient and tolerant, I hope. This is a book about patience that can, in the short run, make cojourneyers feel impatient. This is an unusual book with some counterintuitive ideas that can seem off-putting until they are tried. This is a "read" that demands a slow pace, with rereading. If you really want to reinvent yourself as a more joyful, efficient writer, you owe yourself more than a quick, single reading of *How Writers Journey*.

Acknowledgements

I owe a special debt of gratitude to the hundreds who have traveled through my programs, too many to list here. These bright, curious people challenged my assumptions and practices, informed me of techniques and literature I had missed, and let me know when I moved too fast or needed more examples. I thank my editor, Jim Ice, my copy editor, Jude Grant, and my technical consultant, Jay Williams, at Praeger Publishers for their patience, trust, and help.

Introduction: Long Journeys for Writers

My own headlong adventures prompted the appearance of this book. Two years ago, in what began as an idyllic rock climb on the Appalachian trail, I acted impatiently and injured my jaw. Suddenly, days that had been filled with talking as a psychotherapist and teacher were constrained. I could speak, but only briefly, softly; the pain and disequilibrium worsened if I talked too much. My first thoughts were self-pitying. Then I decided to turn this disappointment to advantage. I would take some of the time I had spent talking to write about my experiences helping writers find comfort and fluency.

I had already published things about my writing programs. But most of my writing on writing appears in little-read scholarly journals and in a slim book for professors who want to be more productive. The writers I had worked with saw the failing. Too much had been left implicit: the long journeys of frustration and discovery for writers; the detailed ways that writers actually change their habits and attitudes; the surprising emphasis in my programs on patience and planfulness. For over a decade, my writers had cajoled me to write about what we actually did together. They said, affectionately, that what I had previously revealed in print failed to help people who lacked the motivation, ideas, and good models for building useful habits and self-discipline. Notably, these friendly critics assured me, my prior stuff lacked the force to instill faith that my programs worked. What I labored so hard to impart week after week hadn't come across in my public accounts.

I liked these encouragements but they frightened me. I wondered: How could readers be expected to endure so lengthy an account and so gradual a procedure? "After all," I said to some recent graduates of my programs, "there are six program steps, each of them sometimes lasting for a couple of months, and innumerable turning points where writers make decisions and draw insights." The answer seemed obvious to everyone but me. "Why not," as one of them put it, "simply do the book the way you do your sessions with us? You've never had problems recruiting people for your programs, despite their ponderous length. Why not act the role of the tour guide, as you so often refer to yourself in the program? Just promise your readers an interesting journey, one that will demand some perseverance but pay some handsome rewards. And, for sure, start off with your usual, light-hearted analogies to comically horrid travel stories that you collect." "Yes," added another writer, "you should let people know, as you did with us, that you offer some odd perspectives but that the journey, once engaged, almost always proves worthwhile."

That was how I conceived this book. As a travel account of sorts. It depicts a succession of journeys with writers looking for more efficiency and satisfaction in their work. It proceeds directly and unpretentiously; I write here much as I talk with my writers. It, like the programs, is a distinctive, unhurried journey through new landscapes, a journey of demanding discoveries; this is no quick and easy jaunt for mere tourists.

WHAT KINDS OF TRAVELERS?

What kinds of writers usually make this trip? They are, I believe, normal writers and normal people (except for their unusually high levels of verbal intelligence and curiosity). Some have serious writing blocks, those enduring silences that come from a sheer inability to get words on paper or screen. Some are graduate students faced with seemingly impossible demands for original, significant writing with too little guidance from their campus advisers. But mostly they are writers who want to be more effective and fulfilled in their work; they are tired of the struggle and they want more success.

The writers I have grown used to share these characteristics: They are stimulating and fun, quick to doubt and to demand magic when I ask them for hard work. They write while hampered by ambivalence and by an overeagerness to demonstrate brilliance. They are curious about the fact that their educations have provided so few clues about finding comfort and fluency in writing.

The writers I depict in this book range from young careerists to retirees. A bare majority of them were in middle age, that period where many writers want more contentment and efficacy in their work. Midlife, in my experience, is a time when writers wish they had learned these things much earlier.

To draw some clear conclusions about what happens to writers on these journeys, I represent fifty-two of them here. This sample comprises twenty-six academic and twenty-six nonacademic writers, half of each group women and half of them men, who completed the program during a span of two decades. (The distinction between professorial and other writers, or between women and men, proves to be so inconsequential that I infrequently mention it.) Each of these writers was picked for her or his typicality among graduates of my programs. Accordingly, the sample includes some who lagged behind their comrades for most of the trip.

In the chapters ahead I present enough samples of what writers do and say so that readers may feel some kinship with many of these fifty-two participants. Ideally, readers will feel like cojourneyers.

Some things about writers in the programs, though, might not be readily apparent in the six chapters downstream. Almost all, for example, had earlier experience in reading and therapy about their writing (this made them exemplary teachers of their fellow journeyers). And all had to work to find me; I never advertise, so they had to have looked deep into the literature or else have talked to graduates of my programs. Still, writers who have made that investment often came to me with an unmistakable skepticism. Because I so often think in terms of travel metaphors, I imagined they had suffered experiences where directions for writing were discouragingly ambiguous. And, deviously, I wanted to begin with an exercise in patience and slow pacing. I hoped to get them to enjoy a pause, amidst their impatience, to consider travel anecdotes like this one about the sense of ambiguity that marks the beginnings of long journeys:

Even in Panama information on travel in Colombia had been almost as lacking as trust-worthy reports on the interior conditions of Mars.... He was a native of Cali.
"Does it rain much in your country?" I had asked him.
"Si, senor, when it rains it is wet. When it doesn't rain it is dry."
"Is it cold?"
"Si, senor, in the cold places it is cold, and in the hot places it is hot. *No hay reglas fixas*--there are no fixed rules."
"How far is it from Cali to Popayan?"
"Ah, it is not near, senor."
"About a hundred miles, perhaps?"
"Si, senor, just about that."
"Isn't it rather about three hundred?"
"Pues, si, senor, perhaps just that."
        Harry A. Franck, *Vagabonding Down the Andes*, 1917

More than a few of the writers who came to check out my program had already grown pessimistic about such ventures. But none quite so dramatically as this traveler by boat:

With the memory fresh upon me of that night of cacophonous horrors, I sought out the purser in the morning to tell him that, like Mr. Dooley, I had determined what to do the next time I felt moved to travel. I should "throw two hundred dollars out of the window, put a cinder in my eye, and go to sleep on a shelf in a boiler works."
        Philip S. Marden, *Sailing South*, 1921

Several newcomers had not found prior writing programs as memorably exciting as they hoped. I wondered: did they expect too much (or, on finding real adventure, would they regret having their wish come true)?

As soon as the Indians cleared the rapids, we would be able to tell if they were gaining on us or not. As they reached the smooth water we measured the distance between us and alas! they were gaining! They came with almost incredible swiftness as they silently dipped their paddles into the water and their strong muscles shot their craft ahead. Slowly but surely they were gaining. I did not dare take time out to fix our propeller. . . . Something had to be done soon; the suspense was almost as bad as death itself.
        John Vanderveer Deuel, *Indians Crocodiles and Monkeys*, 1931

My journeys, I promised, would be more remarkable for their absence of extremes. Then, once the usual groups of four to six writers were launched in my programs, most of us turned to practical problems. As we prepared ourselves, at first in one-on-one encounters, I warned each writer (as I warn you, the reader) about the more mundane pitfalls lying in wait on this trip.

WHAT SORTS OF PERILS LIE AHEAD?

None of us faced the pressures of failing motors or falling arrows (or did we, in a way?). But many writers felt as concerned as travelers experiencing sleepless nights or ambiguous guidance. Almost everyone wanted explicit forewarnings of what could go wrong. In the six chapters ahead I describe the customary obstacles and how writers cope or stumble. Predictable dilemmas arise, for example, when I ask participants to abandon old habits of waiting for deadlines before they write. In the sixth chapter, on resilience, I describe a whole program segment on persistence; it is the stuff that helps writers get past derailing distractions and disappointments. In the long run, all but a few writers who stayed with the plan learned to anticipate most hazards.

Some cautions for prospective travelers need airing now, though. First of all, this is a book about skill, not style. It deals less with writing than with what to do while writing and getting ready to write. I mean to model good habits, not perfect writing. (I try to refuse to pressure myself in ways that lead to writing blocks). No one confuses my writing with the artfully crafted work of, say, Strunk and White's *Elements of Style;* I want to be appreciated as a psychotherapist more concerned about helping people write than with telling them what to write. My goal, stated simply, is to assist writers in finding comfort and fluency. Once writers write with ease, so far as I can tell, issues of style begin to take care of themselves. Some teachers of composition agree with me; for example, Robert Tremmel, whose work I cite later, argues that writers do better to learn the productive habits of successful writers before worrying about esoterics of style.

A second warning: I include a modicum of data herein. Not enough to satisfy scientists. Too much, often, to please humanists. Just enough, in my experience, to annoy almost anyone until the purpose grows clearer. I am a stickler for collecting ongoing assessments and I use them to do two things: To constantly readjust the program to work more effectively. And to help demonstrate program effectiveness to doubtful recruits. Many traditional strategies for helping writers unblock, as we will see, have great appeal but only transient worth. And, strangely, the interventions that prove most helpful here routinely strike writers as most counterintuitive (e.g., the push to begin writing before feeling ready or inspired).

My strongest warning, though, goes to writers who want quick, easy cures for long standing and complicated problems. There are none I know of. In our travels together we will examine alluring curatives that promise magic (hypnotically induced dreaming about writing among them). But this is what we will find: While these things help writers in limited and enjoyable ways, they are no substitute for the steady work that undergirds comfort and fluency.

Fortunately, not all our experiences will be so sobering. In the end, the solution comes close to being excitingly simple; only practice and planfulness are necessary to master the two most essential skills--a moderation in pacing, and a balance between the private and public sides of writing. Still, to achieve this pleasing and productive result often requires a long involvement. Anything less invites impermanence and dissatisfaction.

Writers usually cringe at the prospect of so much study and practice. Why? They often want something that will help them catch up with overdue assignments and unrealized aspirations in a week or two. They may even want the enchanted key that will unlock their hidden genius in but a moment of insight or freedom. And they don't, it usually seems, have the time to indulge in new exercises (this is a normative comment):

You know why I can't possibly do this? There isn't enough time. You don't seem to have an idea how busy I am. Maybe I'll come back and try this when I take a year off from working and when I have nothing to do but write. . . . You have to understand that I have a lot to do already--a family, a difficult job, and much more.

This moment, when writers decide whether to commit to such a major undertaking, is a turning point. Over the years I have learned to carefully list the reasons why writers owe themselves this lengthy, refreshing voyage:

1. While the length of the program (and its emphasis on regular practice and participation throughout) may seem prohibitive, consider this: One of the most highly rated aspects of the program is its time-saving

strategies. Writing and related exercises are almost always limited to brief, daily sessions that do not interfere with more important activities such as social life, professional responsibilities, and exercising. Writers in this program spend less time writing than they expect and get more (and better) writing done than before. In the long run, the program saves more time than it takes. So, I suspect, will this book.

2. Writers often want to put off participation until they have big blocks of undisrupted time. But there is a good reason to learn to write amid already busy lives. The habit of writing in small openings during work days not only produces more writing in the long run (more than writing in big blocks of time). It also helps assuage the anxiety that writers experience in spending day after day without making steady progress at writing. Managing writing as a regular, self-motivated act contributes to enjoyment and self-esteem that cannot be found when writing is chronically put off.

3. Writers customarily tell me that they prefer to wait for inspiration or deadlines that supplant the usual struggle to write. And, often in the same breath, they worry that my program may be premature for them; they may not yet be ready to commit to regular participation. My answer is a bit redundant but no less important then before: Analyses of program components show, beyond a doubt, that writers who begin projects before feeling prepared or motivated achieve more quality and quality of writing. Conversely, writers who wait for inspiration or for big blocks of time achieve far less quality and quantity. Motivation and inspiration come most reliably in the wake of involvement.

4. The writers who worry me most at this point are already writing and reluctant to give up old, partially effective practices. Their attitude is typified by this comment: "Why should I abandon my occasional great binges and sign on for this daily scheduling? I get writing done. I'm successful and respected." In my replies I don't debate the fact that most people write without the kinds of aids I prescribe. (Charles Dickens, for instance, managed enormous success and lasting admiration while working in strenuous ways that eventually killed him in middle age.) The question, instead, is about how painlessly, creatively, and efficiently writers write. Most writers, in my experience, can do better.

5. "But isn't there a quicker way," I commonly hear, "where I could do just a part of it?" "Can't I just do enough to get myself back on track?" someone chimes in. I encourage this tentativeness. I want writers to at least sample the journey before deciding; involvement is the first and most critical step in change. Many of the most persevering travelers started out as doubters who planned to stay on for only a short distance.

Here, then, is what I like to say to writers at this point: "Why not give it a try? Why not see if this unusual and slow-paced approach can begin to help you reach your potential for enjoyable, imaginative, and fruitful writing? Don't you think you deserve a vacation from your usual patterns?"

The experiences of writers who took that leap of faith make up much of this book. I hope to re-create enough of their experience, the ways that they and I interacted, to help readers achieve many of the same benefits. What may appear to be nothing but an armchair journey could prove to be involving.

HOW DOES THIS UNUSUAL PROGRAM TRANSLATE INTO A BOOK?

Readers already know the first part of the answer: The book proceeds in much the same way as the program. It makes for a lingering but, at times, absorbing exploration. None of it, I think, is quite so bad as slogging along through jungle paths with only occasional relief from mud and darkness. There are moments, many of them, that offer new horizons and worthwhile discoveries. Writing adventures, perhaps because they are so rarely reported back to the home crowd, make for compelling reading.

Further on, I attend to details about what needs to be appreciated and practiced in finding fluency and comfort. At every stage, I warn about steps where writers often stagger. And because lasting changes are rarely mastered in a single instance of insight or practice, I am unashamedly redundant.

Another part of the answer (to the question about how the program translates into this book) is this: Along with its length comes a breadth of strategies uncommon to writing programs. We start well before usual beginnings, with considerable attention to finding motivation and ideas for writing. Later, we move well beyond usual pressurings for writing, with exercises for moving incentives inward (as in the chapter on self-control) and then outward (as in finding constructive, supportive audiences for their writing). By the end, we focus on practices that help us endure as writers beyond this long journey, even through great distractions and disappointments. This is the general map for chapters to come:

1. Motivation
2. Imagination
3. Fluency
4. Control
5. Audience
6. Resilience

And this is the usual reaction to the plan. Writers express singular amazement at the part of the program that conveys them into noticing and moderating emotions.   Sometimes, I explain, we will simply observe the emotions that accompany and flavor our writing. Sometimes we will reign-in a generally overlooked but perilous emotion in writing, the near-mania (hypomania) that can bring euphoria, then bingeing, then superficial and hurried writing, then depression. But most of the exertions dealing with emotion take a different tack. They help writers learn and sustain a moderation in pacing, one accompanied by a state of mild happiness that encourages clear thinking and planning.

In the book, as in the program, you may spot seeming contradictions. For example: On the one hand, I will admonish you to follow a rule cherished by writers including Franz Kafka: "Wait" (i.e., before moving into prose). On the other hand, I push you to begin readying yourselves for writing long before you feel fully motivated or inspired.   Another apparent inconsistency: I will admonish you to do lots of regular writing in order to build-in new habits and to manage satisfying outputs. Yet, I will ask you to write almost exclusively in brief, daily sessions, often with no more than fifteen or thirty minutes to accomplish all this.   Ultimately, these incongruities prove to be reconcilable (aided by patience and practice). But to manage this, you will need to negotiate the most difficult demand of the program. (It is one that also, not surprisingly, makes for successful travel).

To an extent, travelers here need to show a modicum of trust; in my experience, they fare better with a willingness to suspend disbelief and go along with the tour. During moments where the trip seems unworthwhile, reminders that others have come to more positive conclusions can help sustain momentum. Trust can also be found in being informed; to an extent, prospective travelers profit in looking over the trip before taking it. In this book form, the journey can be scanned and sampled before commitments are made. Something else helps. My analyses of the fifty-two writers who completed the program show that the writers who traveled most contentedly tended to begin with a decision that they would go along with the trip but on their own terms. They would, they decided early, accept the parts that worked best for them and make changes in the rest to suit their individual needs. They would, as one writer put it later, "humor me."

WHAT DO JOURNEYERS TYPICALLY VALUE MOST?

Earlier we saw one fondly remembered discovery, about ways of saving time at writing and in other daily activities. Another that commonly appears in the comments of writers a year or two after the program is this: The slow, involving pace is one of the most fondly recalled experiences. Why? Because new discoveries were carefully examined and debated. Because strategies were practiced with great patience and support until they worked or not. Because habits were revisited and refined and individualized until they became enduring and satisfying. Because the whole experience proved restful but productive.

A third endorsement from former journeyers is this: things gradually got easier. What began as a near-surplus of new habits turned out to be nothing more than a couple of manageable principles, balance and moderation. These two guidelines, writers tell me, are uncomplicated enough to become daily practices that persist. The fourth common report comes more often during the trip. Writers liked the stirring adventure into new ideas and novel practices. And, in more leisurely fashion, they enjoyed the sociable aspects, of reaching out and making writing a more public and publicly acceptable act.

What about the down side? In the chapters ahead I describe excursionists who left the tour early (and who were, thus, not eligible for inclusion in the sample of fifty-two graduates). They were, by all accounts, individuals who remained marginal and somewhat uninvolved. About half of them opted to rejoin, in a later cohort of writers. After thinking about the program and noticing that they continued to write with difficulty and dissatisfaction, they saw more reason to make the commitment. The other half of leave-takers remained ambivalent about writing programs. "If I am to do it all," one woman said, "I suppose it will have to be the way I have always done it. I don't want to have to become a disciplinarian about it. I want it to be spontaneous and enchanted or I don't want it at all." No one, though, exited bitterly, claiming that time had been wasted. The strongest comment I can recall came from a professional who had wanted to find time to write fiction. He said: "No, this won't work for me, at least. I don't agree with your philosophies or your methods. I don't want to work patiently and I don't really give a damn about finding pleasantness in writing. I don't do things that way."

In two decades of guiding and coaching writers through programs, I have learned to accept most skepticism and criticism. (One program component ahead, on coping with criticism, reflects what I have learned.) I try to listen patiently, to find something I can agree with, and to gradually decide what I might want to do differently. As a result, I have moved to even slower and more detailed strategies for writers. Interventions have grown simpler, to include acts as basic as pausing for comfort and an unhurried search for ideas and motivation. My use of examples has multiplied so that I cite excerpts from journeyers in the program to illustrate nearly every move we make. And, over time, I have summarized more and more of the crucial points as memorable rules. There are thirty-two Rules of Practice to help mark the path ahead (e.g., "Imagination, or new vision, comes most reliably from revision."). And there are many other aphorisms and admonitions to help guide the way. Most often, these bits of wisdom, like everything wise about the program, come from writers participating in the journey. My writers and I have especially enjoyed formulating guidelines that have roots in the observations of ourselves and of our favorite heroes.

When I asked my groups for suggestions of a title for this book, there was surprising accord: It should somehow represent the long, patient journey that writers experience herein. It should mirror the balance and moderation so important to success in the trip. And, above all, it should convey the active, planful waiting that proves so ironically important to comfortable and fluent writing. Several writers suggested a phrase from the poetry of William Wordsworth: "a wise passiveness." (It, alas, proved unacceptable to editors who worry about the cataloguers in libraries who ignore books with vague titles.) Then, we agreed on something more direct and descriptive--*How Writers Journey to Comfort and Fluency: A Psychological Adventure.*

How Writers
Journey to Comfort
and Fluency

1

Motivation

> It was such an environment--a comfortable home, a fragrant garden, an evening walk with gay sisters, an encouraging word from a father who praised and peddled her manuscripts-- that put into Jane Austen's novels a fresh air of peace, health, and goodwill, and that gives to her unhurried readers a quiet satisfaction hardly to be found in any other novels. She had learned that the day itself is blessing enough.
>
> Will and Ariel Durant, *The Age of Napoleon* [1]

When we write with both calm and confidence at hand, we work in an ideal state of motivation, one marked by patience and enthusiasm much like Jane Austen's. Without this combination, writers too seldom find their work appealing and comforting; instead, they force writing with a hurried pace, a lagging confidence, and a lingering malaise. As a rule, poorly motivated writers remain ambivalent about writing and inconsistent at turning intentions into actions [2]. The result is misery, silence, or both.

Consider the reasons why motivation thrives on calm and confidence: First, positive motivations originate in self-assured emotions. Doubt is no friend of motivation. Second, emotion in writing functions best at moderate levels. We do our best problem solving in a state of mild happiness [3].

When I first discuss motivation with writers, their comments reveal what happens when calm and confidence are neglected. Each of the following three excerpts from my notes of sessions is a modal comment (and not just a convenient anecdote):

I haven't written for a long time because the spirit hasn't moved me. In other words, I haven't felt like it. But that's not all of it. I no longer feel confident, if I ever did, that I have anything to say or that, if I did, I could say it well. The mere thought of writing fills me with an odd mixture of dread and irritability.

My writing was moving along nicely until the rejection of my book manuscript came. I had put my whole soul into that thing. . . . Angst is the result. I don't have the will to get back to my writing, so I'm getting further and further behind where I should be. My general state of apprehension is growing day by day; once I get back to writing, the pace will have to be explosive. Still, I'm not sure, given what the reviewers said, that I have the ability to write anything outstanding.

I can always write, always . . . if I'm in the mood, if I'm feeling good about myself. When I write, I write like a firestorm. Unfortunately, it doesn't take much to undermine my fragile sense of self-worth. It's always tempting, at those times [of doubt], to turn to something less threatening, less demanding, less frantic, less tiring.

These same three writers also had something to say about how they might overcome their inertia. They would, they assured me, either wait for inspiration or else force themselves to write. Motivation for them was a matter of extremes; it either seemed fully off or fully on. This note from one of them makes the point succinctly:

I favor waiting until I'm in the mood to write, until I feel I have an original image or idea that will serve me well. Once the tension and readiness reach a certain point, I write, much like a runner off the mark. But, that's the ideal. In fact, I usually have to force myself to write. Or someone else has to. . . . Deadlines work best, even though I hate the agony they bring. Sometimes I can write if I have nothing else to do and *big* blocks of quiet time when I can get on a roll. Problem is, those times are rare.

These two common ways of motivating ourselves to write, waiting and then working under deadlines, speak volumes about writing problems. The first way, waiting for inspiration and mood, symptomizes the most innocent understanding about finding motivation: the belief that good writing must be spontaneous. And so writers wait, passively, for the inspiration that would suddenly make them want to write. The most common result of passive waiting is barrenness. Tillie Olsen, author of *Silences*, provides an unusually memorable description of waiting and not writing:

These are not *natural* silences--what Keats called *agonie ennuyeuse* (the tedious agony)-- that necessary time for renewal, lying fallow, gestation, in the cycle of creation. The silences I speak of here are unnatural: the unnatural thwarting of what struggles to come into being, but cannot. In the old, the obvious parallels: when the seed strikes stone; the soil will not sustain; the spring is false; the time is drought or blight or infestation; the frost comes premature [4].

Olsen also hints at origins. What begins as a natural silence often becomes an unnatural silence because passive waiting invites blocking. The longer we wait without readying and motivating ourselves, the greater the tendency to lose ideas, momentum, and confidence. And as unfruitful delays grow, so does dependence on tense, impatient, and unreliable spurts of motivation that foster eventual barrenness and disappointment.

The second customary approach to managing motivation for writing is forcing. It is, in a way, the opposite of waiting; forcing brings a shift from seeming freedom to obvious compulsion. Forcing implies both coercion and inevitability. When we delay writing to its limits of time available before a manuscript is due, we often necessitate sudden forcing; deadlines may be the most common and powerful kind of motivation for writing. The problems with forcing under deadlines are well known but quietly condoned: (1) With hurrying comes a shortchanging of the reflectiveness and enjoyment essential to good writing; (2) with coercion comes a questionable self-confidence that must be extorted into action or else pushed aside; and (3) with marathon sessions come fatigue and distaste for writing. While sudden forcing often works in the short run, it depletes the motivation necessary for lasting comfort and fluency.

Most of us know the familiar, somewhat diabolical scenario of forcing: We wait until the last minute and then we write at breakneck speed, defying our internal editors (those thoughts and voices representing parents, teachers, and other critics that can make us doubt and revise too soon) to keep pace with our frantic outpourings. We work unceasingly, with the pain of aching eyes, extremities, and minds. And, only so long as the forcing holds sway is the usual struggle of writing held at bay; we may still dislike the task but we make fast work of it.

I know the spectacle all too well. In my trance-like trip through high school, I sensed that anything required of me could be put off and managed later with bursts of serious effort. Even in college. At the same time, though, I understood something else: passive waiting and sudden forcing worked without helping me find happiness or full expression of my potential. Instead, I shifted between depressing lulls and frenzied recoveries, neither of them rewarding over the long haul.

Another problem with forcing is that we tend to practice it reflexively, mindlessly, without quite realizing that it is only rarely imposed on us by others. Closer examination reveals that we generally impose forcing on ourselves, usually by way of waiting for inspiration and then by settling for deadlines:

The only things I have finished during the past several years all got done because of deadlines. . . . One habit that I have established to make myself prepare a paper is getting on the program of a conference where I will have to present the paper in person. At the last minute, sometimes in an all-nighter up in my hotel room, I at last find my theme and I get the paper written. It's the only way I can be productive.

Forcing is problematic in one more way, in its tendency to excessiveness; when writers compel themselves to begin without wanting to, they often have problems working at moderate tempos or, later, at stopping. The euphoria of rushed momentum, where doubts are put aside and where projects may be finished quickly, tends to be self-perpetuating. Technically speaking, great binges of writing take on the addictive properties of hypomania, a state of near-mania with all its excesses including accelerated thought and poor judgment. A novelist in my program depicted hypomania this way (while reinstating some of its mood by talking faster and faster until its usual consequence, dysphoria, set in):

Once I get on a bender, fortified with plenty of coffee and momentum, I become a madwoman on a mission. I set aside whole days and weekends where I do nothing else and write until I drop. I stop only for the most urgent calls of nature or when my wrists cramp up; no one gets through on the phone; I have no idea of the weather outside. When the writing is fast-paced and at its best, I teem with energy and I write without struggle and the writing goes quickly. I've had weekends where I've finished ninety pages, two whole chapters. Sometimes more. I love it. [Pauses and looks away.] Of course, I'm exhausted and disgusted when the elation passes. You know? Sometimes I stay depressed for days afterward; "elation turns to depression," as my therapist likes to say. . . . The shortcoming of my method, I suppose, beyond what it might do to my health, is that I don't always have the openings for these long sittings in my everyday life that I need. Even when I do, I can't face up to the whole outlook; I know what the costs will be, including a complete suspension of any social life.

In even these first few sessions, I encourage contemplation about the costs of forcing and bingeing; one of my preeminent goals is to bring dark, mindless habits out into daylight. Then, given the slightest opening, I begin reminding writers about some of the costs of working under fatigue and tension: irritability and insomnia; suspiciousness; and, again, hurried, under-revised and under-edited manuscripts. Over time, I add more cautions about forcing and bingeing: Both decrease the likelihood of writing again the next day or next week. Both, in the long run, lead to less output and less satisfaction in writing, less quality and originality in the product, and fewer successes with editors than do more temperate, regular schedules of writing [5]. The value of serenity and planfulness in writing is my constant theme.

During our ongoing reflections, my writers usually notice other costs of forcing and bingeing. They sometimes recall that while writing under such conditions they felt less in control of their writing than otherwise. More commonly, they remark on a persistent dissatisfaction about the quality of what gets written under a harried regimen. They remark with emotion on the usual fatigue associated with waiting and forcing:

Offhand, I can't think of anything that leaves me so exhausted, so spent, so much in need of a rest. I'm not sure why.

Another common theme in these statements is a sense of impatience and confusion about how else to manage motivation:

I'm stifled by the uncertainty of it all. I came here knowing something of this sort was wrong and now I'm only getting only a vague idea of what I'm doing wrong. I mean, how does one proceed? What is it that makes a writer genuinely like writing? I honestly don't know. Why is it that, despite my burning desire to write good fiction, I normally feel so unlike doing it? I don't want to have to resort to extremes (wasn't it Proust who had himself locked in a room, sans clothes, until he finished his writing?). I don't want to have to be forced, like a recalcitrant child, to do the very thing I want to do. But I don't have a clue what to do to make it seem more enticing, less involuntary. So, what's the answer?

The same writers often wonder if writing can ever be made less painful:

Am I the only one who finds sitting down to write so gruesome? I doubt it. Am I unique in having to struggle to find a good idea, to wrestle almost every word on paper? Do other of your writers ever get past this enervating, paralyzing, damned inefficient state?

Because many of these writers, beforehand, had no patient listener with whom they could commiserate, these outpourings of private fears and frustrations help provide relief. So do the growing realizations that writing problems are common and not as idiosyncratic as supposed. Many troubled writers, because they tend to work in isolation, come to the program supposing themselves unique for, say, sitting again and again in front of a blank page or screen, searching endlessly for a first word or first sentence. Or for trying to write amidst what seems a full-blown anxiety attack. Or for hating writing but doing it anyway.

As the focus becomes less private and more social, as writing is seen as a shared problem, writers soon move beyond these initial questions. Specifically, they begin to offer tentative opinions about what undermines their motivation to write. Why? Their stimulus comes in seeing similarities and differences in the plights of other writers. Because I consider these writers an admirably thoughtful and verbal lot, I believe that the consensus of their proposals merits a close look.

WRITER'S INITIAL COMPLAINTS AND ASSUMPTIONS

When I discuss this collection of ideas with writers, I notice a temporary shift in mood. It relocates from the excitement and liberation of sharing their problems to an impatience about getting on with solutions; as they begin to consider the general aspects of writing problems, writers react with a mixture of attentiveness and annoyance. They are often behind in their work and eager for quick fixes. They say things like: "This may be interesting, but do I really need this?"

My reassurances often take the form of allusions to travel, my favorite topic of reading (so much so that I assume at least a moderate interest in everyone else). I point out that travellers, like waltzers or other dancers, miss the point if they rush their experience, if they want to finish as soon as possible, if they are not living for the moment. And I note that side trips like this one in our journey have been chosen because the retrospective accounts of prior journeyers indicate the special value of these diversions. In the interest of fairness, though, I do admit that this is the sort of thing that all professors and therapists claim as they lead their trusting "charges" down various paths. ("Ah yes," said one short story writer, "down the proverbial garden path!") In the end, I argue quietly, the excursion demands a modicum of patience and trust. To emphasize my point, I anticipate a fact to be visited later: one of the most powerful predictors of fluency and success at writing is what hypnotists call susceptibility. Writers fare better when willing to suspend disbelief and to immerse themselves, for a while at least, in the flow of the structured experience. There is another reminder that helps engage skeptics in the journey: Our initial exercise of reviewing what keeps us and others from writing fluently and comfortably can be intrinsically interesting. A few, brief examples make my point:

1. The connection between the lack of hypnotic susceptibility just mentioned and a tendency to block.
2. The generally unrecognized shortcomings of bingeing at writing.
3. The usual reluctance of blocked writers to endorse the acts of prewriting (e.g., patient planning, organizing, and conceptual outlining before turning to prose) that accompany fluency and comfort in writing.

To help writers generate insights about what helps and hinders their writing, I coach them in a method with the awkward label of a "retrospective thinking-aloud protocol." That is, I ask them to tell me "what was going on in your head when you found that you didn't feel like writing at some recent time?" Then I ask it another way: "What were you thinking and feeling at the time?"

In their first accounts, writers add two things that confound their descriptions: They fill in missing details, and they explain too soon. With practice, they start with simple reports of what they thought and felt. The first stage (when writers are still more likely to explain than to report) produces accounts that look like this one:

Well, I knew I was too busy to write. I really was! I had a lot of other things to do that conflicted with wanting to write.

This same writer, with repeated prompts to do little more than report her thoughts and feelings, eventually came up with this account of the same experience:

All right, what I was thinking was this: "I want to believe that I enjoy writing [pause] but I know that it is always a struggle." I thought to myself, "God, how much pain, uncomfortableness, and plain hard work writing always is!" And I was feeling the sinking feeling, at the same time, that it probably wouldn't be very good writing. I thought of something I had done recently, a prospectus, that sat around in editors' offices for nearly a year and then, all at once, all three of them rejected me in the same month. The thought of these orchestrated rejections made me think about how risky writing is, about my lack of faith in my ability to produce what editors want. At the same time I felt my motivation, already tenuous at best, ebbing away. After five minutes of this, I decided to leave the room. I hurried away feeling as if escaping something sinister, saying to myself, "I'm not ready."

The value in these more carefully crafted accounts of blocking experiences goes beyond their growing explicitness; they also help writers become better self-observers and listeners. With practice at generating and refining their own recollections of what happens at writing times (supplemented by similar accounts from other writers), they begin to pull away the shrouds of mystery about what motivates or hinders their writing. The result: a list of categories of what stymies motivation. Each one addresses a simple, objective problem.

Categories of Explanations for Failings

Ambivalence. The most common of reasons relate to mixed feelings. Writers yearn to write but find it a struggle and hope to put it off; ambivalence is the primary affect reported in connection with writing, even among writers who manage to do a fair amount of it [6].

As with related states of ambivalence (e.g., procrastination), reticence about writing elicits irony. One clever account depicts writers as seemingly unique among artists--all of whom, but us, actually *want* to work [7]. (My own, occasional psychotherapy with blocked painters, potters, sculptors, and architects suggests that writers are not so unique in their ambivalence as they suppose.)

Waiting. The next most common reason for not finding motivation is diabolical and familiar. It is the periodically successful strategy of passively waiting for it. Silent writers commonly explain their inertia as deliberate, as an act of waiting for inspiration and direction; on closer inspection, though, the waiting is often recognized as inefficient:

Oh, I guess it hasn't served me well. Wouldn't you agree? But, nonetheless, I find the idea of a Muse serving me with great ideas and impulses an attractive one, don't you? [I agreed with this comment and noted a similar fantasy: during my years as a bachelor, I often mused about the unknown women who might suddenly call me, despite my dormancy. About as much came of my fantasy as I had overtly invested in it.]

With continued experience of looking at passive waiting over a month or two, writers' accounts change as they practice the retrospective thinking-aloud protocol. At first, as usual, explanations dominate:

I found myself doing little more than waiting around during that week of vacation. I was waiting because that's how writing comes to me, while I'm doing other things like painting or woodworking. Right? Sooner or later, something happens to make me want to write, something like an integrative idea that will lay out the whole plot line, something that will inspire me to feel that I have something worthwhile to write. It can't be rushed, I know that much.

As I coach writers to begin reflections with more direct, unadorned reports of what they actually thought and felt at the time, clearer and more useful accounts like this one emerge:

Now I know: I thought to myself that I was ready to write. I think I said something like "I'm ready at last, let's go." I also thought a bit on the plot I had planned and I realized that it was only a rough idea. Then came a clear thought and feeling: "I didn't know what to do next." I actually said it to myself. But then I calmed myself by thinking about what I could do to get started. I began to imagine a first sentence. But, nothing came to mind, nothing that worked, and I could sense the panic moving in. I thought, "What if I can't, what if I write something that gets me off-track, on the wrong track?" In a flash, I think I said something else: "I'm going to have to deal with this later. I'll think about it some more then. I'm going to have to hope that I can come up with something clever for the beginning . . . that I'm going to feel more like doing this maybe tomorrow. . . . [later] I sat there telling myself that waiting until I was ready had worked in the past. Still, I realized that I had just talked myself out of writing for no particularly good reason. I asked myself, "So why couldn't you have just taken the plunge to see what you could say? Why couldn't you have made some progress?" Looking back on it, I imagine that is how it usually goes; I just hadn't quite seen it so clearly before. No wonder I don't write much: I'm not well prepared and I feel unconfident. Then I talk myself out of even trying to get something going. Oh my!

With such accounts, drawn and redrawn over several weeks, comes the hint of new wisdom about writing. The most crucial realization is nothing but a clarification of an increasingly familiar idea: that passive waiting for motivation can be unreliable and unproductive. There must be, writers hesitantly agree, a better way.

Still, writers who consider abandoning old habits of passively waiting for motivation usually vacillate. They hesitate and they explore alternatives. One is easing into writing with a preliminary kind of writing called free writing (the oft-used strategy for writing quickly, without pausing to edit or correct, whatever comes to mind). For the moment, though, uncertainty dominates; as soon as these writers feel uncomfortable, they revert to old ways [8]. While they hedge, writers joke about a deeper reason for wanting to hang on to the habit of waiting. Waiting for inspiration, for mood, and for Muses carries the promise of magic and genius:

How nice it would be to have the whole thing, the driving force and a breakthrough idea, breathed into me as a divine afflatus where I would be the amanuensis who gets all the credit and enjoyment. I realize how silly that sounds, but at some level I hang on to it with the tenacity and innocence of a child.

The message that starts to come to the fore in our discussions is this: When we wait too often for magic, we make ourselves vulnerable to disappointment and, in turn, to hopelessness [9].

Disaffection with writing. The third realization about why motivation is not forthcoming sounds like the first. In fact, though, disaffection can be far more problematic than can ambivalence. Disaffection includes, first of all, a cynicism about writers and writing that can distance us from the whole enterprise. Sometimes, for example, disaffection germinates in the perception that our writing and ideas may have grown pedestrian, no longer fresh [10]. Just as often, it stems from a disillusionment with the writer's usual life. We can chafe at years of anger over poor reception of our writing, at seeing other, seemingly less talented writers muscle or maneuver past us:

This is what I was thinking about: "Why write? Look at all the crap that already gets published in the [scholarly] journals; why add more shit to an already bounteous pile? A lot of it is just politics and privilege. The same people who do most of the publishing know each other and review each other's manuscripts. Very little of what they publish is worth the reading.

I was trying to recall where I had read this thing that keeps running through my mind. Writers earn something like $2.50 an hour on the average and that's probably an inflated estimate. I was thinking of something else I had read, I can't remember where, that a successful author, someone like Updike, said that most of us can only waste an editor's time with our poor writing. I thought: "Yeah, he's probably right. Why bother?" It made me think, as I recall, of a book entitled *Rejection*, a collection of horror stories of authors being rejected over and over again. Have you read it?

I had read it. And I had heard many similarly dispirited accounts of what happened to writers getting ready to write. I could even add a related explanation of why motivation for writing can prove elusive. The idea comes largely from critics who suppose that most writers write only because they have unhealthy motives and personalities. In this perverse but persistent notion, we might hope that writers stay unmotivated (and, so, healthy).

The usual logic goes like this: Writers seem less sociable and likable than nonwriters [11, 12]. In fact, writers often treat each other savagely in reviews [13]; in some cases we can be sure that they write for revenge and other suspect motives [14]. They sometimes use morbid compulsions as motivations, or write out of cowering fear, or with the aid of breathless manias, even from the dark experience of depression itself [15]. Thus it follows that writers, if they are as inherently mean and unhappy as they seem, must write only at the behest of their personal demons.

Little is said, in this lurid literature, of healthy motives; cynics seem little disposed to find them, even in their own writing. Nonetheless, writers can use these pessimistic characterizations to advantage: When their writing is rejected, they can attribute the reason to having written something too healthy, too true to appeal to the shadowy forces who keep the gates of publishing. Similarly, when writers cease writing, they can congratulate themselves on putting aside a tempting vice. They can even muster a ready explanation of why others show more success at writing then they do.

I often see some of the same pessimism as my own writers practice the retrospective thinking-aloud procedure. When, in about the third week, I ask, "How did you feel when you last wrote without forcing yourself or the writing?", the first replies run, predictably, to explanations and not reporting:

Well, I haven't written that way lately; that just doesn't work. That isn't how I write. I'm not normally driven to write. I've even thought that I can't succeed at writing because my temperament is all wrong. I'm not angry enough, not depressed enough to want to be writing all the time. I want to write, but for ordinary reasons . . . with normal motives.

Over time and with closer reflection, writers settle down to second approximations of recollections that pull back from earlier incriminations of motives for writing. This eventual recounting of an unforced stint of writing is typical:

I hadn't thought of it before, but actually it was quite a nice experience. . . . Not a peak experience, maybe a flow experience. I recall it as though it were a nice dream. At the time I was unhurried and I was having a good time. Maybe it was a dream [laughs]!

No, it was real but uncommon. I was, as I moved along, not talking to myself, debating with myself as I usually do when I write. I was just writing things as they came to mind, guided by little more than a broad sense of where I was going. As I wrote, I paused to see if it needed clarification or elaboration and to see where I would be going next. At several points I felt so good about my progress that I stopped to congratulate myself. An all too rare experience. . . . [Later:] When I think back on my own best writing experiences, I have to wonder about supposing that writing draws from depression or some other state of mental illness. I'm inclining to believe that writing, easy and good writing, depends on a state of well-being. But I'm not sure about that because it goes against so much of what I have read and heard about writing.

Of course, not all stymied writers come up with insights like this one, at least not until writing more regularly. As a rule, writers just beginning to understand their lack of motivation and confidence continue to look for causes more consistent with their current moods. The next category illustrates that tendency.

Paradoxical reasons. The fourth most common reasons are excuses that commonly take the form of humor and paradox. While such reports sound defensive and anxiously self-conscious, they are informative and intriguing. This sort of thinking and emoting has produced a large and entertaining literature, one that laughingly justifies silences, procrastination, and other maladaptive writing habits. Although excuses may not help motivate writers in effective ways, they can relieve tension and promote playfulness.

One kind of paradoxical humor about writing is of the gallows variety. Every once in a while, otherwise staid scholarly journals publish an imploring title (e.g., "My Latest Attempt to Overcome My Writer's Block") over an otherwise blank page. The empty page beneath the title bespeaks the dilemma of many aspiring writers: Attempts to unblock seem doomed to failure. Curiously, none of these journals seems aware of the precedents in printing blank pages to represent the difficulty of writing for publication. No matter. Each repetition seems to meet the need of the moment for release from the usual, humorless pressures of contesting for always scarce pages.

In another, more readable genre, writers fantasize about what could have been accomplished without distractions and usual human failings:

"And now to work on my book," I almost said to myself. . . . Or would have, except that it was just about time for the mail. . . . It meant neglecting My Work, but I waited and watched. . . . As it emerged, I saw it was a bright red halter, worn by what appeared to be a young Chinese woman, in short shorts carrying a clipboard . . . working her way through college by selling subscriptions. . . . So we went upstairs, and in a series of steps, she showed me what she had in mind. . . . Anyway, that's the real reason my summer in 1973 was less than productive. You don't have to believe it if you don't want to [16].

Other humor is more obviously antagonistic and carries out the main mission of aggression, of enforcing conformity. It generally chides writers who annoy colleagues by producing too much writing, or it complains about civilians who tell writers what they should write [17, 18, 19]. Writers employ a similar irony to publicize injustices in the editorial system, as did Jerzy Kozinski by exposing the unsuspecting editors and reviewers who rejected the resubmission his old and already successful manuscript [20]. Of course, in our readiness to reject the gatekeepers who reject our work, we might wonder how well we would do in recalling something published years earlier by someone else (. . . or even ourselves?).

At its strongest, humor is used defensively; writers have a singular genius for transforming a lack of motivation for writing into a lovable weakness [21, 22, 23, 24]. The arguments usually go like this: First if it is true that, left unattended, many problems solve themselves, why bother to keep up with the letters, memos, assignments, and other nuisances accumulating on your desk? (In fact, according to these popular accounts, most missives opened long after their receipt no longer require action.) Or, with obligations like writing that cannot be avoided, why bother to act now when the act will come more easily later? Second, procrastinators, especially those who display casually disorganization, seem more endearing than their overscheduled and compulsive counterparts. And it follows, if these less zealous individuals do accomplish something, we can admire them all the more for managing it because they were not openly trying or caring. In the main, humor about procrastination works; it provides a needed occasion for fun. I have file folders bulging with newspaper and magazine briefs that report on imaginary meetings of procrastinators where schedules are not kept but where everyone had a splendid time. Most are creative and hilarious.

Yet, there is another side to all this. Humor about procrastination and writing pushes aside the realities of graduate students who do not finish dissertations [25], of women and minorities who too often do not find success in writing [26], of writers who fail to make good use of that dearest of all commodities, time. The reasons why we neglect the realities of procrastination are not hard to find. Such reminders create discomfort. And, by themselves, they do little to induce change.

Better solutions emerge as writers look more and more at why they fail to find motivation. They do this by way of recollections, by way of reading the literature on writing problems. The same journeyers who had seemed vague about their writing problems begin to present impressive insights: They talk about having worked at writing in states of habitual nonreflectiveness (one writer likened it to something he had seen described as working while half-awake [27]). And they contemplate what kinds of deliberate acts will provide surer and more lasting motivation for writing.

What Writers Suppose Might Improve Motivation

As a rule, writers journeying through these exercises generate ideas about enhancing their motivation in three successive waves. In the first swell, they express a clearer sense of what they had earlier wanted to say but had been unable to articulate, about wanting writing to be unconscious and effortless:

At the time I was thinking: "I don't want to have to think about it. Thinking about it will get in the way." I thought . . ."[I] don't even want to know where it comes from. [I] don't want to impede it. I want it to come in a sweet rush that will become apparent to me only as I realize that I am already writing fluently, cleverly, quickly." . . . Now I see the problem in the script I commonly impose on myself. While I was busy reassuring myself that I wouldn't have to work hard or suffer, I could have been getting some writing underway. I could have been doing things to get myself ready to write instead of just telling myself not to think about how I do things. Think of it!

So, reflections in the first wave show not only an awareness that wanting writing to be effortless and completely spontaneous can be counterproductive, but they also suggest reasons why.

The second wave of writers' suggestions for enhancing motivation mirrors the growing interest of participants in the literature, especially its charming claims about finding mysterious energies that motivate writing [28]. This prospect, of finding so easy and painless an impulsion, seems a nice alternative to passive waiting where nothing happens. "Perhaps," as one writer put it, "the Muses still exist. I hope so."

The most compelling prospects in our readings depict a "will to write" that can be hypnotically induced; in these accounts, impetus and ideas are provoked by way of a mere suggestion [29]). Almost every writer I have known imagines hypnotic strategies as nearly perfect solutions to establishing motivation. Why? Because hypnosis appears to work painlessly by implanting an idea (e.g., "you will dream of your project and your dream will provide you with a creative solution") that induces the motivation (e.g., "after your dream, you will feel impelled to verbalize and act out your solution"). My writers even kid me for not having yet provided something so easy and effective:

You have to admit that using dream induction sounds a hell of a lot better than your apparent prescription for regular, hard work at writing. Maybe your short-sightedness is the product of your Calvinistic, rustic upbringing. Hypnotists somehow seem more urbane, more inclined to find ways around hard work.

I agree. It does sound better, and there are days when I might like to appear more urbane.

I listen patiently and supportively to these enthusiasms and traditional beliefs. For one thing, *I* want them to be true. For another, I suspect that most of my writers will soon become aware of some of the reasons why hypnosis generally disappoints seekers of motivation: not all writers can be hypnotized; even those who are hypnotized typically have dreams that bear no resemblance to plans or actions for writing; and, most problematic, inductees are no more likely to write and persist than other writers [29].

I hold off on emphasizing this discouraging news about hypnosis. Instead, I hypnotize many of my patients at this stage with the optimistic purpose of inducing dreams with both inspiration and motivation for a projected manuscript. The usual recounting goes like this one:

The idea was so compelling. Under hypnosis, I was commanded to find ideas and forces for finally getting on with my project. I fully believed it would work. Lord knows, I wanted it to work. Even though I didn't seem to have the dream that we had projected, I certainly felt more motivated to write for the next day or two. Pumped! . . . But by the end of the second week or so, reality had set in for me. I still wasn't on track. Somehow, I realized, I still didn't have the habits or the discipline to make a go of it. My fantasy that the hypnosis would make me do it was only a fantasy. The hypnosis was fun but I can't say it did anything permanent, even when we tried it a second and third time.

Nonetheless, even as we uncover more of these limitations (again, by way of reading, and via my practice of occasional hypnotic "induction"), I emphasize the benefits of hypnosis. At the least, as we have already seen, the very readiness to be hypnotized ("to go along with the suggestion, to take the leap of faith") helps immerse writers in the act of writing. Susceptibility also helps create a trusting style that doesn't mire writers in a focus on the immediate correctness of words and sentences. And, a related practice, of preprogrammed daydreaming conducted during lulls in the day, can provide rich associations for writing projects.

The outcome of our first venture into hypnosis, then, is both disillusioning and educational. The disenchantment in not finding motivation through hypnosis stimulates many participants to revert to an older solution for motivating themselves. They see a renewed appeal in deadlines and binges. Yet they report newly implanted doubts about magical solutions. I use the occasion, this moment of exceptional openness, to encourage a new perspective on the problem. It may be, I remark with a bit of optimism, that we can salvage some parts of waiting and forcing.

REFRAMING THE PROBLEM

Here, there is a distinct change of pace and format as my writers and I begin to meet weekly in small groups of four or five people (readers of my preliminary accounts of this book told me they did much the same, on their own). So here I move from my role as a traditional therapist to one more like a group facilitator. But first, before getting groups to do more of the work, I indulge in a bit of teaching. As a long-time professor, lecturing comes all too easily; I have to watch it. As a safeguard I ask the group members to take on my former role, of listening attentively, of stopping me for clarification, of challenging me to explain and reexamine my assumptions. They do.

I start by sharing a list of assorted realizations that have come to me gradually over my two decades of interest in writing problems:

1. The most successful writers, like John Updike and Louis L'Amour, while often complaining about the difficulty of writing well, emphasize the importance of regular work in daily sessions, regardless of mood [30, 31, 32]; that is, they don't struggle with motivation beforehand but, instead, rely on the regular habit of writing to provide the needed impetus; what might have begun as forcing became an effortless habit.

2. The exceptions to the rule of regular, hard work are just that, exceptions [33]; writers who claim otherwise have understandable motives in making it seem that they write quickly and easily, without discipline (notably the chance to impress us with their genius [5, 34]); when writers disguise the sources of their motivation (e.g., a habit of regular writing) they make themselves appear more brilliant and they misdirect our own efforts to mimic their success.

3. Some writers do find prosperity with occasional binges of writing, but they pay a price; where we look closely at individuals who managed motivation by working in great marathons (like Ayn Rand and Anthony Trollope), we see evidence for unhealthy exhaustion, induced depression, and unfulfilled potential [35, 36].

4. We can learn about little-known aids to motivation from teachers of writing, composition professors; they help students find incentives by teaching them to solve the right problems (e.g., not supposing that a lack of time is the problem but, instead, finding ways of making better use of available time [37]).

5. And finally, we can solve the problem of motivation by becoming involved first and motivated later, by seeing writing as a matter of joining an ongoing conversation where we listen first and feel like talking later [38]; in the last analysis, optimal motivation depends on moderated kinds of waiting and forcing.

What do writers get from this preliminary discussion? The point about finding motivation through patient but active involvement is that it generates the most immediate conversation and hopefulness. Writers like the analogy of joining a conversation as a first step in managing motivation. The idea, first of all, provides a sense of relief. It suggests that the primary task of writers consists of little more than tuning in on the ongoing conversation in one's genre, an act that doesn't seem to demand a lot of immediate energy or decisiveness. It even suggests a basis for confidence. By listening and noticing, we can somewhat effortlessly discover the essential themes, who creates them, and how they are best expressed.

Second, the idea reveals a practical way of mustering more and more motivation. As we read, listen, and notice, we ready ourselves to do what we would do in any social conversation: Ideally, we want to enter with a variation of our own, one that takes the conversation into account, one that is motivated by having listened and prepared until we feel impelled to contribute. (Either that or we eventually discover that we are in the wrong conversation.) Realistically, we might not feel motivated about entering the conversation until we learn the issues and detect something worth saying.

Third, the idea of treating writing as a conversation suggests that the skills we need to find motivation are learnable, not magical. Consider an example of a simple principle that writers most readily grasp about the social skills of writing: Common social intelligence tells us to hold off on speaking out (or on writing for public consumption) until we first, join the group, listen and read patiently, and inform ourselves enough so that we are inevitably prepared and inspired to make a contribution to topics under discussion. When this is done with moderation, the waiting becomes less passive and the forcing becomes less active.

When we involve ourselves while waiting before actually writing for public consumption, several things happen. Soon we come to know what the major and most respected conversations are and who makes them. We gain a sense of the larger conversation in terms of tone and content (something that editors routinely conclude is missing in the work of failed writers). We gain a sense of where the conversation is leading and where the most exciting new conversations will emerge. We collect a growing set of notes and thoughts about what is already in print and about what could be said. And then, again, we become so involved and informed that motivation and confidence eventually impel our speaking out.

Does this phenomenon hold true for all kinds of writers? Even in fields where authors seem publicly disconnected from each other (say, in mystery or romance writing), writers help themselves by paying more systematic attention to what succeeds, to the styles of leaders, to the trends of topics, even to instances of breakthroughs by unconventional authors. Many seemingly reclusive writers claim to work entirely alone, perhaps in their attics surrounded by nothing but banks of file cabinets. Only on closer examination can we see that they are constantly involved in the conversations of writers and editors in their genre [39].

There are, again, exceptions. But why, I say to my writers, look to exceptions and enhance the risk of making an already difficult task more so? Or, I ask in another way, why deprive yourself of a proven, practical method for improving your writing and the motivation to do it? As writers ruminate on my queries, they often make comments like these two:

I see, I think. See if I'm right. Writers who wait to enter these conversations properly do more than just waiting. They are supposed to be actively reading and listening and letting themselves become more involved and ready. . . . Then, as the excitement builds naturally about having something worthwhile to say, they move toward the center of the group and say something that fits in, that adds something worthwhile. Right?

What I'm realizing is that I've approached my writing as a very private matter, as something I do entirely on my own, as something quite independent of what other novelists are doing. I do want to be original, but I also realize that I could do a lot more to discover what others are doing that works. In a way, I know [what works]. I know what I like and admire. But I haven't taken the trouble to look carefully at what makes them successful . . . at what I could, not copy, but maybe emulate. What hadn't occurred to me at all is talking to writers at this stage. I had imagined, I guess, that only when I had managed my success would I enter any conversation with them. . . . If there is a lesson, it may be that by not being a part of the conversation, by not feeling that excitement or confidence, I have made it harder to motivate myself.

Impressive as these insights are, they don't always translate into action, at least not immediately; the reframing exercise just depicted more often does nothing but plant seeds for thought. At this point, I push only for a questioning of long-held beliefs and habits such as passive waiting and forced writing under deadlines. Inevitably, I note a conversation like this between two writers in the group:

I still don't get what you mean by joining a conversation. Exactly what are we supposed to do when we join?

Maybe I can help. I think it has meaning at two levels. It means learning about what is being published and thinking of the writers who publish as carrying on a kind of conversation that we can learn from. We can listen to what is topical and how it is said in ways that succeed. On the other level, I think, it refers more to raising our consciousness about writing, to conversing with ourselves and with other writers, any writers, about writing. . . . I think it means coming out and getting involved and using that experience to build natural motivation.

While this germination is underway, my writers and I discuss related ideas. The more parallels we can see to a new insight, the surer its adoption into mindful practice.

The following list depicts the most common discussion points that follow: (1) We talk more about the conversation metaphor, about the wisdom of entering a conversation without unnecessary baggage (e.g., impatience, cynicism, perfectionism, pessimism). (2) We look for kindred ideas in our literature gleanings (e.g., Lynn Bloom's claim that the most readable and memorable writing is witnessing about one's purpose and message, a style that offers readers the prospect of friendliness and enthusiasm [40]). (3) We find solace in beginning to understand how incubation (the supposedly passive waiting that courts inspiration) in writing really works: mostly by way of inducing a refreshing pause that follows the formulation of a problem in ways that allow us to notice connections and better ways of saying things [41]. (4) We begin to generate a tough resolve by facing up to the realization that the demandingness of writing [42, 43] is no good reason to put it off or dread it; we agree that we already know how to put such apprehensions aside (e.g., from experience in self-discipline borne of necessity, as with daily habits of going to work at a regular job with a minimum of struggle). (5) We take a preliminary look at how our usual pessimism or optimism affects our readiness and confidence to write [44]; expectations weigh heavily on motivations. (6) We remind each other that current problems of pressing deadlines are separate problems. That is, we should not wait to catch up on overdue projects before practicing brief, daily sessions of generating motivation for manuscripts that can be managed more sanely in the long run. (7) And, finally, as groups begin to grow visibly weary of all this talk, we finish with the timely topic of moderation. We conclude the discussion by recognizing the possibility that ideal motivation comes with compromises between forcing and passive waiting. That is, we recall the famous writers who employ a modicum of forcing moderated by habit ("they just do it because they are used to doing it") and of waiting enhanced by preparing ("by the time they start, they are already doing it").

This, then, is a reframing session. None of these exercises takes long, usually about fifteen minutes. None provides complete answers or quick cures. Reframings merely help move writers away from old, unreflective practices that may have made finding motivation and confidence difficult. Reframings also become exercises that writers practice on their own, as part of slowing down to think more about what they are doing.

In the next session we revisit many of the same old points. Slowly, surely, writers are entering a conversation about writing; they are listening to writers and thinking about writing more fluently and comfortably. The following favorite points turn up again and again, as new groups of writers pass through this stage:

1. Passive waiting has been shown to be ill-suited to solve thinking problems in general [45]; writing is, essentially a matter of solving thinking problems.

2. The most effective incentives for writing are internally generated (e.g., as in writing for the sake of the joy of discovery [46, 47]; when we properly join a conversation, the motivation to participate becomes internalized and, so, less forced.

3. When we wait for the unconscious to provide motivation and materials, we probably err because the most efficient and effective writing has conscious and deliberate origins [48]; this is all the more reason to be thinking and preparing while waiting.

4. Motivation and inspiration follow, not precede, the practice of regular, accumulated work [33]; thus, gradual and somewhat painless involvement in public conversations (eventually in public expressions) builds a gentle force for writing; said another way, we err in waiting for motivation that impels us to write.

5. Motivation, as with any other skill, relies on moderation, on getting more from less; it also requires enough patience and noticing so that we solve the right problems [37]; that is, we would do better to make writing a regular, daily practice instead of waiting for big blocks of undisrupted time.

6. And, again, mild happiness facilitates problem solving. (This said, we come full circle to the first point in our discussions.)

Mind you, these are merely topics of lively discussion, not necessarily of conviction, at this point. Old habits and beliefs change slowly. They prove especially stubborn in the face of such seemingly counterintuitive notions as these. You, the reader, might expect much the same.

A curious thing invariably happens about here. Writers realize that to settle questions about what works and what doesn't, they will need to move to experience. We are, after a month or so of talking together, ready to sample some strategies for finding motivation. Our conversation has conveniently grown to the point of compelling more active involvement and discussion.

As I demark this transition point for groups, tension levels rise temporarily. We all know it has been easier to talk about new approaches to motivation and writing than to practice them; we all grit our teeth at the prospect of putting these new ideas into action. Doing so, we realize, probably means hard work or at least discomfort. Once again, old habits such as rushing to meet deadlines seem temptingly familiar and adequate for our writing; it is, predictably, a time for joking. Writers almost smile as they say things like "This had better work, or else I'm asking for my money back." I usually smile back and respond with a single word: "Patience."

TREATMENTS THAT MOTIVATE

Treatments are, in some ways, harder to describe than the conversations that precede them. Treatments are, after all, experiential; recipients often internalize new strategies without much external comment. A lot of quiet time is spent thinking and rehearsing. There may be a parallel to difficulties in describing any such treatment: we know a lot about pioneering psychotherapists including Carl Jung but little about how they actually did their therapies. So it is, perhaps, that most experts on writing tell us far, far more about problems than solutions.

Nowadays, though, we have advantages. One of them is the retrospective thinking-aloud protocol that we have already encountered. It affords us a useful record of what writers think and feel during treatment sessions. The resulting reconstructions provide part of an apparently complete picture of what happens as writers become more fluent and comfortable.

Rationales for Specific Treatments

Planning treatments for motivation presents a special quandary; popular therapies almost no clear precedents for enhancing motivation and yet this is probably the most crucial intervention. How, I routinely ask, do most practitioners manage to induce motivation? As groups help me answer this question, I ask them to consider two examples of solutions. In the field of teaching improvement, program directors generally limit their efforts to faculty members already motivated to seek treatment [49]. In the field of literary study, attention may be given only to the blocked writers who have already proven their talent by writing successfully; a lack of prior and significant fluency is seen as proof of a deficiency in talent [50]. I wonder aloud as I ask a related question: Could this general attitude (about only wanting to provide motivation to those already motivated to seek it) explain why well-established domains of treatment such as smoking prevention attract less than 15 percent of the people who need treatment?

Even in the best-developed of schemes for generating motivation, where psychologists teach ways of building "self-efficacy" (e.g., via advice about arranging success experiences that will increase expectations of efficacious recovery after failures), the actual mechanisms remain vague [51, 52]. Overall, then, what we can surmise from current literature and practice on psychotherapy is disappointing. In the main, therapists seem inclined to treat people who conjure their own motivation.

Nonetheless, writers are good at recognizing some promising clues. For instance, we know what not to do to optimize motivation: neither passive waiting nor impatient forcing. And we know what to do. We are already into habits of gradual immersion and sharing (in writing that is carried out habitually and in calm moderation, without rushing or bingeing; in writing that is less private).

So it is, for example, that my recent groups of writers have settled on the conversation metaphor as a pivotal strategy. This is how the sequence might be conceived initially: First, we would shift to a stance of more listening than talking, of seeking interactions with successful authors, and of reading up on their genres. Then, having established more mindfulness about old habits of waiting and forcing, we would begin to work at motivation with more planfulness and regularity. The central strategy has, by this point, become quite familiar: We plan to move away from passive to active waiting by joining a conversation and by expecting involvement to precede motivation. Still, while these planning sessions are generally seen as easy, not everyone who participates makes it past this point. But those who stay become even more involved and motivated.

What predisposes some writers to drop out at this critical turning point? My exit interviews with drop-outs suggest a combination of impatience about taking so much time with prewriting exercises and a discomfort with making writing a more sociable activity. While traditional personality measures of traits such as introversion do not predict dropping out, newer measures of pessimism linked to low self-esteem, cynicism, and procrastination born of anger do.

The next step, for that majority of participants who stay on, is a formal intervention. It is one that we have already been practicing informally.

Stage 1: Learning about Tacit Knowledge from Experts

In this first formal step, writers agree to spend regularly scheduled time as readers and listeners. The result is impressive; writers often take only weeks to uncover what took me years. They quickly discern, for instance, which of the writers in their own genres have the most of offer. Donald Murray, a patron saint among composition teachers, is a favorite in the genre we share as group members--the one where writers write about writing. Indeed, Murray has written so long and well about how writers can improve their lot that he merits especially careful reading:

When I get an idea for a poem or a talk or a short story, I feel myself consciously drawn away from it. I seek procrastination and delay. There must be time for the seed of the idea to be nurtured in the mind. Far better writers than I have felt the same way. Over his writing desk Franz Kafka had one word, "Wait." [53]

In our discussions of Murray, groups take pride in seeing the subtlety in many of his points. He doesn't, for example, really mean procrastination in the sense of passive or counterproductive waiting; he means waiting while getting ready, while nurturing and organizing ideas. In describing himself, elsewhere, as a "seeker of interruptions," Murray relates a way of taking pressure off himself. Groups extend his ideas, often as in this interpretation: When writing is not rushed, when its progress is actually fostered by disruptions that give time for more reflection and preparation, writers work at a more comfortable pace.

Many of Murray's points require no interpretation; he is, for example, nearly unique among writers in speaking directly to the problem of finding motivation. He calls it force. When groups share the exercise of paraphrasing his thoughts on paper, the outcome looks like this:

1. Get interested in a subject and collect information about it; become an avid collector of details, facts, thoughts, anything including references. As collections build, so will interest--to the point where it takes hold of the writer.
2. With immersion in a subject, the next step, wanting to order and organize the information, comes naturally. So does the following step, wanting to share collections with other people.
3. The ensuing inevitability of sharing what we collect takes form as writers become aware of a waiting audience for the materials being amassed and organized; the realization emerges that much of what has been collected and clarified is unknown to others or else misunderstood by them. The will to write requires more than a desire to communicate; it also wants the arrogance of believing that the communication is worthwhile.
4. Finally, after rehearsing the material in their minds, writers impose a plan and a schedule as the last step for moving on to more direct action.

In our discussions of Murray's script, we agree on several points. We are surprised that, given the near absence of directives for finding motivation in the literature, Murray's seem so wise and practical. We like his presentation of ideas in a clear sequence of acts that we can practice, one that takes the mystery out of conjuring force. And we appreciate the cleverness with which he has sold us on his approach; motivation, we imagine, requires a certain amount of merchandising. From all this we draw the first guideline or rule in the program, one that proves ubiquitous:

RULE #1: Wait.

Then, with this clear directive in hand, another predictable mood of somberness settles over groups. The reason is that we see an unfamiliar task ahead: collecting and sharing material for our writing before we have decided on what, exactly, to write. With these doubts and frustrations in mind, groups lapse into doubt. From this momentary fall-back, though, we generate useful realizations. We recognize that progress will probably come slowly, haltingly, amid some uncertainty. We sense that unforeseen risks and difficulties lie ahead, much as in any journey. And as we regain our course, we agree that above all we need to practice patience and a willingness to try things. My notes from the repetitions of this stage include someone saying:

I'm a control person and while that makes this all the harder, it makes it all the more useful. Why is this? Because, I think, I can proceed at a comfortable pace.

To reinforce the point about the value of taking a leap of faith, I add a brief explanation of "involvement theory." It says, simply, that learning and success depend, more than anything else, on involvement. For students, this means that immersion in campus events and facilities, in conversations and collaborations with faculty members, does the most to ensure success in college and in careers afterward [34]. For writers, this means that involvement in the regular practice of reading, of collecting and organizing, of writing, and of conversing about writing leads to prosperity. In a way the insight here seems simple: Involvement is tantamount to motivation; one reinforces the other. But in a way the insight is complex: Involvement precedes the calm, lasting motivation we are discussing here; so it is that we must find ways to begin before feeling fully ready or inspired.

The point just made becomes the second memorable rule:

RULE #2: Begin before feeling fully ready or inspired (because motivation comes most reliably in the wake of involvement).

As we proceed, we often refer back to these rules. At the end, we work from little more than the accumulated list of reminders. (The concluding chapter of this book relists the rules so that you can see look ahead to the signposts for this long journey.)

Having agreed on a couple of general rules and on the need to immerse ourselves in preliminaries, writers tell me they feel even readier to enter the second step of formal treatment programs for motivation. Indeed, as participants often note about the ensuing step, we are once again beginning before usual and formal beginnings--a good way of ensuring motivation. Readers may have to work even harder before feeling ready.

Stage 2 of Formal Treatment: Building a Calm Focus

My second formal emphasis, after building a conversation, is on patience, the other essential component of reliable motivation besides involvement. Without it, we cannot make good use of beginnings before beginning. Without it, writers will not participate fully in conversations or adaptively prepare their contribution while waiting to make public statements. And, without patience practiced as a calm pleasureableness, writers make the act of writing too aversive to maintain the desire to resume it. Consider that two predictable characteristics of blocked writers are reclusiveness and impatience. There is, as you may sense, another rule at hand:

RULE #3: Remember that impatience blocks writers by associating writing with rushed, incomplete work. (And that the opposite of impatience, patience, is a form of active waiting.)

Our exercises in fostering patience start with a lessening of the emotional tension that commonly accompanies writing; we begin with relaxation because impatience is essentially tension. So long as writing remains tense, writers are hard-pressed to exhibit patience or to enjoy writing. To convince writers of the maladaptive connection between writing and tension, I spend time with each of them in individual sessions where they write (if possible at their usual writing site and at their customary writing time); if they cannot write during my observation, I assign a simple task of paraphrasing from something in print. I then watch from the background (before long, writers learn to ignore my presence). Where writers are too inhibited by my presence to write at their normal pace, I obtain their permission to drop in, unannounced, during a scheduled session when they will already be working. Sooner or later, we recreate the reality of writing as though working to complete a normal assignment.

Once these writers have momentum, I stop them occasionally, say every five minutes, for tension checks. What I can see as they write reflects what they tell me during pauses. As a rule, they write in uncomfortable postures (often hunched over a keyboard), with their backs, necks, and foreheads strained. Over time, as they write at a faster pace, tensions increase and writers grow more and more reluctant to pause. Once writers gain momentum, they hate to relinquish it.

At the ends of these sessions, I ask writers to recollect what they thought and felt during the half-hour of my presence; this is a variation of my usual reliance on thinking-aloud techniques. Writers' most salient recollections concern the novelty of being stopped again and again while writing; participants at this stage of the program rarely welcome interruptions because impatience and brief pauses are incompatible. The other outstanding recognition at this point relates to the tension, discomfort, and rushing that usually accompany writing. Writers express surprise at their observations:

At one point I thought, "Wow, my neck and seat and arm are really sore. I wonder why I work this way? I don't need to." I thought, "I guess this is how I always do it." Then another voice shot in and said, "So what kind of reason is that?"

I thought about two problems immediately. One, I wasn't at all comfortable. Two, I was on such a roll that I had already lost touch with my outline and plans.

The same kinds of discussions reveal commonalities among the diverse writers that I attract to my programs. Only rarely do these scriveners display already entrenched habits of pausing to relax, rarer still of periodically getting up to stretch. Evidently, writing is usually practiced as an endeavor where we labor without pauses, ignore discomfort, and rush impatiently to conclusion. Writers are more likely to stick to their chairs than to their plans.

Surprisingly, even fewer writers take the simple precautions that alleviate eye strain (by pausing to distance-focus) or wrist-arm fatigue (by stopping to stretch, flex, change position, and ensure physical support for forearms). And, even in the midst of these interventions, most fall into old habits of hurrying and of abandoning blueprints for writing. Why?

Well, it certainly isn't something I devise consciously. I can't remember any ongoing thinking or feeling about working so fast and without any concern for my comfort. But I can recall what I thought when you stopped me: "I don't want to stop because I don't want to lose this thought, I want to stay on this roll, I want to get finished as quickly as possible." Now that I think on it, no wonder that I so often finish feeling exhausted and then discover that what I have written is disjointed.

The consensus of other writers who had just observed themselves rushing and not resting has been much the same. Many of them had supposed that once writing, they should work to finish as much as possible because motivation and ideas might never again be so accessible. Almost all these writers could recall an even more primitive feeling: once underway, they did not feel like stopping until they were out of words and energy. "Spent," as several writers termed it. "The hell with outlines or comfort once I'm on a roll," said another.

But exhaustion and straying are not the sole outcomes of impatience and rushing. Only as we persist in reflections does something else become apparent. Intensity produces tension that makes stopping difficult and transitions to other activities awkward:

Come to think of it, this is always how I feel when I finish my bouts of writing. I'm wired. It's hard to quit and about all I feel like doing is writing some more, even when I can write no more. I always have trouble dealing with this, what should I call it, leftover nervousness. I guess it's one of the things I don't like about writing.

Other writers at this point talk about residues of tension from bouts of rushed writing that included irritability, insomnia, and drinking. As we talk individually and then in our groups, we begin to express an understanding for famous authors, F. Scott Fitzgerald among them, who abused alcohol in their efforts to relax after writing.

At the same time we agree on something else. Working with high intensity and without relaxing pauses is not the only source of tension in writing [54]. Some of us bring already established fears (of failure, of success, and of other things) to the table. Still, we also concur, it makes sense to begin by paying attention to how we generate maladaptive pressures of the simplest sorts: by working amid impatience and deadlines. First things first. So long as we work at writing in a forced, relentless pace, we make ourselves susceptible to problems of motivation.

To combat the powerful habit of working under tense impatience, I coach writers in what I call comfort exercises. We take a few moments to begin practicing methods for instilling moods of calm and patience. As we do so, a predictable thing happens. The same writers who have tolerantly listened to weeks of talk about writing now suppose themselves too busy to practice comfort exercises:

I don't know about spending much time on this. Surely, there are other people here who are as far behind schedule as I am. When do we get on with writing?

The continuing theme of such comments is usually this: if patience and calm have a use, why can't they be mastered later, once writers are caught up? Here is an instance where I act forcefully. I remind writers that comfort exercises take only a minute or two from most writing sessions, that such practices make writing more pleasant *and* productive, and that putting off basics imperils our long-term success because of their links to motivation. The result is usually a grudging agreement to give comfort exercises a try (even while finishing up other overdue tasks).

Exercises

Comforting. We start with the most basic of exercises, of enhancing bodily comfort while writing. The strategy begins with self-observations of discomfort, a foreign experience for most writers. The assignment produces immediate results.

When they are cued to stop every five to ten minutes to monitor their comfort, writers express surprise. After only the first half-hour, sitting positions may have grown uncomfortable; buttocks and lower backs are already sore, often throbbing; crossed or cramped legs may be numb; eyes ache. There is also surprise at how easily these discomforts are allayed. Corrections demand little more than minor shifts in posture and positioning. A related observation: When minor corrections are not made over time, larger discomforts become apparent; stiffened backs, tensed necks, clenched wrists, and tightened foreheads grow more and more painful. Once well established, these usually neglected aches are not so easily vanquished with postural shifts and calming thoughts.

Then they demand more extensive interventions and rest. A simple principle of relaxation applies here and later: the earlier the detection of tension and the earlier its relief, the better.

With just a few trials at self-monitoring, most writers evidence real changes in mindfulness about attending to comfort. One change stands out. Old patterns of indulging tension to the point of near irreversibility are generally abandoned (or at least moderated). Writers tell me that what helps them change these personal habits is social pressure; thus, we contract among ourselves to continue to schedule pauses for such checks and adjustments every five to ten minutes while writing. Later, we report our compliance to each other. Even the people who initially need to rely on timers and signals to remind them of check points soon establish the habit of regular pauses.

Soon after, by the next week, we add two new elements of monitoring to our pauses. The first occurs with every pause: a deliberate, far-reaching stretch while adjusting sitting postures, extending extremities to full length and flexing them. It includes taking deep breaths (and following the next few breaths as they move in and out through airways). It ends with resettling and restarting. The second element of self-monitoring comes every half-hour and takes writers out of their coveted chairs for standing stretches. Both exercises work and both elicit curiously strenuous resistance once writers begin putting them into practice. Why? The first objection relates to the blocked writer's best friend, impatience. The message is by now commonplace but worth reconsidering because it is so likely to crop up:

Listen, this is interesting, and I don't doubt that your intentions are honorable, but I have serious writing to do. I don't have time for this nonsense. No offense, but I'm exactly two months past my editor's deadline. I want you to help me get started.

The second source of resistance is also familiar by now. It is only just coming to clear expression. It concerns another close relative of impatience, control:

No, no. [pause] I can tell you that won't work for me, and for a very good reason. If *I* stop, even long enough just to make myself comfortable, I could lose my train of thought. Before you know it, I'll be blocked again. In other words, if and when I am lucky enough to get started, I'm not going to be making any unnecessary stops.

I listen sympathetically and then respond, patiently. These are, I acknowledge, customary and important concerns. I address them with a set of serious rejoinders like these: First, I have tracked over a hundred writers through the unaccustomed experience of scheduled pausing, and trains of thought are rarely lost because of them. Second, where writers are immersed in a complex idea or anticipating a series of points, they can preserve and even clarify them by making a note of them as their first act in stopping to pause. While the ideas are fresh in mind. Third, when trains of thought and momentum are indeed lost, they are easily regained. One useful strategy for refinding our voices relies on free writing (the method of writing whatever comes to mind without stopping to edit).

Another is related and can be called recollective rewriting: it has writers reinstate old cues by rewriting the last few sentences already visible on paper or screen. And yet another strategy is more a matter of planfulness. An effective method of ensuring easy restarts consists of never stopping at the ends of paragraphs . . . even sentences. Unfinished tasks tend to stay nearer the forefront of our memories and motivations than do finished thoughts. In contrast, restarting with new sentences or sections places a much tougher demand on writers. New starts are more likely to be eyed without the confidence and momentum of knowing what precedes them and without fresh thoughts of what comes next. Cold starts invite avoidance.

Finally, patience is easier planned than practiced. Simply knowing that impatience is the single most important predictor of writing blocks is not enough. Nor is an appreciation that impatience pushes writers to write without proper motivation and readiness (i.e., the enthusiasm that comes from joining a conversation and the confidence of knowing what is worthwhile to say). And, to complete a redundant point, it does not suffice to merely know that underlying factors of patience, including comfort and skillfulness, make writers better motivated and more productive [5]. What matters most in the long run is making patience, the act of slowing down and making use of planfulness, a regular habit. The mechanisms for establishing motivation and patience are closely parallel.

When I have said all that, most groups react with quietude. After a moment or two, they say that they sense the need to get on with practice. Some writers are ready to resume or begin a planned manuscript. Others will work more readily by making notes from literature related to their intended projects. A few suspect they can do no more than rewrite manuscripts left unfinished or in need of revision. Even the most blocked writers find they can manage to paraphrase or transcribe an admired manuscript. The point is to establish a habit of writing regularly, accompanied with calm and scheduled "comfort stops." We even find ways around usual complaints about time. Because busy schedules are a common problem, we agree to begin with sessions of no more than ten or fifteen minutes a day.

Something interesting accompanies this preliminary regimen of daily writing. It is an extension of the social contracting we are already practicing. Each of us arranges to stay in daily contact with a partner who is not only attempting to manage a similar schedule but who will also coax us to write (or to do something related to writing) during each planned period--and, of course, to make pauses and comfort checks habitual parts of those sessions. The most essential part of coaching may be motivating people to do what they already know. Coaching also depends on reminders, something that readers may miss if they do not arrange conversations where they give and receive guidance.

Daily practice of this routine for at least a few weeks produces three crucial realizations in writers. First, they begin to see that a regular habit of brief sessions of writing is not difficult to manage, even in the midst of busy days. Second, they report a sense of proud accomplishment in maintaining their writing on a daily basis, especially amid the most demanding of daily schedules. Third, they revel in discovering that in the "partners program" they can help themselves by helping other writers:

It is one of those things I should have been doing already. (I always feel that way about any worthwhile discovery.) I have already come to like the idea of the regular pauses. In a flash I can see what is wrong and make amends. And at the same time I feel good about taking better care of myself and that makes me happier. I can't remember having been a happy writer many times before. . . . I can tell that the pauses are doing something for my imagination too. Just stopping and then thinking about what I've just done gives me new ideas, more than I can recall coming up with in my usual work.

The big surprise is being able, despite my own profound inexpertise, to help someone else. Or that she, being in the same boat, can help me. All it takes, a lot of times, is knowing that a call is coming and that it would be easier to be able to say, "Yes, I've done my little bit of writing today" than to have to whip up excuses.

Relaxing. After we have moved through just a week or two of practicing comfort pauses, I ask group members to add the next logical step in establishing patience, relaxation. This request elicits far less consternation than the initial push for comfort; writers are already in the habit of pausing and of benefiting from it. Moreover, relaxation exercises are familiar to many participants, most commonly in the form of meditation, muscle tensing-untensing, or physical workouts that reduce tension. The only problem in these usual familiarities is this: most relaxation programs teach tactics that are too complicated and demanding to persist in everyday practice. This common experience leaves veterans skeptical about reengagement. Consider, for instance, the widespread and potentially effective method called progressive relaxation. Its requirement of tensing and then relaxing each of the major muscle groups, of having to stop all other activity for many minutes, eventually inclines people to abandon its practice.

A more practical strategy, in my experience, consists of making the exercise brief, noninterruptive, but "applied" (i.e., applied to the ongoing task that generates tension, not practiced separately from the ongoing act). The simple act of keeping one's tongue relaxed and at the bottom of one's mouth is a good example. ("This proves that truth is stranger than fiction," said one writer.) The check for position and tension takes only a moment, and neither the check nor the adjustment need interfere with any activity except talking. Tongue checks (jokesters have great fun with this one) work because they help ensure a fundamental kind of relaxation. Here's why: when we are tense, we keep our tongues at the roofs of our mouths, as though ready to speak in a millisecond. When we relax our tongues to the bottoms of our mouths, we quietly stimulate a larger series of relaxation components: untensing our jaws, releasing sustained inhalations and noticing our breathing in and out of our noses, loosening the muscles of our necks and foreheads, and so on.

Tongue checks work because they can be practiced almost anywhere and during almost any activity (e.g., while driving, a great generator of tension for many people) and with immediately obvious results. In studies where I have asked writers to practice tongue checks during each of their comfort pauses, to maintain that pose while writing, and then to self-rate their tension after writing on a ten-point scale, the individuals who report the most reliable practice of tongue checking also evidenced the biggest gains in tension reduction.

The writers who fare best at this strategy generally add an elaboration on their own. Each time they relax their tongues, they say something relaxing to themselves like "Calm down, slow down," and they practice a moment of meditation by counting the inhalations and exhalations passing through their noses. Easy as they sound, tongue checks and meditational pauses require months of regular practice before they become automatic.

While habits of pausing for comfort and relaxation make surprisingly large contributions to reliable motivation, there is more to ensuring a wise passiveness in writing.

Stage 3 of Interventions: Establishing a Regular Habit of Writing

The third step works especially well when formally introduced at this juncture. Writers already know about some of the benefits of establishing regular habits associated with writing; the pattern of regular pauses for comfort checks is an example. Writers already have an appreciation of the potential role of habit in ensuring motivation; they know, for instance, that many established writers have equipped themselves with a daily routine of writing, one that requires no struggle because it has become customary. And writers in the program bring another useful anticipation to the addition of a formal stage of habit in writing. They are already doing it, as part of the practice of comfort pauses and relaxation exercises. There is, once again, real benefit in beginning before beginning.

At this point, then, we contract with each other for an even more explicit commitment to brief, daily sessions (bds) of writing-related activities. Still, most groups make the pledges in preliminary fashion; it takes time to experiment with times of day and lengths of sessions. We start off with a set of guidelines based on what has worked for scores of writers who preceded us:

1. Begin with truly brief sessions, perhaps no more than fifteen minutes; the point is to establish the habit of regular work related to writing.
2. Be content, for now, with any activity that contributes to writing; reading with note-taking, rereading of old writing, planning, and the like, all augment the motivation and ideas essential to eventual success.
3. Practice the habit of regular daily writing while maintaining the sense of joining a conversation and while continuing to exercise patience.
4. Continue the social contract of having your partner monitor your regularity at bds (brief, daily sessions) and related commitments.

Then I add a pair of related cautions: First, expect this effort to establish a new habit to work imperfectly, certainly in the short run. And, second, plan to forgive yourself for failing to supplant old, entrenched habits with ease.

Soon after, groups generally press for the addition of a rule about the value of habit:

RULE #4: Practice a regular habit of writing to instil reliable motivation.

With this in mind (and in practice), we agree to remind ourselves over and over about the key ingredients in establishing new and more useful habits in writing: Patience and beginning before feeling ready.

Stage 4 of Interventions: Combatting Special Forms of Impatience

This next step guards against another aspect of impatience, excessiveness in carrying out activities. Learning to stop is more difficult and important than starting.

Exercises

Recognizing hypomania. Habits of pausing regularly to reestablish comfort and relaxation protect us against the frenzied, nonstop writing that turns into hypomania (that lesser form of mania). But in reality, even writers with habits of patience already in place continue to face occasions where excessive hypomania can take precedence. Sometimes the very nature of strong momentum, the seductiveness of continuing with the euphoria of ideas and the delight of not having to struggle to write, reinstates hypomania. Sometimes the difficulty of breaking out of a slump or a depression seems to make the alternative of euphoric rushing a necessity. However it starts, the elevated mood of bingeing and strong hypomania distances us from inclinations to pause for comfort checks and relaxation exercises.

What helps temper hypomania? The habits of calming and slowing are only a start. Writers fare even better with the addition of constant reminders about the perils of bingeing (e.g., it launches unprepared writers into rushing and, so, risks failures).   Something related also helps in a preliminary way--a combination of planfulness and proactiveness. Once hypomania gains force, it is difficult to stop.

My writers and I begin the practice of planfulness by looking ahead to customary times and circumstances where bingeing of writing may be most likely. There are strong commonalities in these personal scripts (and many of them hold true over the course of a year or more). Binges are most likely under deadlines, when motivation is hardest to conjure, when we are already upset, and when large blocks of time are found or forced:

Well, I haven't quite put this in words before, but I can see a pattern around my past binges. Something where history will repeat itself. Usually I binged because I had to. I had run out of time and I had to make the best of what little was left. In projects where I worked more steadily toward my goal, I didn't need to binge, at least not to that extreme. . . .   I guess the other opening for binges came when I didn't have effective and realistic plans for all the things that needed to be done and for all the time that I would need. In one incident that comes to mind, when I should have been finishing a revision of my book manuscript for my editor, I got caught up in roofing my house (something I should have let the roofer do without my help). In another one, I used the circumstance of my family being gone for a weekend to write in a grand binge almost day and night. Not a fond memory . . . it wasn't my best work and it took me a week to get back to normal. My wife said, when she first returned home, "What have you been doing that was so tiring?" I could at least say it was nothing she would consider immoral.

I think that I binge when I'm feeling least secure, when I'm worried that if I don't do a lot in one sitting, I will never make any significant headway on the paper. It's when I'm feeling my most impatient, when I seem to have the least confidence in my ability to write again.

Something really critical is finally starting to occur to me in this talk about bingeing. Learning to stop is as important as learning to start.

Groups show special appreciation for the insights that emerge now. This is a distinctive point of enthusiasm and wisdom. In particular, we share a keen realization about an important preventative of hypomania: learning to stop on command. Repetitions of this comment help consecrate it as the fifth rule in my programs:

RULE #5: Stop.

This rule means stopping at the end of a scheduled writing time, despite the temptation to add the sentence or two still in mind. Learning to stop is an ultimate exercise in patience; the urge to continue includes a big component of impatience about not being finished, about not being productive enough, about never again finding such an ideal time for writing. Stopping is also an exercise in building confidence and trust; without establishing enough self-esteem to stop midstream we deprive ourselves of chances to find confidence and control. And, finally, learning to stop is a fundamental exercise in time management. The most difficult but fundamental lesson about time use is learning that important tasks (especially those we tend to delay) can be carried out most efficiently in brief, regular periods.

Stopping. Time management, done well, means allotting no more than the necessary time to any one task per day (even reading this book) and then, while still energetic, stopping and moving on to other important activities including rest. In the case of writing, limiting ourselves to brief, daily sessions of, say, no more than thirty or sixty minutes (or to three or four hours maximum for professional writers) means that writing cannot interfere with more important responsibilities such as social life and exercising.

This is one of those times in the journey when groups tend to fall silent while listening intently. To encourage their reinvolvement in active conversation, I change gears. In the midst of this discussion about the advantages of stopping in punctual fashion, I stop to summarize the main points in a list of brief points designed to stimulate discussion:

1. Timely stopping keeps us from staying with a project too long, until it takes on fatigue and the excesses of hypomania including rushed and nonreflective thinking.
2. Timely stopping permits us to move on to other planned tasks and, so, reduces feelings of busyness and overscheduling.
3. Stopping on schedule, compared to persisting in binges, produces far more quality and quantity of writing in the long run.
4. The habit of timely stopping, again, is as essential to building optimal motivation as is timely starting. (When we stop with ideas and enthusiasm still at hand, we carry more impetus to the next writing session.)

Brief, daily sessions (bds). Then, as comments start to emerge, I slow down to preview a related notion. I distribute a list of some of the advantages of the timely stopping that permits writing in brief, daily sessions (bds):

1. Bds reduce warm-up time to near zero; the usual prospect of warm-up time (usually spent trying to reacquaint oneself with material no longer fresh in mind) often undermines motivation; when we approach resumption of a project knowing that we must begin with hours of review and rethinking, we may put it off.
2. Bds keep writing fresh in mind so that writers notice connections within and without their projects throughout the day.
3. Bds moderate hypomania by simple virtue of limiting session lengths and, in turn, reinforce the habit of writing with calm and confidence.
4. Bds alleviate pressures for rushing to meet deadlines because they help ensure that writing will be completed and revised on (or before) schedule.
5. Bds help establish the regular habit of writing, regardless of felt mood, in a way that makes motivating ourselves easier; strong habits kept pleasant are tantamount to compelling motivations.

Still, implanting a habit of bds may not be enough; we can hardly overestimate the potential of hypomania to supplant ongoing habits and moods. The final step in combatting binges, then, takes us back, briefly, to the practice of pausing while writing to monitor for comfort and relaxation. To check for warning signs of hypomania, my writers agree to add monitoring for signs of rushing and impatience. It doesn't take long.

Checking for rushing and impatience. This is the sort of interim reminder I give to writers already practicing comfort checks: Consider first, as part of planning to make such checks, the nature of full-fledged mania. Its tell-tale signs are a loss of appetite for eating or sleeping and a disorganized passion for communicating; mania is also marked by tendencies to take impulsive risks and to display grandiosity. While most of this pattern sounds out of bounds for ordinary writers ("that's not me, though I might wish it were at times"), we can spot the approximations as hypomania emerges, even amongst the least colorful of us. During rushed and extended writing, hypomania takes the form of lessened appetite for pausing, for planning, and for slowing down to relax. And as the faster pace and euphoria of hypomania dominate, we take unnecessary risks and we experience delusions of grandeur. Any part of this complex ensures problems in durable motivation for writing. Nonetheless, bingeing and hypomania offer enough short-term benefits (e.g., excitement) to make them difficult to abandon.

The solution for writers who want to cling to the euphoria and ease of bingeing and hypomania has two parts. One part is implanting in them a growing awareness of the limitations of excessiveness. The other is eliciting a willingness to try moderating hypomania with the limited time available in bds. All but a few writers agree to humor me.

Fortunately, hypomania is easily spotted in its formative stages. One proven method consists of looking, during already established pauses, for signs of: (1) a growing impatience about pausing because we want to continue our writing without interruption; (2) a quickening pace of writing, one that may exceed our ability to type or write without an increase in mistakes (e.g., mistyped words), one that leaves us feeling nearly breathless and definitely hurried; and, (3) a heightened state of tension and discomfort that demands harder work for its moderation with relaxation exercises. (Please notice something similar. Did you rush to get through this overly long sentence?)

What should we do upon spotting these symptoms? The best first move is making ourselves stop for each scheduled pause while reminding ourselves of the dangers of continuing to rush (e.g., fatigue that makes writing aversive; impatience that leaves writing unskillful). Just as we learn the importance of beginning regardless of mood, we soon see the profit in learning to stop irrespective of mood.

The second move is a matter of redoubling efforts to reestablish comfort and relaxation, particularly during the last minutes of planned bds for writing, when we are most tempted to rush. This could mean adding a minute to usual efforts at stretching, at tongue and jaw untensioning, at distance focusing, and at self-talk that helps calm ("I want to do my best work, and rushing won't help meet that goal"). When the onslaught of hypomania is strongest, writers tell me, the best countermeasure is this: to get up out of one's chair and to stand, stretch, walk around, take deep breaths, and deliberately decelerate one's thinking by talking it aloud.

The most telling advantage learned in standing away from acceleration seems to be a matter of regaining control:

I think this works because it is practice in stopping, in saying "no" to that part of me that wants to carry things to excess.

I can make the standing-away work because I use those few minutes to calmly retrace what I have already done and [to] think about how it can be better. Then, when I sit down again, I restart with some revision and honing. That sort of deliberateness relieves some of the impatience that had crept into the writing. Later, about a page or so later, when I get back to where I was, I'm working at a more reasonable pace and I know I'm doing better work.

As usual, not everyone shares these insights and enthusiasms. A few writers continue to object to the regular pauses and to the seemingly endless list of exercises to be performed (even while admitting that the whole assemblage takes less than a tenth of each writing session). Some writers wonder if I have ever really known the delights of hypomania and productive binges, events that no seemingly ambitious and sensuous person would want to give up. And, again, there are concerns about our time being spent on what appear to be slow-moving and indirect solutions to immediate, pressing problems. For many writers in this stage, our journey seems to proceed at the pace of a Long Island post office.

In my experience, the most effective rebuttal to these reservations consists of summarizing the case histories of writers who accomplished far more comfort and fluency with patience, calm, and bds than without. Conversely, I reinforce the point with accounts of writers who did *not* abandon impatience and bingeing: Some continued to write sporadically, few if any with pleasure or confidence in doing their very best work over the long run. Knowing how difficult this struggle is for many writers, I breathe a sigh of relief when even the most disconcerted participants make partial concessions like this one:

Yeah, OK, you may be right. And you may well be wrong. I do know that I need to do more here than just get started and finished on one manuscript. It might, I don't know, be nicer to write every day, even bad days. I suppose that we all need to quit bickering here and just get more absorbed.

Disputing worries. As groups settle into practicing bds and their built-in pauses and checks over the next few weeks, a reassuring calm often settles in. Only one more concern emerges for the moment. Some writers, upon experiencing unhurried prose for the first time, worry that something essential is now missing:

I'll tell you what worries me. It's a thing that makes me feel that I'm going to be a more placid but less creative writer. I know that true creativity depends on a kind of deranged, out-of-control approach to writing. (I once heard that garlic is to salad what madness is to art.) Any potential for all that is long gone from these calmed-down, too-short sessions. Here's what I suspect: Serene writers must be dull writers.

My responses at this point have grown predictable but no less important, I believe. I remind doubters of the advantages of patience and of our agreement that giving bds a chance is the economical thing to do. (After all, old patterns may not be maximally efficient.) And I overview research showing that calm, planful, and regular writing may be more creative than either bingeing or other sporadic outputs [55].

Then I make a point that derives from rule #2. Just as involvement precedes the most reliable and effective motivation, regular practice of calm bds precedes conviction that the strategy works. It is what the business world calls the "results-first" approach, of leaping in and trying a strategy instead of first debating it at length. After all, I note, much of what blocks writers is a fear of failure or a pessimism about being able to make alternative strategies work [56].

This moment in our voyage, where some writers experience the doldrums, provides a chance to introduce one more brief conversation and exercise. Appropriately enough, it confronts the problem of occasional emotions and moods that halt our progress. In this incarnation, the exercises are only preparatory, just enough to ensure adequate motivation for later encounters.

Supplanting negative emotions and moods. We already know too well, my groups and I agree, about these sorts of hindrances to motivation. They include breakdowns in self-esteem, prospects of public embarrassment, reinfections of perfectionism, and so on [5, 57]. As we discuss these blocking agents in a preliminary way, I make a couple of points. First, we will reencounter these same concerns in later stages of the program, at the point where already motivated writers become blocked. Second, consistent with our general approach, we will begin solving these problems well in advance of their formal location in the program; indeed, we have already been doing so. For the moment, then, we may need to do little more than acquaint ourselves with negative emotions and moods that can undermine motivation. Within limits, we can practice some simple curatives for putting things like writing anxieties aside.

This step in ensuring motivation, too, relies on periodic self-monitoring. Writers who especially need help in this regard take up the habit of checking, before, during, and after writing, for maladaptive mood states. Doing so takes practice, particularly for those of us unaccustomed to noticing our moods. When the mood is mild happiness, we can congratulate ourselves on having managed an ideal state for motivation. When, in contrast, the mood is anxious, angry, or depressed, we need to take quick action. One efficient method for detecting and supplanting the causes of such moods utilizes a variation of the thinking-aloud protocol seen earlier. In this case, writers simply make notes of what they have been thinking and feeling during the last few moments before starting to write [58]. For example:

First, the facts: I suddenly felt jumpy. I had suddenly started ruminating about my boss at work. I just had to tell myself, calmly but firmly, to put off worrying about that until later. In a moment I was able to clear my mind of that worrisome stuff and get on with writing. But if I hadn't, who knows where such a lovely thought would have taken me?

There is another, equally simple curative for interloping thoughts and emotions. Again, we identify the likely stimulus (usually a worry, often about something other than the writing at hand) and essentially stop it (often with nothing more than an implicit command to "STOP"). We can then help reinstate the calm that was disrupted by way of already familiar moves that precede a return to writing: stretching, resettling, distance-focusing, and, of course, lowering our tongues. In either case, the goal is the same. The ideal mood for motivating ourselves to do our best writing is one of mild and optimistic enthusiasm.

Together, these two preliminary tacks for managing mood resemble the strategies we have already learned in this chapter and they hint at something more general in the principles. To truly master interventions like relaxing and comforting, we must learn to apply them to a variety of different situations.

Writers tell me that as they develop an ability to better control their tensions, moods, and planfulness, they sense a growth in self-confidence; more and more they feel like writers in control of their writing. With this confidence comes a calm that marks the end of the first and most difficult part of our journey.

My groups welcome the end of this segment of the program as a chance to rest and decide what to do next. Generally, three things come to the fore: One is the shared sense that we are now more ready than ever to get on with writing projects; in a way we want the next segment to be action- and results-oriented. The second consensus is more surprising; there is a sudden interest in conducting self-assessments about blocking tendencies; writers show an interest in learning more about which of their problems remain to be solved. (A self-assessment device, the Blocking Questionnaire, is one example [59].) The third interest at this juncture relates to building expertise as self-motivators. M o s t writers at this point have not yet mastered motivation; we still need much more practice and support. While we express a special commitment to Donald Murray's steps for building motivation step by step, we share a final bemusement. We still want writing to be magically painless.

SUMMARY

When we have finished our formal, concentrated work on finding motivation and confidence, I distribute a brief, written summarization of what I suppose we have learned. Each such missive is subject to correction and elaboration.

Foremost, I think, we have seen that usual means of conjuring motivation (waiting passively, rushing under deadlines, and bingeing) work unreliably and inefficiently. In the short run, these traditional methods of motivation can leave us ambivalent and our writing incomplete; in the long run they can undermine our confidence, enthusiasm, and growth as writers.

The key insights, some of them seemingly counterintuitive at first sight, were condensed into five rules: The first and second said that we err when we wait passively and then force motivation for writing; the most reliable and helpful motivation comes in the wake of gradual, patient immersion in broadened conversations about writing and in regular habits of working at writing. The third rule specifies impatience as the principle villain in distracting writers away from the kinds of involvement they need most before launching most efficiently into prose. When they jettison impatience, writers can assume the moderate pace they need for clear thinking and creative expression. The fourth rule is about habit; a regular, productive habit of writing in brief, daily sessions pushes aside excuses of busyness and instills a powerful kind of motivation that comes from writing out of custom, without struggle. The fifth rule says that timely stopping is as necessary and important for stopping as for starting. When we cannot stop on schedule, we binge, we rush, and we associate fatigue with writing (and so, lessen the motivation for writing again). By developing the self-discipline to stop for pauses and at the end of regular, brief sessions, we help minimize impatience, exhaustion, hypomania, and unreflective writing. And by learning when to stop, we become better managers of both our time and our motivation because we stop when we still have some of each left for other, more important activities such as our social lives.

Which rule is most important? As we move ahead, writers tell me the first rule matters most. It is an admonition that resembles the advice from many great writers to wait before moving into prose (not passively but actively--while generating involvement, ideas, and interest).

What image is most salient from this first leg of our journey? Again, the first. At the beginning of this chapter we pictured Jane Austen working with a fragrant garden and quiet satisfaction at hand. By the time we reach this resting point, I hope that all journeyers have begun to experience that picturesque mood for optimizing motivation. When we travel with patience, comfort and involvement, we find the peace, health, and goodwill that motivate more travel.

REFERENCES

1. Durant, W. & Durant, A. (1975). *The age of Napoleon.* New York: Simon and Schuster, p. 411.

2. Brownell, K.D., Marlatt, G.A., Lichtenstein, E. & Wilson, G.T. (1986). Understanding and preventing relapse. *American Psychologist,* 41, 765-782.

3. Oatley, K. & Jenkins, J.M. (1992). Human emotions: Function and dysfunction. *Annual Review of Psychology,* 43, 55-85.

4. Olsen, T. (1965). *Silences.* New York: Delacorte Press, p. 6.

5. Boice, R. (1993). Writing blocks and tacit knowledge. *Journal of Higher Education,* 64, 19-54.

6. Hartley, J. & Knapper, C.K. (1984). Academics and their writing. *Studies in Higher Education,* 9, 151-167.

7. Redmon, C. (1979). (quoting Merle Miller in) The agonies of authorship. *Washington Post,* May 24, p. 85.

8. Flower, L. (1990). Negotiating academic discourse. In L. Flower, V. Stein, J. Ackerman, M.J. Kantz, K. McCormick & W.C. Peck (eds.), *Reading-to-write,*

pp. 221-252. New York: Oxford University Press.

9. Bowers, P.G. (1983). On not trying so hard: Effortless experiencing and its correlates. *Imagination, Cognition and Personality*, 2, 3-13.

10. Hatterer, L.J. (1965). *The artist in society*. New York: Grove Press.

11. Rothenberg, A. (1990). *Creativity and madness*. Baltimore: Johns Hopkins University Press.

12. Garfield, E. (1989). Creativity and science. Part 1. What makes a person creative? *Current Comments*, 43, 3-7.

13. Bauer, B. & Moss, R.F. (1985). Feeling rejected? *New York Times Book Review*, July 21, 1, 29-30.

14. Sheppard, R.Z. (1983). Goodbye, Nathan Zuckerman. *Time*, November 7, 88-89.

15. Holkeboer, R. (1986). *Creative agony: Why writers suffer*. Bristol, IN: Wyndom Hall Press.

16. Gurney, A.R. (1977). *Entertaining strangers*. Garden City, NY: Doubleday, pp. 110-121.

17. Goldsmith, B. (1984). "You know, I could write the most wonderful book." *New York Times Book Review*, September 30, 35.

18. Parini, J. (1989). The more they write, the more they write. *New York Times Book Review*, July 30, 10, 24-25.

19. Spurgeon, B. (1991). Why they write . . . and write . . . and write. *Los Angeles Times*, May 12, 1, 12.

20. Peters, D.P. & Ceci, S.J. (1982). Peer-review practices of psychological journals: The fate of published articles, submitted again. *Behavioral and Brain Sciences*, 5, 185-192.

21. Baker, R. (1983). Creeping on at a petty pace. *New York Times*, May 7, 23.

22. Haberman, C. (1975). Better late than never. *New York Times*, March 7, C20.

23. Hamada, R. (1986). In defense of procrastination. *University Magazine*, 8(1), 28-29.

24. Maddocks, M. (1982). In defense of procrastination. *Christian Science Monitor*, January 7, 22.

25. Sternberg, D. (1981). *How to complete and survive a doctoral dissertation*. New York: St. Martin's Press.

26. Boice, R. (1993). New faculty involvement for women and minorities. *Research in Higher Education*, 34, 291-341.

27. James, W. (1911). The energies of men. In *Memories and studies*, pp. 229-264. New York: Longmans Green & Co.

28. Nixon, H.K. (1928). *Psychology for the writer*. New York: Harper.

29. Barrios, M.V. & Singer, J.L. (1981). The treatment of writing blocks: A comparison of waking imagery, hypnotic imagery, hypnotic dream, and rational discussion techniques. *Imagination, Cognition and Personality*, 1(1), 89-109.

30. Goldiamond, I. (1977). Literary behavior analysis. *Journal of Applied Behavior Analysis*, 10, 527-529.

31. Sanoff, A.P. (1986). Conversation with John Updike. *U.S. News & World Report*, October 20, 67-68.

32. Jacoby, R. (1988). The writer as worker. *Los Angeles Times*, June 17, part II, p. 7.

33. Asimov, I. (1981). *Asimov on science fiction*. Garden City, NY: Doubleday.

34. Astin, A.W. (1985). *Achieving educational excellence*. San Francisco: Jossey-Bass.

35. Brandon, B. (1986). *The passion of Ayn Rand*. Garden City, NY: Doubleday.

36. Glendinning, V. (1993). *Anthony Trollope*. New York: Alfred. A. Knopf, p. 280.

37. Flower, L. (1990). The role of task representation in reading-to-write. In L. Flower, V. Stein, J. Ackerman, M.J. Kantz, K. McCormick & W.C. Peck (eds.), *Reading-to-write*, pp. 35-75. New York: Oxford University Press.

38. Olson, G.A. (1992). Publishing scholarship in humanistic disciplines: Joining the conversation. In J. Moxley (ed.), *Writing and publishing*, pp. 49-69. New York: University Press of America.

39. Asimov, I. (1979). *In memory yet green*. New York: Avon.

40. Bloom, L.Z. (1992). Writing as witnessing. In J. Moxley (ed.), *Writing and publishing*, pp. 89-109. Lanham, NY: University Press of America.

41. Perkins, D.N. (1981). *The mind's best work*. Cambridge, MA: Harvard University Press.

42. Burka, J.B. & Yuen, L.M. (1982). Mind games procrastinators play. *Psychology Today*, January, 32-44.

43. Tremmel, R. (1989). Investigating productivity and other factors in the writer's practice. *Freshman English News*, 17(2), 19-25.

44. Seligman, M.E.P. (1991). *Learned optimism*. New York: Alfred A. Knopf.

45. Flower, L. & Hayes, J.R. (1977). Problem-solving strategies and the writing process. *College English*, 39(4), 449-461.

46. Flower, L. & Hayes, J.R. (1980). The cognition of discovery: Defining a rhetorical problem. *College Composition and Communication*, 31, 21-32.

47. Hall, D. (1973). *Writing well*. Boston: Little, Brown.

48. Singer, J. (1988). Sampling ongoing consciousness and emotional implications for health. In M.J. Horowitz (ed.), *Psychodynamics and cognition*, pp. 297-348. Chicago: University of Chicago Press.

49. Eble, K.E. & McKeachie, W.J. (1985). *Improving undergraduate education through faculty development*. San Francisco: Jossey-Bass.

50. Leader, Z. (1991). *Writer's Block*. Baltimore: Johns Hopkins University Press.

51. Bandura, A. (1977). Self-efficacy: Toward a unifying theory of behavioral change. *Psychological Review*, 84, 191-215.

52. Landino, R.A. (1988). Self-efficacy in university faculty. *Journal of Vocational Behavior*, 33, 1-14.

53. Murray, D. (1978). Write before writing. *College Composition and Communication*, 29, 375-381.

54. Rabinbach, A. (1980). *The human motor: Energy, fatigue, and the origins of modernity*. New York: Basic Books.

55. Boice, R. (1983). Contingency management and the appearance of creative ideas. *Behaviour Research and Therapy*, 21, 537-543.

56. Rothblum, E.D. (1990). Fear of failure. In H. Leitenberg (ed.), *Handbook of social and evaluation anxiety*, pp. 497-537. New York: Plenum Press.

57. Boice, R. (1992). Combining writing block treatments: Theory and research. *Behaviour Research and Therapy*, 30, 107-116.

58. Boice, R. (1985). Cognitive components of blocking. *Written Communication*, 2, 91-104.

59. Boice, R. (1990). *Professors as writers* (see section entitled "Blocking Questionnaire," pp. 129-149). Stillwater, OK: New Forums Press.

2

Imagination

> To capture what you experience and sort it out . . . you must
> set up a file . . . . Whenever you feel strongly about events
> or ideas you must try not to let them pass from your mind, but
> instead to formulate them for your files and in so doing draw
> out their implications, show yourself how foolish these
> feelings or ideas are, or how they might be articulated into
> productive shape. The file also helps you build up the habit
> of writing. You cannot "keep your hand in" if you do not
> write something at least every week.
>
> C. Wright Mills, *The Sociological Imagination* [1]

The second major destination in this expedition (once routines are in motion for finding motivation through patience and comfort) is imagination. Imagination, like motivation, comes by way of regular involvement in activities that we may not ordinarily associate with writing. The most important work in writing occurs before we write.

Where do we find imagination? One answer lies in the advice left for intellectual explorers by a forgotten pioneer in sociology, C. Wright Mills. We would do well to join the small audience still following in his way; Mills' directives for a habit of formulating and filing ideas get to the heart of this second chapter.

When my writing groups and I discuss Mills' recipe for finding imagination, we recognize its familiarity. It resembles Donald Murray's scheme for eliciting motivation by finding and collecting ideas (Chapter 1). With Mills, though, the emphasis rests more on furthering imagination than on mustering force; in the long run we must arrange both a reliable source of motivation and ideas to sustain writing. Until writers learn to trust themselves as a faithful source of inventiveness, they continue to hesitate and doubt.

In this first glimpse at finding originality, I remind writers of encouraging points. First, we already know some ideal conditions for motivating ourselves to be imaginative: patience, comfort, and involvement. And second, we appreciate what misleads many writers into believing that they do not have strong imaginations: they have not learned that regular involvement in conversations and in information collecting precedes imagination. Neither motivation nor imagination has any good reason to appear out of the blue.

Then I add a caution or two. In some ways this transition from motivation to imagination is more demanding than it appears. While both tasks rely on regular habits of listening and preparing, imagination demands more effort and risk than does force. As we collect and arrange ideas for writing, we make planful, risky decisions about how to interpret and what to exclude. In particular, we notice patterns and associations with special promise. Imagination takes diligence and decisiveness.

Still, my experience tells me that this second major task won't be as difficult as most participants might imagine it. Once writers are involved and enjoying the stimulation of new ideas, they hardly notice the increased demands. Instead, most writers tell me that they are bothered more by old impediments--the temptation to wait passively for imagination, or to suddenly try to hurry and force it, or to simply put it aside while rushing to finish current tasks. These familiar embodiments of magic (passivity and impatience) are the demons hardest to exorcise from writing.

There is even more reason for optimism when we look closely at the alternatives to these problematic tendencies. When we give up passivity for more active, generative waiting, we shift naturally to listening, then collecting, and then imagining. And when we can do this while putting aside impatience, we encourage the conditions for creativity. New ideas come from old; new associations come with repetitions made from varied, playful perspectives.

Once I have stated and restated the rationale for finding imagination, I pause to reinforce the timeliness of this second task. Few writers, even those with their motivational routines working smoothly, have yet moved beyond learning to muster force at will; the confidence that they will almost always have imaginative things to say lies down the road. My role here, I usually note, is to guide them on one of the shortest, surest paths to that point.

For the moment, though, our new destination seems vague; the prospect of displaying imagination summons up insecurities. Inevitably, one or two people in a group restate a common and destructive prejudice that inhibits writers:

Now I can tell you what has been bothering me all along... I've been thinking that just about anyone can create enthusiasm and motivation--even patience and whatever. But when we get to the bottom line, maybe some of us will not be up to having anything to say. We might draw blanks. When I've blocked in the past, it hasn't been so much a problem of not feeling like writing as of not really feeling that I had something worth saying.

Somewhere I heard or read that the reason that most writers don't write is because they have nothing to say. I'm all too ready to agree that it applies to me, an unimaginative type if there ever was one.

With this sort of thing said, groups ventilate and commiserate. We have come, suddenly, to a blocking factor that hasn't yet found direct expression. We ask (much as you might): How can we write if we are unimaginative and uncreative? As a cloud of uncertainty begins to settle in, I try to move the discussion in a sunnier direction. I start by contending that we will not know how imaginative we can be until we involve ourselves in a set of proven strategies for arranging imagination. This is where C. Wright Mills and his kin come into play.

Mills on Finding Imagination

Groups at this juncture begin to work in concert, efficiently. Without much prodding from me or each other, they assign pairs of writers to each develop just one or two of Mills' ideas. The usual result, after collaborative editing, is a list of suggestions for building imagination like this:

1. Adding things to your idea files, at least weekly, helps keep projects fresh in mind and creates a regular habit of working at writing.
2. Collecting ideas cultivates the imagination; summarizing and rearranging them loosens the imagination and brings surprises (e.g., combinations of ideas that had seemed unconnected).
3. Fitting ideas into files tests their compatibility with developing themes; practice at inclusion and exclusion builds more decisiveness and lessens inclinations to suppose that everything known or read must be included.
4. Integrating new and old materials into files can be aided by playfully casting ideas into types, by finding new types via games (e.g., looking for extremes and opposites in materials; by cross-classifying ideas).
5. Making the habit of collecting into a daily activity leads to an ever-growing imagination.
6. And, in turn, a burgeoning set of ideas seduces writers into writing projects that have no formal, abrupt beginnings. Imagination involves writers in prose before they fully realize that they are beginning to write.

Reactions. Curiously, some of the writers who have already become the most involved in extracting lessons from Mills offer the most forceful reservations about them. This is a common hesitancy:

It might work, but only in fact for academic writers like Mills. They have to be current and scholarly, right? Professors have to know all the arguments and nuances and then come up with new twists on them, right? But my writing isn't at all like that. Science fiction writing is bounded only by the imagination, not by borrowing from other writers.

At least one other group member usually reinforces the point. People working at mysteries, scripts, detective stories, children's tales, novels, biographies, and technical writing have expressed similar skepticism. Do you, dear reader, take after writers who suppose that cautions and correctives apply to others but not to themselves?

This conversation also, inevitably, includes reservations about time and effort. The most vocal complainers in this category are the professorial writers:

Perhaps some dissertation writers need this. I don't. I know what I need to write. Sure, I will spend some time doing a computer search to see if I'm missing a relevant source. But I don't see myself taking time every week to work up a set of file cards and notes. . . . I don't intend to beat myself to death with a lot of busywork.

With these two kinds of reservations stated (about academic writing and about busywork), we quietly begin to share our perceptions about some limitations in what we have just said. The two writers just quoted illustrate the tendency toward reconsideration:

Well, for one thing, it isn't true that I don't worry about not being more imaginative. No doubt, I could benefit in paying more attention to ideas that I see in news articles and collecting and developing them. Instead, I think, I've launched myself into things where I had a good idea for a story line but too few of the details and creative links worked out. It seemed that those things should just happen as I wrote. They didn't, always. . . . You know, I actually made a move in this direction a few years ago. I began cutting out articles and newsclips with scenes and discoveries that I thought I might fit in with some of my ideas. I just threw them in a drawer. The problem was, I can see now, that when it came time to use them, I hadn't prepared them in any way and I didn't feel like plowing through the whole pile when I was trying to write.

Yes, I there is some [pause] irony in what I said earlier, about not having the time or needing more imagination. Who am I kidding? As things are right now, I'm still having trouble feeling that my writing will be original and innovative . . . and appealing. And the ten minutes or so that filing and annotating would take now and then, I could manage. I think now that a lot of my exception was a matter of not wanting to have to make writing so disciplined, so Prussian, so lacking in spontaneity.

When writers have provided their own arguments and counter arguments in this brief debate, there is a welcome recognition. They are, they realize, becoming better at spotting impatience and its close relation, insecurity. In this upbeat atmosphere, we feel confident in assigning ourselves a sampling of Mills' scheme.

Collecting and Casting Ideas into Types

We begin with a trial run, a communal task of collecting and organizing ideas with general relevance to all of us as writers. And, appropriately, we focus on ideas about finding imagination, as though we were readying ourselves to write about imagination. The following example of one group's file helps illustrate a simple solution to making sense of the myriad material we collected. What started as a seemingly disconnected assortment of ideas, each summarized on a separate page, began to fall into three general types:

1. First type = ideas about methods for notetaking.
2. Second type = notions that collecting leads to a more fluent imagination.
3. Third type = idea that work on imagination encourages clarity of writing.

How did we come to decide on labels such as these three for categories? Simply by drawing key words and associations from the sentences collected in our notes on ideas about imagination (" I like to decide by listening to how they sound, especially when I list them together; some fit in, some don't"). How did we settle on these three categories, at least tentatively? Merely by checking to see that they accommodated all the ideas that we wanted to categorize and that the headings usually encouraged placement of an idea in only one category. A typology that has no room for new ideas on the general topic is too narrow; a listing that does not help sort ideas into separate categories is of little use in drawing more general themes from distinctions and patterns.

Consider this sample of the methods we used to cast a large set of materials on imagination into the three types just listed (and its organization into semi-outline form):

1. Methods for translating notetaking into imagination

a. One strategy for notetaking while reading is called the double-entry method [2]. In its most exacting form, it has writers enter the essence of what they are reading onto the left half of their note pages and what they think about the reading on the right side. There are two complementary tasks here: summarizing what has been read on the left side, and entering succinct responses and associations to each left-hand entry on its right, specifically about how an idea relates to themes and planned projects.

The double-entry format helps writers (1) to make decisions about what is important enough to list from readings, (2) to add reflections about what makes those entries useful (perhaps using a format of free writing), and (3) to institute dialogues with themselves about how their readings and ideas tie in with other material. With practice at summarizing essences and provocations (with the aid of inner dialogue as an ongoing conversation about ideas), writers become skilled notetakers, annotators, and marginal commentators.

And with practice, something else happens: Most writers decide that not all of this formality is necessary once double entries are mastered; instead, many writers can manage by simply reading and noting their comments, initially in the margins of photocopies of what they are perusing, later upon separate pages to be filed, categorized, and cross-referenced.

b. Another strategy for note-taking that builds ideas and imagination is called the gist-and-list method [3, 4]. It helps us find the essential points in what we read: by way of playing with ideas, nutshelling ideas and then "teaching" them, treeing ideas in diagrams, and looking for cue words amongst sentences. In addition to these familiar notions of finding imagination, the list-and-gist strategy adds more: pushing ideas into new formats, new diagrams; pausing to consider where the scheme can go awry; imagining how audiences will react to the arrangements; and reading someone else's writing as though we had written it (and imagining how we would change its key points in a rewrite).

2. How patience translates into useful ideas

a. Successful writers learn time-saving ways of keeping collections of ideas and information from becoming overwhelming; imagination works best in moderation. One of the best ways to avoid "datacide" or "ideacide" relies on imagining audience responses to what we are writing and then, later, actually soliciting others' input about which ideas are most and least essential for delivering our message [5].

b. Research shows that the most creative, imaginative individuals display unique talents for avoiding premature closure; they put off final decisions about organizing ideas while maintaining high standards for

(1) the quality of the materials they collect and for (2) the purpose of collecting them [6]. In other words, they wait.

c. The point just made can be stated in yet another way: the most efficient writers learn not to give up too soon in searching their memories, in forming associations between memories and new ideas, and in forcing novel arrangements of ideas [7].

d. Imagination flourishes with regular exercise that extends beyond note-taking and writing; it also profits from everyday practice of mental imagery and inner speech (about outer things) as ways of seeing things differently (e.g., as opposites; from the view of someone with a very different style; even in terms of ideas organized as rhythms or melodies [8]).

3. How imagination leads to simplification including greater clarity

a. As writers practice noticing, organizing, and associating ideas, imagination becomes more controllable. When writers abandon the fiction that imagination lies hidden within them, they make room for a more manageable notion: that they can cultivate their imaginations with conscious acts of doing and collecting. This, in turn, means that writers can relax and make meaning when they want it, much as they find it, much as it reveals its own associations once on paper [7].

b. Collecting and organizing grow naturally into planning, and planfulness lies at the heart of clarity and purpose. One historical hero of clear writing, Count Georges de Buffon, supposed that planning not only dissolves confusion about where to begin projects but that it also brings special ease, pleasure, and a sense of life to writing. Another old hero, Alexander Pope, modeled the use of noticing and restating to achieve unusual compression of expression. Consider his clarity in depicting how imagination becomes originality: "What oft was thought, but ne'er so well expressed." [9]

c. With the planfulness of collecting and organizing comes encouragement for outlining. Outlines can be kinds of shorthand that help organize emerging ideas into visible, coherent wholes. As we see patterns, we can further enhance their clarity (e.g., when writers take care to develop ideas by alternating concrete cases and generalizations [10]). This act of collecting ideas into simplified patterns also provides a crucial aspect of imagination already mentioned, an enhanced sense of control over the material [11]. (Just ahead, I demonstrate one way of collecting and controlling material, by showing the vestiges of the outline, with its enumeration still visible, from which I worked.)

d. With control and expertise comes a sense of ownership; as writers manipulate the information they collect to suit their own purposes, they help make it their own [12], principally by simplifying and clarifying it while integrating it into their already existing collections. And as the ideas become more integrated and personalized, something even more curious happens. Writers become less concerned about finding and expressing perfectionism [13] and more ready to take risks in expressing themselves and in changing their plans. Why? Evidently because perfectionism thrives on an inner focus and diminishes when we turn from thinking to doing.

e. Finally, regular habits of cultivating imagination encourage efficiency of action; writers are prompted, as they attend to what works and what does not, to concentrate more on productive sources of ideas while "satisficing" elsewhere on activities that deserve no more than cursory attention [6]. Along with that tendency to sort out the useful, comes another act of easement. We not only become selective about the people to whom we look for ideas; we also become more tolerant in assuming, at least momentarily, their points of view [8].

Reactions. This exercise is no small matter. Nor does it promote immediate lucidity; the ideas just presented often generate confusion and doubts. The first reaction of writing groups, once having pared and presented a list such as this one, is always the same. The list seems overwhelming:

This bothers me because it seems like I'm back in college again. There seems to be too much to learn, to remember . . . and even then, it really isn't done. It still needs restating . . . or something.

Wouldn't everyone agree, this is too much? I had as much fun as everyone else putting together our list, but now I wonder if we have bitten more than we can chew.

Nonetheless, writing groups, once they have complained, move to a more patient and optimistic stance:

We're overreacting. We just need a break. There isn't so much to this list, not so much that is new. Think about it: If we do what the exercise prescribes, if we look for links between the list and what we already know, the whole thing seems less threatening, less overwhelming.

I don't think this can be any more confusing than what I've already been doing. Once I get used to it, I think, it can only help.

And, tellingly, other group members reinforce the need to proceed more confidently:

_____ is right. She is! Almost nothing on this list is totally novel. Look at it: Planning is old hat. Eh? So is collecting and note taking. We might not have called it delaying closure before, but it certainly fits in with our theme on patience. I wonder what we are so afraid of? Why are we so quick to back off and imagine that we can't hack it?

I agree. All that makes the conceptual outline difficult to read is that we still have to fill in some of the transitions and connections to what we're doing.

This series of interactions is a especially gratifying for me. Groups and individuals are slowly but surely "getting it." They are constantly stopping and challenging new ideas but then finding ways to incorporate them to tasks at hand. I remind myself that this sort of educational experience is what keeps me involved with writers. And I tell them much the same thing, particularly that I appreciate their hard work and openness. Then, with the groups having already done much of the work, I add two more points to the discussion about finding imagination.

In the first point I examine the reasons why writers typically do not know the rules of finding imagination. The roots of this unawareness, I argue, owe to usual practices of keeping tacit the most crucial knowledge about fluency [14]. Clearly, few of us were explicitly taught the skills of imagination in school. Yet we can easily envision how much easier and more instructive our formative writing assignments might have been had they focused on, say, beginning with systematic collections and conversations. What seems less obvious is why our schools leave topics such as motivation and imagination untaught, why they seem content to leave most writers struggling.

My own conclusion about this neglect is this: I believe that our society tends to see writing, when it can be managed with seeming spontaneity and mystery, as the ultimate test of brilliance. The true mark of genius and creativity, seemingly, is the ability to master imaginative writing without instruction or hard work. Writing, more than any activity I know, can bring out the elitist in us; we may expect only the very smartest and most talented of people to succeed at it. Accordingly, most of us who write fluently do little to share our knowledge about finding motivation and imagination.

In my second closing point, I offer a related reminder. When we put exaggerated value on writing that is managed quickly, spontaneously, independently, and brilliantly, we burden ourselves with unnecessary emotional baggage about writing. Such writing is possible but rare and it is, in fact, no better than more deliberate writing.

Elitism is a powerful constraint against adopting practical and visible methods for summoning up imagination. And, as a rule, it turns into insecurity and procrastination.

My own cautions elicit ready accounts of similar experiences from writers, stories that reveal a growing awareness about the perils of elitism:

When I can't write as fast and effortlessly as I want, I worry about not being as bright as some of the writers I admire. When I have to putz around figuring what I want to say, I feel that kind of impatience that is accompanied by the little voice that says I shouldn't have to struggle if I'm truly creative and smart.

So the point, then, is this? If we're going to do a good and patient job in the exercises for imagination, then we have put aside our old fears about being deliberate and hard working, right? . . . We may have to become geniuses the hard way. Pity.

EXERCISES FOR FINDING IMAGINATION

A reminder: The first set of treatment interventions (Chapter 1) focused on enhancing comfortable and patient involvement in writing contexts. The same exercises continue to hold importance here; motivation is as essential to prewriting tasks (such as collecting ideas and imagination) as it is to writing prose. This means that the same cautions about guarding against passive waiting and rushed forcing apply to finding imagination. And it means that the same strategy of progressing gradually and recursively remains in place; at times, the program moves with what seems the speed of the Long Island Railroad. This, I warn my writing groups (and you), demands loads of patience and involvement--in a word, motivation.

You may already know a reason for optimism in this leisurely pace of travel; if things go according to plan, we will end up with materials so close to written prose that the next transition will be easy and enjoyable. Typing the first draft will seem as much like rewriting as writing. And there is a method to this madness of gradualness; the plan is both simple and somewhat familiar, one designed to demonstrate its effectiveness with only the briefest of initial exposures. As usual, my groups launch themselves with brief discussions.

Discussions about Combatting Impatience

Consider what some writers find especially difficult at this point. Most of us would rather conjure single, quick drafts of what we want to write than spend a lot of time at prewriting. Writers, in my experience, need a way to put both short- and long-term benefits in perspective. We pause, my groups and I, to collect and list (what else?) what we have learned about impatience:

1. Rushing interferes with the calm and happiness essential to optimal problem solving (and, after all, finding imagination is a task in problem solving).
2. Writing without careful planning imposes the extra strain in composing of having to discover what can be said *while* saying it.
3. Trying to write before having established an involvement in ideas limits motivation for writing.
4. Richness of imagination, and of its relative, creativity, depends on delays in closure that are best filled with patient searches for ideas and plans.
5. Rushing is fatiguing and wasteful.

With this resaid (much as though we have just reformulated a set of ideas, with some slightly new ways of expressing them), we revisit one more crucial consideration: Pacing. We agree, my groups and I, that an ideal gait for prewriting will have at least the following properties: It will afford comfortable, reflective, and productive outputs. It will be moderate and steady, but occasionally variable. And an optimal pace for an entire project will properly be set now, during prewriting activities.

This, I add, is where we might profit in looking briefly at the data I collect about writers I find who are exceptionally comfortable, fluent, published, and admired: These exemplars have a unique predisposition. They, unlike, most other writers, generally spend as much time in formal prewriting (i.e., note-taking, filing, playing with ideas, and planning) as they do in writing and rewriting prose. My point, my groups graciously agree, has the quality of a memorable rule:

RULE #6: The most fluent, efficient, comfortable, and imaginative writers spend as much time at prewriting as at prose writing.

There is, in this sixth working rule, a nice reaffirmation of the value of patience. Writers generally agree it carries a ring of truth. But there is also a familiar worry here. Many of the writers I have known wonder, again, if this advice can be meant for them; after all, they may be as likely to dawdle while starting as while finishing a manuscript:

Oh, this might not work for me. No one could imagine how much time I can spend, once I'm nearly finished, looking again at the literature and worrying if what I have said has already been said or if I have plagiarized someone or if I have left something important out. Or how much time I can devote to making sure, before I even start in the first place, looking and relooking to make sure that I haven't missed anything remotely relevant.

:oncern doesn't prove too difficult for groups to counter; group
vo handy responses. One addresses the implicit assumption that
ng must be time wasted:

u're spending that time at the beginning or at the end doing really
constructive things--like planing or reviewing--it isn't so bad. Just spending it worrying,
of course, could be a waste. No one here, I think, is giving you license to spend lots of
your writing time worrying and obsessing (even though most of us may be guilty of
doing it at times).

The other response is just as simple:

One of the key things in Rule 5 is balance, I think. The idea is to spend about as much
time on preparation as for writing . . . . When you get to the point where the putting-off
of starting or finishing becomes disproportionate, you know you're out of bounds. That
you need to find help.

In the main, these answers help settle the fears of writers who are being
encouraged to take even more time with the peripheral aspects of writing. We
agree that we won't know how well we can curb old excesses until we immerse
ourselves in exercises on imagination.

Something else happens: The more we prewrite, the more we collaborate.
Over the years, writing groups have helped me produce a set of fairly consistent
steps for finding imagination.

STEPWISE EXERCISES FOR FACILITATING IMAGINATION

We start with familiar directives (e.g., moderation and balance). And, we
acknowledge that the written set of steps is only suggestive; different writers and
different tasks may require flexibility. From all this, we settle on a direct, blunt
writing style (one that provides a bare outline for individual elaboration):

Step 1: A scheme for depth and economy at notetaking.

Read and take notes in the kind of comfortable, scheduled format that we
have already practiced in generating motivation. Begin (ideally, but not
necessarily) with a new project, at the stage of involving yourself in the
literature and other conversations of the topic/genre. Make the practice of the
following subtasks a regular part of brief, daily sessions.

1. Ask other writers (by phone, writing, or in person) already in the
   conversation of your genre for suggestions of a reasonable reading list
   for you as a new entrant into a specific domain of writing. For

instance, ask for indications of readings that model excellence in terms of clarity, readability, or creativity; ask for hints about what writing is at the cutting edge in the field (or for classics); ask for examples of writing that have misfired. At the same time, share a sense of what ideas and themes you might pursue; most writers can provide you with ideas and sources especially relevant to your interest. And, many writers (especially leaders in the field) can give you a sense of whether or not you are on track with your ideas for a project.

From this preliminary exercise in collecting, make a reading list, and next to each entry add brief notes about why colleagues recommended each of the readings.

2. Take the stance of reading-to-write, as Linda Flower calls it [12]. That is, read with the conscious purpose of readying yourself to join the conversation of your genre. In this mode, practice the style of highly efficient readers who scan most copy and devote careful attention to only the most relevant sections of the material [15]. Add occasional checks for the thoroughness of your perusals by rescanning the reading to see if you select the same passages as most relevant.

Experiment in deciding what kinds of passages will be most useful to you as a writer. Some writers collect examples of prose that model clarity or insight. Some writers look for ideas that resemble their own, some for things that could be related but only with reflection. And some writers look for contraries to serve as reminders of what not to do, or as prompts of how they might think differently.

3. As you read-to-write, take notes to use in the writing. Some notes might well be excerpts, copied word-for-word, that capture the mood or style of a source (always, of course, set in quotation marks and with the page numbers for the quote entered at the end of each quote; most plagiarism owes to poor bookkeeping). Some notes can condense or translate the essence of what you are reading, usually but not always in terms of its relevance to what you will be writing (interpretations of what you are reading and thinking can come later). And some notes will consist largely of reminders of what you may want to do in your own manuscript. When you reread these notes, you will be stimulated to think of things beyond the material in front of you. But without setting down enough cues to remember what you are thinking now, whole trains of thought can be lost with unsettling swiftness.

Many writers like to vary the format for note-taking: Common practices include writing pages of notes by hand (sometimes with diagrams and sketches), pausing while reading to make entries on a word processor, retyping scribbled notes onto note cards, or reentering notes into software systems that help file and organize collections. In the long run, at least in my programs, writers tend to settle into one main format, of handwriting notes on note paper for later filing and marginal notation. The usual goal in making these notes is to limit them to a single, readable page of entries.

4. As you read-to-write, engage in a writerly conversation with yourself. Carry on a dialogue by responding to what you have noted and written with still more notes [perhaps by entering asides and afterthoughts in brackets].   Reinsert the notes you had made earlier about why colleagues recommended readings and about your reactions to their ideas.   Look back at related notes and add comments about interconnections. And allow yourself the luxury of entering occasional bits of the prose that you may eventually write. Substantial, crucial collections of interconnections belong on separate pages.

5. Set fairly firm limits on how much time you will devote to reading and capsulizing a resource. Common allocations run from five-fifteen minutes for news articles to one-three hours for a book. But keep guidelines flexible; encounters with particularly rich resources may merit far more time and many more revisits.   Other sources may deserve no more than the minimum--full bibliographic citations at the top but only a few words as a reminder about why the sources seemed unimportant.

   Set limits about lengths of notes; working within a usual constraint (say, one page per resource) helps focus notes on the most essential ideas. Some writers take this limit so seriously that they revise notes by editing out all but the most indispensable entries (often while adding more reflections of their own).

6. Put all notes into a standardized format with the source fully listed at the top. Enter classification codes at the top of each page to permit easy indexing. And, make copies (via photocopy or printing from microprocessors) of your note pages so that you can carry your collections with you for reading and annotating during free time. Many writers find unique perspectives when they take collections of note pages to quiet places (e.g., the special collections room of libraries), to the outdoors, even to discordant contexts (e.g., to train or taxi rides).

7. File collections according to categories that prove most inclusive and useful. Experiment. If new material cannot be incorporated, file labels might need expanding; if, again, materials commonly fit in more than one category, the categories may be too indiscriminate; if resulting subcollections do not suggest new ways of seeing associations in collections, the typologies probably are not imaginative enough. Writers often find that they can judge the usefulness of filing systems in another way, a kind of exteriorizing, of putting the typology and

brief descriptions of the contents of each into a visible format (even a drawing or diagram); when the elements seem to fit together in a sensible, useful pattern, the scheme is working.

8. Make summary lists of sections/categories based on only the most crucial ideas and begin to add notes about overall themes and special details that can become a part of your writing. In other words, begin looking for story lines or patterns of argument at local levels and then combine them into a larger plan. At the same time, record your thoughts about useful particulars such as scenes or insights that will help bring direction and substance to the general plan. These acts initiate the transformation of a simple outline (i.e., one that merely lists) into a conceptual outline (i.e., one that lists and gists).

9. Explore alternatives in notetaking--for example, try free writing as a method for generating essences of what you have just read. This is an instance of notes made as an aside, on scratch paper by a writer in the program:

I'm reading this and I know somehow that it must be relevant, but how? I need to concentrate. Look for things that impress or puzzle me. To imagine what this writer could teach me about writing a biography about a public creature. Could it be that this biographer seems at times visible and at times invisible? At just the right times? What he does well, I imagine, is to use the supposed narrative of two friends to talk for him. As when they are planning the trip. This covers his speculations about things that don't seem contestable, that are easily imagined. Then when he, this fluid biographer, steps back into view it is to present more the credibility of documents and records, to let readers sense the digging that lies behind his interpretations.

And, use alternatives in notetaking to get past some usual writing blocks.

10. Finally, alternate prewriting with prose writing to avoid the danger of staying in prewriting too long. Even while immersed in the beginnings, occasionally pause to put your ideas into approximate prose. Free write. As you proceed with notetaking, move more and more outward away from overreliance on prewriting. Constantly remind yourself not to remain in prewriting too long (and that you need take notes on every possible source before moving toward prose).

Writers not only become stuck, in a way, by perfectionistically staying in the notetaking phase too long. Just as often, in my experience, they flounder when trying to make order out of a collection of complex ideas. When this happens,

outlines do not work. At those times, I ask them to list and gist while talking
aloud about their reflections on what they are reading. I listen and I encourage,
taking notes on what they say that could be useful, and read them back for
transcription. Just as often, someone else from a group assumes my role. An
example [with the coach's abstracted record of what the writer was saying while
thinking aloud during the procedure] appears next:

*[Let's see what is here; I like to look for the three main points. Two of them are obvious
because they appear in the title and in the major headings. What's first?]*
   1. Diets are a national institution
   --dieters spend a fortune; some programs are longstanding
   2. Diets have never been proven effective for most dieters
   *--most dieters actually gain weight as they move from diet to diet, bingeing to regain
what they have just lost and more*
   [Now, now what? Oh, the conclusion can be the third point, I think.]
   3. The best known alternative to dieting is not dieting
   --nondieters not only gain less extra weight over the long run, they can feel better

This is only a first approximation, but it suffices to show how easily the process
works. Once observers read back their notes on a writer's thinking and
noticing, the next steps come naturally. The writer can continue to think aloud
in subsequent sessions while reorganizing his or her notes into more elaborate
lists and gists, gradually taking over the role once played by an external
observer. If that proves temporarily awkward, we add the convenience of a tape
recorder from which ongoing thoughts can be transcribed once gisting and listing
are completed for a session. Readers, in my experience, can practice similar
exercises, alone or with a partner.

Consider the real-life example just depicted. By the next session, with the
writer herself assuming the tasks of internal and external observer, that list grew
to four main points (the new, penultimate point, became one of why diets
commonly fail) and to include many more supporting gists. She was, to
paraphrase Donald Murray (Chapter 1), writing before writing.

A final example of useful alternatives in notetaking is journal keeping. Daily
entries, typically made during reflective moments in evenings, include thoughts
about what was written earlier and about what lies ahead. These musings, many
writers assure me, create special opportunities for imagination that can be used
directly or indirectly. This example is from the journal of a novelist in the habit
of journaling near bedtime:

I've just imagined a chorus of faces, all the people who have given me quotes about what
it is like to be a writer on leave in a university. I can, more or less, hear them all at
once, in near concert. They have a special message for me. I must listen. I must listen.

The crux in becoming more imaginative is practice and openness; imagination requires a regular suspension of disbelief. It also depends on regular recordings of the thoughts and stimuli that lead up to writing. Without recordkeeping, we may fail to notice things, we may forget what we do notice, and we will certainly shortchange our potentials for imaginative juxtapositions. One more thing helps. The writers who seem to fare best as note takers take the biggest risks. Reconsider the example, just cited, of the writer who is thinking of her interviewees as a collective chorus (this time, as spoken to me, a week after she had made that entry):

What amazes me about having entered and then using that wonderful image, is this: even as I first made the note, it frightened me. I almost hesitated because it isn't, wasn't, the sort of thing I usually put down in writing. . . . This is how I am becoming more imaginative.

Because notetaking is, in some ways, novel and discomfiting, I take special care to coach writers through its practice. I sometimes sit with individual writers, usually at their own writing sites, and ask them to talk aloud as they work at taking notes. Eventually, after a session or two, I assign this role of observer/recorder/encourager to partners in twosomes or threesomes from the writing groups. Curiously, even writers who have not yet put this insight into effective practice can provide useful prompts for others. In the next subsection, I sample the accounts of writers struggling with the steps just prescribed for note taking.

Reactions to exercises for notetaking. Every writer I have known has struggled with some aspect of these exercises in notetaking. Every writer, upon struggling, expressed surprise at laboring over what had seemed so simple a directive. Each clustering of assignments (see list above) and their reactions deserves its own, brief mention.

1. About asking other writers in the conversation for suggestions of useful reading: Many writers spoke of reservations about taking the time for such requests or about imposing on others:

This was the hardest part for me. I don't like to impose on people. Not on busy, successful writers like Henry or Gardner.

But as one or two group members reported success (e.g., appreciative acceptances of colleagues put to the request), this barrier was quickly overcome:

When I thought about my own reaction to being asked for help I realized that I am always, almost without exception, happy to oblige. Then too I realized an old pattern in myself. I always feel reluctant to ask for help of any kind. That is just plain stupidity. All three of the people I wrote and then called gave me lists and then said that they enjoyed the task. They found it stimulating. Something they should do themselves.

2. & 3. About reading-to-write and extracting only the most relevant ideas: This directive produced frequent resistance and inclined some writers to suppose that it was nothing but an exercise in superficial scholarship. Most commonly it produced apprehension about being able to scan and quickly spot the essentials. Signs that such concerns were being resolved came in comments like these:

Why did I stop complaining that this method was tantamount to shallow preparation? Easy. I found that, if anything, it kept me more on focus and more in depth. When I gave my closest attention to only a few ideas, there was more depth of understanding than I expected. Before, I always tried to read too much. I took reams of notes, most of it useless. [In response to my question, how did you get past the obstacle of not being able to decide quickly on what to note in your readings?] Uhm, I think I know. What helped was a thing that got brought up in group, about reading like a reporter who has to gather a quick but accurate picture. This is how it worked for me: As I read along, I imagined myself, while I scanned every paragraph, keeping up a running commentary about the plot line and what the interesting interludes were. . . . It really wasn't hard, once I gave myself this imaginary reporting job.

4. About carrying on dialogues with oneself in response to what was being read: The strategy just depicted (of becoming a reporter for imaginary readers) and others like it (e.g., imagining oneself as the author of what is being read and making inferences about how some things were done commendably) work nicely. There are few lasting bewilderments about this exercise.

5. About fitting notes into usual limits of one page and one brief time period of working: This assignment produced the most resistance of any step in notetaking. At first, disbelief dominated:

Initially, you know, I couldn't believe that *everything* of note could be portrayed in a page or less. I believed that my own careful efforts would end up as pages and pages of notes, just as always. Immediately things came to mind, whole series of passages from Truman Capote, that could not be fairly represented in such a niggardly allotment of space.

But once writers were induced to try pulling out essences of ideas, reports almost invariably changed:

I'm glad you suggested a compromise. I felt pretty stubborn about not sacrificing or artificializing some things. But as I saw that I could refer to the essentials with a brief characterization (and page numbers) that would encourage me to look back at the original, something else became clear. It turned out that for most purposes, the briefs work more than well enough. Sometimes better, because they put me more into the role as interpreter, translator.   Not to mention how much easier they are [than indiscriminately expansive notes].

6. About transferring notes to pages that can be carried about for reflection in varied settings: No one objected to this assignment.   But the majority of writers in my programs put off its actual practice; few writers are in the habit of making writing portable.   Even over the next month or two, only a few brave souls made a custom of carrying their collections with them for contemplation and annotation during their forays away from homes, offices, and other familiar writing sites.   Some of the nonpractitioners sensed the reason that kept them from making their writing more portable:

It's basically compartmentalization.   I, for one, like to keep my writing separate from other things.   It's something I had done only in a few specified places.   It's something that can come to seem manageable only on a word processor; it has for me.   (At one point, I actually wondered if I could still do much writing by hand.)   The act of fitting writing in among the other things I do, while I'm sitting on a park bench, would seem strange, almost indecent.

6. & 7. About indexing and filing: These exercises, predictably, elicited complaints about time and busyness.   In the end, two things helped writers adopt practices of indexing pages and then sorting them in constantly revised file categories.   One aid came as testimonials from experienced writers who were brought in from outside the writing groups.   These people spoke, among other things, about the long-term value of notes that can be used over and over again in new projects.   The other thing that helped grew from reports emphasizing the stimulation value of categorizing materials into types of ideas:

I'm basically so lazy and filing makes me concentrate on how things differ and resemble each other, and on how they interrelate.   It has proved a pleasant surprise because it really works to make me more ingenious and it is fun.

8. & 9. About making notes on notes and experimenting with formats of notetaking: These difficult assignments evoked only moderate resistance, perhaps because writers were already involved in note taking by this point. Something else may have contributed to the popularity of these exercises; they produce ready results:

Not until I was making summaries of what was in the notes for certain categories did it all become useful and make sense.   This is a surprisingly neat way to see patterns and to straighten out my thoughts.

Maybe this isn't what I'm supposed to say but what I like best is journal keeping.   Each evening I make a kind of report about my progress as a writer--progress as a person and progress in my story. This writing has provided my first real feeling of peacefulness and imaginativeness as a writer. That's important, to me.

10. About pausing while notetaking/collecting for occasional forays into prose: This caution produced deceptive results for a long time. Writers who reported general success sometimes proved to be far behind other journeyers who had essentially put notetaking behind them. The specific problem wasn't that writers were doing nothing but notetaking. Rather, they were reporting other activities (e.g., outlining; prose writing) but still feeling unable to move beyond never-ending notetaking. When this hidden pattern was at last uncovered, the reaction was usually a mixture of guilt and surprise. Writers in this dilemma agreed about what helped most: the act of occasional pauses to free write how notes would turn into prose.

Step 2: Shaping ideas into imagination.

With a good set of notes abuilding (and without waiting for a complete, perfect collection), the time for Step 2 is already at hand. While the mechanical act of collecting and filing ideas produces many new perspectives, we can do more. The prescriptions we saw earlier from C. Wright Mills help orient us in a chart for further action:

1. Use brief, daily sessions (even five-ten minutes in the midst of daily schedules) as times for deliberate exercises of revisiting, annotating, and reorganizing your notes. This time is not usually meant for entering new notes; it is more for noticing and planning.
2. During these brief sessions, experiment with schemes for organizing ideas into diagrams and themes that can become outlines and/or plot lines for manuscripts. Draw actual designs and maps to see how things fit together; use free writing to find out what themes you can express.
3. Make a conscious effort to delay closure in these sessions. Practice patience by spending more time at playful reconfiguring, particularly at times when patterns and themes seem settled upon. Post a sign, like Kafka's, that says "Wait."
4. If you get stuck at organizing your ideas, work up a second, related project; the cross-transfer of ideas may help unblock you. Or the experience might convince you that the first project is abandonable.
5. Set deadlines for cutoff points where, ready or not, you will go public with your working materials. While you should caution your friends and colleagues that your ideas are still formative, you can legitimately ask for useful feedback about what works and doesn't in your schemes. In particular solicit specific comments about what you have

done well (compliments are valuable) and about what you might do better: Have you missed something? Are you right in suspecting that some ideas aren't fully developed or interconnected at one point or another? Does the organization seem obvious, and involving?

6. If you want to work at the task of collecting on your computer, find someone knowledgeable about software packages that file materials and ease the task of accessing and rearranging them [16, 17, 18, 19, 20]. But, at the same time, set firm limits on time invested per day in learning and practicing computer technologies; both software and journal keeping have remarkable potentials for engaging writers in habits that become ends in themselves.

Reactions to Step 2. Resistance to this second step comes typically in two parts. One relates to demands for another regularly scheduled session each workday, no matter how brief the exercise. The second concern is about exposing one's ideas, still provisional, to public scrutiny. Both reservations, curiously, come down to one basic issue, of taking the practice of writing outside its usual bounds. There is, for instance, no real problem in finding another five minutes during afternoons for sessions in imagination. Instead, the strain lies in distributing writing as bits and pieces (in between doing other, quite different things). A related concern is about usual needs for warm-up time:

You can't really expect me to shift gears into my writing so suddenly when I've just been directing a meeting. I need some time to get back into the mindset of a writer and that takes a lot more time than five minutes, I can tell you.

As usual, practice makes for belief; as writers show a willingness to try brief, daily sessions (bds) for finding imagination, I hear more reports of rewarding discoveries. At the same time, writers make two other points: First, even in so brief a format as the imagining sessions, there is time and need for exercises in relaxation and pacing. And, second, yet another thing saves time that might have been spent in warm up: when writers re-create summary notes and diagrams and combine them with new jottings and sketches, they reimmerse themselves in a project within moments. Together, these reflections lead to an important realization about what helps:

I want to mention the thing that matters most. I have become so involved in my writing and my imagination exercises that I often find myself thinking about ideas and plans during other parts of the day. It's quite pleasant, really . . . far better than the usual stuff that creeps into my consciousness. Anyway, the point is that because I think so much about the project, I need no time for warm-up.

Not only don't I need warm-up time any more, but I find myself getting excited about spending my little times on organizing. It reminds me of having a nice afternoon affair.

I'll tell you all something funny about this. It can have a downside, one that doesn't bother me too much. I think that I may seem a little more absent-minded as I walk around deep in thought and reverie.

Two other practices help foster imagination, in my experience. In group meetings we make a point of checking up on each other's regular involvement in afternoon imagination exercises. So, when we have trouble staying on schedule or making progress, we arrange social contracts for daily calls to partners. And, as usual, we look to published sources of strategies for finding imagination. We often settle on the book *Thinking on Paper* [21], as one guide. Its authors, V.A. Howard and J.H. Barton, begin with a familiar format, a version of free writing that directs readers to literally think on paper. Carrying out this kind of free writing illustrates what can be said readily and what still needs to be said. Howard and Barton also suggest additional moves in organizing the outflow of ideas. All of the moves are based in planning:

1. Plan to devote at least one paragraph to every major idea or argument;
2. plan necessary concessions to the opposition as soon as possible (e.g., find ways to suggest that you understand and accept at least part of the resistance you face); and,
3. plan connections and transitions between paragraphs and sections.

We also, my groups and I, resort to our old habit of looking for scholarly bits of advice. An example: Joanne Kurfiss' conclusion that experts draw general themes and plans first, before addressing specific details such as sentence wording [22]. "What that means is," as one writer put it, "that experts not only delay closure, they also solve the right problems." That level of understanding calls for a move to the next set of exercises.

Step 3: Preparing useful outlines.

I always stress the word "useful" when discussing outlines. Most writers, I learned early on, associate outlining with mechanical listings that were unpleasant to assemble and unlikely to find much willing use. What we need, most of us, is a reintroduction to outlining as something that flows naturally and helpfully from collecting and imagining.

Like any other prewriting habit, outlining works best when kept moderate and approximate. Useful outlines don't try to do too much; optimally, they need provide little more than intermediate summaries of what we plan to do and say (when we move to prose). The easier and more obvious the access to ideas and themes, the easier the actual writing will be. Thus, outlines properly begin in tentative fashion, as lists and gists; with some elaboration, they present cues about our own slant on ideas and some ordering for presenting them [20].

Outlines can be made especially useful by rewriting them to approximate, more and more closely, the prose they foreshadow. To capture the essence of an idea, many writers simply imagine that they have been assigned the task of verbally describing it to a friend, simply and succinctly. After they actually speak their synopsis, they write it. And when they have done much the same for each idea, they repeat the process as a way of expressing how ideas fit together into paragraphs, sections, chapters, and so on.

The result is a format for outlining where each listed point is accompanied by a brief description of what it means and how it connects. It becomes a conceptual outline. For example:

B. The immigrant experience for Chinese women can be separated into three generations.
--i.e., while the three successive groups of women are not really different generations of mothers and daughters, each is a separate cohort that regards the other as definitely of a different time and mentality

   1. First generation daughters were . . .
   --i.e., they experienced America through the eyes of . . .

Three things seem especially helpful in drawing out this sort of elaboration. One is perusing notes and recollections about a point and using that information to free write a first, crude approximation to what you might say in prose. Patience helps encourage the crucial act of waiting while we figure out what can be said. The second aid to elaboration is just as simple; outlines profit in rewriting. Done properly, each revision becomes more elaborate and closer to actual prose (e.g., see the "i.e.," under "B," just above), all the while retaining the freedom for change. The third and most important facilitator is a tolerance for proceeding without having completed some points. Temporary voids (actual holes in outlines) exemplify the rule of proceeding before feeling fully ready. These voids do deserve close attention, however; writers work efficiently when they at least enter a note about what thoughts had come to mind while being unable to make sense of an idea or cluster.

As I present these notions of conceptual outlining to writers, I include a variety of examples. No matter how winsomely I do this, though, most writers struggle and resist, often with what seems like amazing density to me. Often they don't begin to catch on until I immerse them as onlookers in my own writing.

For readers of this book, I offer an analogous experience in duplicating an actual conceptual outline. It is, prior readers have told me, a peculiar but helpful experience. In what follows, I share this section of my outline in whole. I also include the asides that I entered both at the time of outlining, and later, during reflective periods. [Those dialogues with myself appear here, just as they do in my outlines, in brackets.]

A Sample Outline (from this section of the book)

3. Step 3. Preparing Useful Outlines (emphasize the word useful; most writers write without outlines or ignore them):
--most writers learn to use and dislike outlines as stiff, mechanical devices [so much so that many of them may not read this part]

a. Useful outlines demonstrate two familiar principles:
1) the value of moderation and approximateness
--the best outlines are intermediate summaries easily accessed during writing (see Kozma, 1991) [20]
--the easier and more obvious the access to ideas, the easier the writing
--outlines need not do too much, just list, gist, and cue
2) outlines become more useful when they are rewritten for clarification and expanded to descriptions of what will be said [is this point valid in the saying, or do I need to add more explanation about why it is true?]
b. Even when writers are convinced that conceptual outlining can be useful, they express uncertainty about how to proceed
[acknowledge what a real, nuisancesome sticking point this is]
--model some outlining of this sort, first from a program participant, then, perhaps, from my own writing [Will this disrupt the flow of the chapter? Check later to see.]

3. Step 4. Striving for Balance
--the point is to extend the notion, just presented, that balance and moderation apply here, to outlining, just as much as to other parts of writing
--related point: make this a summing-up, a set of prompts about prewriting that readers will want to look back at

a. first priority: maintain collecting and rearranging as an enjoyable task
--see Marshall & Durst, 1986, re. writers who find pleasure in triggering associations as part of preparation [23] . . . and re. readers who prefer writers able to project a voice of active involvement
b. second priority: aim for increasing clarity
--see Gopen and Swan, 1990, for a message about the import of planning every unit of discourse to make only a single point [24]; too often as we rush, we try to insert a complex of ideas into a single unit
[problem: should I present an admonition that I am not sure I follow myself? I guess I could say that I'm trying and that I'm learning as I am doing and clarifying things]
--add a participant's comment in excerpt here, something that addresses the awkwardness of proceeding with this rule (e.g., see notes, #87-17-98, re "not wanting to work with another composition teacher")
c. third priority in outlining: continuing to build involvement/motivation
--Bloom (1992) argues for involvement augmented by witnessing [an idea I introduced earlier, briefly . . . check to see where]; i.e., we should write only on subjects that fully engross us, that invite readers to join in on our excitement, that impel us to take

risks as writers and that invite readers to take risks as readers [25] [good wording, keep some of it . . . but make sure it's mostly mine]

--Bloom, an intriguing, imaginative, risky writer, adds a bit of self-disclosure about what all writers aim for in a quote from Joan Didion: "listen to me, see it my way, change your mind" [26]

[I like this quote, but what does it mean here? Does it demonstrate or witness the risk of coming out and admitting why we write? Is it really true, for me at least? I guess the point has something to do with putting provocative ideas into the outline that can make me think and re-see. I'll solve this problem by inserting a representative quote or two from the groups and see how this clump comes out. I'll have to check back to be sure of what the groups thought of Didion's confession.]

[I checked: they loved it for its disarming honesty, "something worth aiming for, from time to time, in an otherwise boring task." #91-3-51]

d. look back and plan ahead while outlining [and enter marginal notes for future reference]

1) i.e., periodically revisit the general diagram of your plan and consider if you are on track in terms of making your points clearly, economically, and in a stimulating arrangement

2) at the same time, plan for likely roadblocks in building imagination

[one possible example: if I do carry out my thought of inserting this particular outline material into the text, will I have presented enough of what I am thinking and feeling that might help illustrate how conceptual outlining actually works for me? I guess the potential roadblock I could demonstrate with this concern is not working with clear goals in mind. I need to more clearly work with the goal of presenting just enough and making it clear]

--Flower & Hayes (1977) provide instances of likely roadblocks: reader's negative attitudes, and gaps in our own knowledge [4] [how should writers address these obstacles while outlining? By acknowledging them; by continuing to work at reading/notetaking and, so, adding essential information; and by tying in the new material by using the exercises in imagination for contrasts and comparisons, etc.]

--another point about anticipating roadblocks: most writers, in my experience, can predict the spots where they will stumble with surprising accuracy (like dowsers?)

-- to illustrate, depict the list provided by one group that worked together communally to outline some points about likely hurdles in outlining:

a) first roadblock--at the beginning of outlining, editing and looking for perfection too soon;

b) roadblock at the midpoint of outlining--wearying at the prospect of long projects and of having to imaginatively organize a lot of material; and,

c) toward the end of outlining--beginning to rush and run out of motivation, succumbing to temptations to binge at outlining or to turn to something else that has been put off during outlining.

d) at any point--impatience.

--add groups' communally derived solutions (combine the two sets on note page four) for planfully preventing these predictable problems, all of them already part of the

program (i.e., patience, pacing, comfort, and more patience . . . but, most of all, discovering that this act of constructive waiting pays off).

--Several good quotes from participants come to mind. Locate them and make sure that they are representative of the larger sample. [later: when assembled, they don't work; what follows seems sufficient]

--a related insight reported by many group members: learn, even during outlining, to spot catastrophizing and to replace it with wise passiveness; i.e., when panicking about making too little progress in the face of a large task, simply take pleasure in doing something constructive with the moment, such as noticing your progress in conceptualizing ideas and plans; when panicking about not making sense of something, pause, relax, and think back to recent successes at finding essences and links. Think, "How did I do it then?" If that fails, free write.

e. bds

--close out this section with a reminder of what may seem most unnatural here: approaching outlining as an extended, oft-revised act carried out in brief, daily sessions (and not, for the most part, in one or a few bursts of quickly forgotten planning).

--an equally important point is about establishing the regular habit of outlining and prewriting; add Tremmel's observation that writers don't feel like writers until they practice writing regularly [27]; evidently, the same feeling grows with regular practice at conceptual outlines.

--and, allude to Perkins, conclusion that regular immersion in thinking and noticing increases the probability of seeing connections and gaps, etc. . . . of becoming imaginative and creative [6].

--and, possibly, add some of the rules for finding creativity here; outlining is not too early a stage to begin arranging for this outgrowth of imagination

[later: maybe not; while the point about installing the conditions for creativity early (e.g., not identifying too closely with initial ideas, maintaining high standards of excellence for the product) is valid, this may overload writers who are still struggling with conceptual outlining. On the one hand: I can't include every interesting idea that comes to mind. On the other hand, this is the best place to begin to build creativity.]

--perhaps, as in the program, the mention of finding creativity here could be preliminary . . . just one point with obvious application to outlining:

1) Rothenberg (1990) on "janusian" processes as conscious and rational and essential to creativity: "multiple opposites are simultaneously, either as existing side by side or as equally operative, valid, or true. . . . What emerges is no mere combination or blending of elements . . . a leap that transcends ordinary logic" [28 (p.15)].

[notice that his wording is initially confusing . . . deliberately?]

--i.e., this kind of juxtapositioning can be practiced deliberately in outlining, perhaps more readily than anywhere else; Rothenberg claims that without it, writers cannot be creative.

--groups, I see in my notes, had interesting reactions to Rothenberg's notion; quote one or two of them (at least the one that typifies the sense that we only need the vaguest sorts of appreciations of how to find creativity at the moment; "are not our creative efforts at imaginativeness a good beginning?" # 88-2-190)

[do I need to worry that this quote sounds too articulate to have been spontaneous? No.]

Reactions to this shared outlining. The strongest reaction to interspersing my outlining into my finished prose, in early drafts of this book, was my own. I disliked having to put the conceptual outline into the prose that it portended; it was too redundant, even in a book full of repetition. Early readers agreed with me and, so, I have deleted the prose version of most of the foregoing outline. I am told that the outline, fittingly, works well enough to say what I would have said in more usual sentences and paragraphs. (It also reminds my groups and me of the growing sense among academic and technical writers that the terse and enumerated style of some foreign-born authors writing in English may be the format of the future. It suffices, it permits ease of reading, and it offers a ready sense of organization. But does it lose heart?)

You may sympathize with the reactions from writers most recently engaged in these exercises for finding imagination. Salient was its initial foreignness:

It created some discomfort. It reminded me of the things you see where you learn how special effects were made in movies like *Star Wars*. It can be disillusioning, or maybe boring. Not as good as discovering who the wizard is in Oz. . . . But this is admittedly a bit different because it is helpful to know how a writer actually plans and carries out this conceptual outlining.

A related anxiety was about disclosiveness:

Doesn't it worry you that you have made the mechanisms of your writing so public and so, well, simple? It might me. . . . You, have, in a way, exposed a vulnerable part of yourself to us.

Before I even try to answer, group members take on the responsibility; I am relieved. Here is what becomes the consensus: This a time when we realize, all of a sudden, that self-consciousness of this sort is no friend of writers; we anticipate that there is much to be gained in making our prewriting public. As we continue our discussions, we do the next logical thing. Most of us share our conceptual outlines and talk about how the material will translate in prose. In a flash, it seems, self-consciousness is displaced by interest about the variety of ways in which writers approach conceptual outlining. There is a fascination over the ease with other people can see different, and often better, ways of making our points.

Some surprises inevitably emerge about the elaborate but generally useful planning that a few writers carry out. Two participants from my recent groups sketched drawings of scenes and characters as parts of their conceptual (and visual) outlines. Two built casual scale models, both unknowingly in the style, more or less, of Sinclair Lewis modeling his *Main Street*. And one other put his plot lines (with parenthetic descriptions) on a continuous roll of brown wrapping paper (knowingly like Jack Kerouac writing *On the Road*). Still, for all the liberation and imaginativeness that conceptual outlining can bring, it continues to elicit serious questions at this point in the journey. Six types of doubts stand out in the aggregate of groups' discussions on this topic:

1. *Is it all necessary?* Questioners begin by asking, "Is this all indispensable, all this writing of preliminary stuff, where nothing is left to the imagination once you get down to writing?" And, they wonder if some of the description and detail couldn't more economically be left in their heads, to be poured out as prose, to be refined in rewriting.

This hesitation is so predictable that I have a well-rehearsed answer at the ready, one based on my own research studies with prior sets of participants: When writers take the time to concoct thorough and stimulating outlines, they spend less time completing projects overall than they do on projects with minimal prewriting. To reinforce this last point, I cite the comments of writers who have, under my unrelenting scrutiny, tried projects both ways. For example:

The reason that the outlining with approximations works better seems simple once you've tried it once or twice. When you have done the conceptual outlining well and imaginatively, the writing is a snap. It's really just rewriting because you don't have to struggle to find ideas, just to say them a bit more clearly.

2. *How do you know what is best to say about points when you've only just thought of them?* I advise writers to use the strategies we have already seen. I model for them how I imagine (by thinking aloud my imagination) that I'm reporting to a notetaker. As I list points, I make tentative guesses about the relevance of why I am adding ideas. As I gist the ideas themselves, I put them in my own words. In this first approximation to an outline, I aim for little more than getting a few words or associations in place to guide a re-draft.

Then I add an important pair of points while thinking aloud to the group: Rewrites are always easier, if properly prepared, than first writes. And when we wait before conjuring more definite statements, we delay closure.

3. *Why take the trouble to note asides?* This question is the most direct of many queries about why we shouldn't leave more to our memories. Here too, I have data to buttress what will eventually be more obvious. Writers who talk-aloud asides while outlining (so that I can record their thinking) but who do not write them down, forget far more of them by the time they write prose than when they record asides. Outliners who enter thoughts and ideas into written notes and outlines always have reminders at hand, and almost always remember their relevance. The few moments spent making extra notes pay handsome

dividends because notes are far better sources of imagination than are our unreliable memories.

4. *Isn't so thorough and extensive a plan constraining?* This is a good question; outlines can limit and even misdirect. So it is that many of us have learned to distrust them. But this memory often ignores the reality that decisions about directions and goals must be made sometime. Conceptual outlining simply advances some of the task of decisiveness to an earlier stage, one where alternatives are more visible and more likely to be tried and retried.

This objection also overlooks the outcomes of extending outline revisions/refinements into regular sessions for reflection. Done efficiently, outlining and planning continue, on a modest level of a few minutes per day, even as we involve ourselves in prose writing. When writers do this, they discover two things: how well the plan works; and new ideas.

In practice, then, conceptual outlining can provide even more flexibility than does its absence. And, again, it encourages a reasonable limit on indecisiveness about settling on themes and directions. It even, with its carefully laid plans, helps limit the sidetracks that distract us and our readers.

5. *Should outlining await the completion of collections?* Asked another way, this question addresses the problem of how we will know when we have enough ideas to begin outlining. My own studies indicate that writers need wait no longer than having enough material to create an inviting scheme for categories and for making sense of them. Most writers, in my experience, can generate impressive outlines simply by speaking aloud about what they will probably do.

My advice here, oddly, is not to wait. It is never too early to join a conversation in the sense of planning what we may say and interesting ways of saying it. But what then, I am typically asked, about the distraction of working with so many gaps in our plans? Here too, you probably know, the answer is already familiar, one that needs occasional restating. Where the growing outline indicates holes in our knowledge or understanding, we have an economical sense of what more we need to read and note. Where the outline doesn't fall into coherency, we know that we need to work more at collecting and imagining...or that we may need a new scheme for organizing.

The essential point here is this: We get better results from outlines when we stop thinking of them as discrete acts limited to one stage of writing. At their best, outlines develop gradually, expand and vary as the task changes, and serve as checks for staying on course as we proceed through the writing. At their most imaginative, outlines prompt unusual associations. Some writers I know insert cues to remind them of colors, sounds, emotions, and smells that can become a part of final presentations.

6. *Isn't this deception of sorts?* Or, asked another way, "Why not just admit that all this is just a first draft in disguise?" Here, because this question is more troublesome than the others, I enlist the group, including the questioners themselves, to provide most of the answers. In fact, we come to agree, prewriting is different from prose writing in important ways. Prewriting is generally more informal and tentative and, so, takes less time and energy than a prose version of a manuscript. For a similar reason, because it is less demanding and anxiety provoking, it is less likely to block. And, because conceptual outlines only approximate prose, the act of rewriting them is more fluid than rewriting from formal prose. Finally, prewriting encourages us to hold onto cues about alternatives and plans longer than does prose. The more farther we are into the writing, the more distant the landmarks and instructions with which we were launched.

The real dilemma here, it seems to me, is whether writers should work consciously or unconsciously. While prewriting does offer the romance of discovery, it promises less of the magic of unbidden spontaneity. In the end, we must decide to find inspiration or else hope it finds us; we must decide between deliberate work or unreliable bursts of imagination.

But fortunately, this is not the end; it is still nearer the beginning. As we have broadened our views of imagination, we have also agreed (at some point near here) to devote the bulk of our bds (brief, daily sessions) for at least the next several weeks to our listed exercises in collecting, filing, outlining, and revising. As a rule, writers contract to spend fifteen to sixty minutes per weekday to prewriting (and another five minutes, later in the day, for perusal and noting).

Hereabouts, more than at any other point in the program, confidence is unsteady; imagination can still seem distant. Aplomb about having something significant to say is one of the most difficult qualities that writers can assemble. As a rule, writers keenly anticipate the importance of building-in gradual success as part of recruiting confidence. The other keys to arranging certainty--balance and moderation--remain less accessible for awhile.

Step 4: Striving for balance and moderation in prewriting

This fourth step becomes a part of prewriting only when the prior three steps are underway. After about two to three weeks of bds devoted to little more than prewriting, once collecting and its offshoots have become productive and enjoyable, groups slow down to help prepare a checklist of reminders about ways of ensuring balance and moderation:

1. Practice prewriting as a regular habit accompanied with comfort; work without struggle, in calm, reflective fashion. Balance the excitement

of immersion with the patience of checking for comfort and reflectiveness.

2. Set limits on preliminaries by working in bds, each with a clear and reasonable goal such as taking notes on a single source, or filing notes into a new set of categories, or summarizing the notes in a category, or beginning to assemble summaries of connected ideas into outlines, and so on. Balance the drawing power of anticipating what lies ahead with a quiet thoroughness in completing your goal for the session at hand. Know when you've done enough for the day.

3. Ensure momentum and spontaneity by plunging into stages (notetaking, filing, etc.) before feeling fully ready. Practice patience at proceeding with at least a few holes and uncertainties in plans and outlines. But not, as a rule, more than a few at a time. Use the appearance of voids to focus searches for ideas and sources to be carried out during other brief openings in the day, not to halt ongoing work on imaginativeness. Balance the need for thoroughness and perfection with the flexibility of delaying closure and of moving ahead, for the moment, with the chain of ideas. Prewriting is, after all, just prewriting.

4. Promote both motivation and imaginativeness by maintaining conversations about your genre and about what you are setting out to do, even as you work privately to draw some of your own insights and directions. With too exclusive a reliance on internally generated force, without the social stimulus of reading and talking, prewriting loses much of its potential impetus. A similar point: Balance the need to make discovery entirely your own with the reality of checking for receptiveness of your audience.

5. Balance the open-endedness of exercises in imagination with regular acts of decisiveness about categories, probable themes, workable plots or interpretations, and how things will be stated. But temper that decisiveness with a readiness to change and abandon ideas that do not prove out; as confidence and imaginativeness grow, stubborn attachment to plans lessens.

6. Always include acts of notation about what you think and plan (as marginal jottings, as summaries, as approximations of the prose that lies ahead). But keep asides brief and to the point; make sure that they do not dominate your time or distract you from meeting most daily goals.

7. When you have finished a step, no matter how decisively and confidently, revise it at least once. Herein lies a typically neglected but powerful source of imagination. Balance the impatient but provident impulse to move on when you have finished with the other

extreme--an awareness that you may not have prepared as imaginatively as you might.

The last reminder has proven so valuable that groups like to make it a rule.

RULE #7: Imagination, or new vision, comes most reliably from revision.

With more occasions for reviewing these points, we see another general principle for imagination related to balance and moderation.

RULE #8: Prewriting distributes the usual suddenness of having to generate our best imagining and wording at once.

Said one writer, wryly, after she and her group had hammered out a version of this eighth rule: "I guess this rules out my favorite vice, churning out single-draft books with the mark of facile genius." We all agreed.

OUTCOMES

How do we know, for a fact, that prewriting works? It takes more than the satisfaction of the moment, more than occasional anecdotes, to make a compelling case. Writers who pay to participate and who work hard want evidence that the program delivers results. All of us taking the leap into new and sometimes frustrating tactics profit in seeing evidence of effectiveness. So it is that I routinely collect a variety of data about the habits and attitudes of writers moving through the program. This is a moment (while writers actively practice the unaccustomed exercises of prewriting) where proof is particularly encouraging.

Some writers want quantitative facts; others require little more than factually based abstractions of what works and for whom. Assuming similar tastes in readers, I try here to provide both in brief and mutually palatable form. In the main, I focus on what distinguishes the most and least successful participants on a variety of measures. Here I portray the results from the sample of fifty-two participants described in the introduction to this book.

Quantitatively Based Indices of Progress

Exemplars. Slightly less than half these writers evidenced the progress they and I had expected, of moving from low self-ratings of motivation at the beginning of prewriting sessions (a mean score of 2.4 on a 10-point scale) to moderate levels (4.9) within one month of regular work in motivation exercises

(Chapter 1). By the end of the third month, they evidenced moderately high motivation (7.0) that coincided with at least a month of regular involvement in conceptual outlining. Over the same period, the journal entries of exemplars about their thoughts at writing times indicate a drop of nearly 40 percent in negative self-talk about the task at hand or about writing in general.

To add more systematic ratings about progress, I analyzed the spoken and written comments of participants according to an index of optimism/pessimism [29, 30]. This measure proved to be complex but interesting. A significant portion of exemplars, eight of twelve, began as mild optimists (i.e., they explained causes of failures at writing as impermanent, as nonpervasive, and as nonpersonal) and then stayed at that level. Others improved slightly but no one in this subgroup evinced declines in optimism.

A measure of imagination completes this picture for the moment. To compile it I regularly asked writers to nominate each instance from their prewriting sessions that constituted a new (1) meaning or connection, (2) insightful rearrangement, or (3) idea that would translate into a crucial transition or point in prose. The exemplars mentioned above began with modest outputs of imagination, with a mean of 4.8 recorded instances per week while still working at motivation and at collecting and notetaking. By the time exemplars were practicing conceptual outlining, counts had risen to a mean of 12.0 per week.

Problematics. Only 11 of the 52 writers fared poorly, by their judgment and mine, after sticking with the program for these three months. They too shared a common pattern, one worth noticing. Their self-ratings of motivation began at a low level (mean = 2.1) and, while fluctuating, often sank lower (normative range = 1.9-2.9). Their journal entries of negativism began at a level higher than that of exemplars (mean per day = 4.8 per writing session vs. 2.9) and showed no reliable decrease over this time. Examples of negative self-talk: "I have no creativity, why kid myself?"; "Reviewers can always find fault with my writing."

Pessimism was the strongest, most consistent characteristic of problematic participants. They began the program with the highest level of pessimistic statements (e.g., "I'm not an imaginative person and I never will be because that's the kind of person I am, plodding, careful and uninspiring"; "this might work for other writers but not for me") and they clung resolutely to their negativity over the first three months. They were also strikingly unlike other writers here in another way. Problematics reported frequent bouts of mania and depression associated with program exercises, usually in association with great binges of prewriting or writing. These were writers who complained loudly of a lack of time for writing, of busy work-lives and home-lives that prevented writing. Nonetheless, their own monitoring (complimented by some of my own) of their daily time expenditures showed that they regularly had sufficient time, at least one hour per day of combined segments for writing on the schedules prescribed.

One more fact about this problematic pattern helps make the point about a powerful set of handicaps; almost two-thirds of the 40-plus writers who quit the program before this point (and who are not part of group of 52 under continuing analysis here) had demonstrated a similar profile. (The other nonstayers simply did not get involved in the exercises.) All but three nonstayers displayed high levels of busyness (i.e., feeling too busy to write).

Qualitatively Based Indices of Progress

To provide this more personalized kind of accounting, I used my regular notes of individual and group sessions with writers to portray their progress or lack of it. The majority of participants, whether working in or out of academe, rated these qualitative accounts as more valuable. My portrayals of writers (much as with the excerpts that appear throughout this book) provided two insights. One was the reassurance that problems were not idiosyncratic:

That's a relief, seeing that others actually work themselves into a frenzy over their ambivalence and their inability to think of anything worth saying.

I sometimes imagine that I alone could want to write and *not* want to write at once. Thank god, I'm not alone. Misery loves company.

The second advantage in representative anecdotes lay in their specificity; writers could see in them examples of what to do or not to do:

That one, of the guy whose wife didn't approve of his writing until he himself approved of it, makes a good point. We give others lots of signals about whether we want them to discourage or encourage, or to approve or disapprove, don't you think?

You know I'm really surprised that anyone else would be dumb enough to think that a [alcoholic] drink right after writing is the way to wind down. When I did that, in the past, it set off a whole series of events, not one of them helpful to my writing. I need to make sure that I don't fall into that kind of slip again.

The thing I needed to hear the most was how somebody made the habit rule work. I tend to make plans and then not carry them through, so there was a good idea in hearing that the "exemplars" actually call each other at prewriting times to, what should I call it, spur each other on to maintain the habit.

We do more than find reassurances and a few specifics for thriving. We work hard to come up with sets of general principles.

Unadaptive styles and attitudes. Four characteristics distinguish participants who make slow and unsatisfying progress in finding motivation and imagination:

Problematic writers, first and foremost, do not fully join the conversation about writing. They are not ready and enthusiastic participants in the discussions and problem-solving efforts of writing groups. They seem distracted and do not listen patiently to what other writers experience or to their suggestions for new strategies. They seem to persist in seemingly self-centered and isolated efforts as writers.

They, more than other writers, persevere in mystical and maladaptive beliefs about writing, particularly in supposing that good writing is more a matter of awaiting magic than of making meaning.

They stubbornly insist on maintaining old habits of arranging motivation by way of passive waiting or hurried forcing. They are especially likely to claim they are too busy to work at writing in bds.

They, more than other participants, dislike the regular, routine work of prewriting. They are least likely to be collecting and arranging ideas, to be discussing and sharing plans, and to be incorporating approximations of prose into their plans at this stage.

Some problematics face up to the characterization being presented; some are not yet ready to admit what is now obvious. To help put these peripheral members at ease, I encourage everyone to share instances where we have, even in the midst of successes, exhibited some or all the patterns just listed. The message is again one of common travels as writers; we all share the same tendencies to undermine ourselves and we can all learn from and help each other. Out of this comes a bigger relief from looking at our foibles. We cheerfully agree that we can learn more from observing adaptive patterns.

Adaptive styles and attitudes. We do, in fact, find more cause for optimism in the accounts of writers who moved quickly to adaptiveness. Why? Because all of their acts can be emulated without undue effort. Five factors seem to make the difference:

First, they are involved. They work at patience and at suspending disbelief, as evidenced in this comment from an exemplar:

What was most important for me [was] to stop complaining and finding excuses. I needed to do more listening and doing. More, I had to find out that getting involved would provide the inspiration and ideas that I needed.

Second, they didn't necessarily stop being romantics, but they faced up to unromantic realities about regular, conscious, planful work:

I hated to give in to my arcane belief in the Muses. Once past my indignancy, though, I could appreciate what works better: A belief in myself and my own abilities . . . in the routines and habits and ideas that I create. Not in my impatience and dreaminess and my misdirected efforts to show how smart I am. Besides, after all, I finally had to admit that I wasn't getting anywhere the old way. A sometimes lovely, sometimes tortuous road that went nowhere.

Third, exemplars minimize reliance on a passiveness followed by hurrying; they begin to replace this reliance with more planful but calm habits of regular writing:

No one was a better example of a procrastinator and binger than I. I waited for perfect conditions and perfect moods. I ended up working with deadlines hanging over my head. In marathons. . . . I didn't get it, the stuff about calm and comfort, until I had done it for awhile. I had thought, "If this works, fine, who knows?" I wanted to be pleasantly surprised and I was. And then, but not before, I understood why my waiting and bingeing had worked so badly. Now my writing is becoming easier *and* calmer and better.

Fourth, exemplars become connoisseurs of collecting and refining ideas to suit their own purposes. And they become observers and noticers of their writing, of themselves as writers, and of the things around them that can become a part of their writing.

What seems to work for me is, how can I say this?, avoiding an overly inward focus. Not too much self-focus. I do better, as we're saying here, by doing than I do with just thinking about doing.

Fifth, exemplars don't wait for colleagues and coaches to provide the whole stimulus for improvement as writers. They continue to read and to collect their ideas. Some exemplars blended the conclusions of Linda Flower and of her collaborators [3, 31, 32] with Mills' Rules. Others, after reading Flower's findings, made abbreviated lists of their own that included points like these:

   a. Imagination flowers with knowledge of strategies (e.g., the WIRMI
      device: "What I really mean is") to generate concepts;
   b. we respond to the problem we pose, so we should pose a careful,
      consciously planful problem;
   c. lack of imagination owes mostly to lacks in strategies for "reading" a
      situation, setting appropriate plans, and assembling the ideas and
      organizations to carry out those plans;
   d. plans work because they break big tasks into manageable subproblems
      and specify the sequence of problem-solving strategies; and,
   e. inexperienced writers, unlike experts, fail to detect problems in under-
      standing because they do less monitoring, use fewer plans and

strategies, and generate less elaborate representations of the problem beforehand.

In the end, writers agree, we have learned the most from an interesting combination, the exemplars in our groups and from groups' exemplars including Linda Flower. We are increasingly reminded that while our daily practice can help provide fluency and comfort, the mix of social support in which we learn makes much of the difference. When we isolate ourselves as writers, and when we are not masters of normative discourse and ideas, we may remain on the periphery of the very conversation we most want to join [33].

SUMMARY

In this second stage of finding comfort and fluency as writers (Chapter 2), we took the exercises we had learned in finding motivation (Chapter 1) to their next logical step. Earlier, we saw that involvement precedes and generates motivation; here we worked our way through even more planful exercises that precede and generate imagination.

It turns out that imagination requires little more than regular habits of collecting writable ideas, of taking stimulating but practical notes, of filing and rearranging ideas until they suggest outlines and plans, of elaborating outlines with approximations of how we will express ideas and transitions in prose, and of patiently revising outlines and plans until our readiness has drawn us painlessly close to prose.

Chapter 2 presents the first evidence for the effectiveness of these prewriting strategies. Writers who immersed themselves in the regular practice of generating imagination evidenced more motivation for writing, more imaginative discoveries that could be used in writing, less mental discomfort with the writing context, and well-formed but flexible preparations for writing prose. Compared to more problematic participants, writers who involved themselves in the exercises prescribed here helped corroborate the three rules added in Chapter 2:

#6: The most fluent, comfortable, efficient, and imaginative writers spend as much prewriting as writing (i.e., they work patiently and productively at generating motivation and imagination before and while committing to prose).

#7: Imagination, or new vision, comes most readily from revision (i.e., imagination is a matter of patiently re-seeing, rearranging, and restating ideas).

#8: Prewriting distributes the usual suddenness of having to generate our best imagining and wording simultaneously (i.e., prewriting builds ideas, directions, and even wordings that become a part of prose, thereby lessening the pain of moving from planning to prose).

With motivation and imagination operating efficiently, we are ready, more than ready, to move from prewriting to writing. To a surprising extent, I have found, we no longer have to struggle for motivation or for ways to say things and organize them. And, in my experience, many of us are by now teeming with ideas while remaining unhurried about getting them into prose. More and more, it seems from my vantage, we are settling in to the pace of our journey.

I too have an exemplar I enjoy invoking again and again, the naturalist Buffon. He wrote (the historians Will and Ariel Durant concluded) as though freed from want and dowered with time. He labored as carefully with his words as with his specimens and, so, produced a leisurely ordering of ideas vitalized with feelings. And, to manage his motivation, clarity, and insight, he trudged to his tower and worked at his planning and writing every morning, regardless [34]. Buffon was, in a way, a local traveler who went far.

REFERENCES

1. Mills, C.W. (1959). *The sociological imagination*. New York: Grove Press, pp. 196-197.

2. Berthoff, A. (1992). Double-entry notebook form. In J.M. Moxley, *Publish, don't perish*, pp. 41-42. Westport, CT: Praeger.

3. Flower, L. (1990). The role of task representation in reading-to-write. In L. Flower, V. Stein, J. Ackerman, M.J. Kantz, K. McCormick & W.C. Peck (eds.), *Reading-to-write*, pp. 35-75. New York: Oxford University Press.

4. Flower, L. & Hayes, J.R. (1977). Problem-solving strategies and the writing process. *College English*, 39(4), 449-461.

5. Galagan, P. (1986). How to avoid datacide. *Training and Development Journal*, 40(10), 54-57.

6. Perkins, D.N. (1981). *The mind's best work*. Cambridge, MA: Harvard University Press.

7. Flower, L. & Hayes, J.R. (1980). The cognition of discovery: Defining a rhetorical problem. *College Composition and Communication*, 31, 21-32.

8. Downey, J. (1918). A program for the psychology of literature. *Journal of Applied Psychology*, 2, 366-377.

9. Durant, W. & Durant, A. (1965). *The age of Voltaire*. New York: Simon and Schuster, pp. 573, 164.

10. Garver, E. (1983). How to develop ideas: The contribution philosophy can make to improve literacy. *Teaching Philosophy*, 6(2), 97-102.

11. Tarshis, B. (1985). *How to write without pain*. New York: Plume.

12. Flower, L. (1990). Introduction: Studying cognition in context. In L. Flower, V. Stein, J. Ackerman, M.J. Kantz, K. McCormick & W.C. Peck (eds.), *Reading-to-write*, pp. 3-32. New York: Oxford University Press.

13. Olson, G.A. (1992). Publishing scholarship in humanistic disciplines: Joining the conversation. In J.M. Moxley (ed.), *Writing and publishing for academic authors*, pp. 49-69. New York: University Press of America.

14. Boice, R. (1993). Writing blocks and tacit knowledge. *Journal of Higher Education*, 64, 19-54.

15. Sternberg, R.J. (1988). *The triarchic mind*. New York: Penguin.

16. Drakeford, (1983). Sorting notes with MailMerge. *The Portable Companion*, February/March, 28-31.

17. Keillor, G. (1983). If Robert Frost had an Apple . . . *New York Times Magazine*, November 20., 81-84.

18. Kellogg, R.T. (1984). Computer aids that writers need. *Behavior Research Methods, Instruments & Computers*, 17, 253-258.

19. Kintsch, W. (1990). The personalized journal. *Psychological Science*, 1, 345.

20. Kozma, R.B. (1991). The impact of computer-based tools and embedded prompts on writing processes and products of novice and advanced college writers. *Cognition and Instruction*, 8, 1-27.

21. Howard, V.A. & Barton, J.H. (1986). *Thinking on paper*. New York: William Morrow and Company.

22. Kurfiss, J.G. (1988). *Critical thinking*. Washington, D.C.: ASHE-ERIC Higher Education Reports.

23. Marshall, J.D. & Durst, R.K. (1986). Annotated bibliography of research in the teaching of English. *Research in the Teaching of English*, 21, 398-421.

24. Gopen, G.D. & Swan, J.A. (1990). The science of science writing. *American Scientist*, 78, 550-558.

25. Bloom, L.Z. (1992). Writing as witnessing. In J.M. Moxley (Ed.), *Writing and publishing for academic authors*, pp. 89-109. New York: University Press of America.

26. Bloom (1992). Writing as witnessing, p. 92.

27. Tremmel, R. (1992). Investigating productivity and other factors in the writer's practice. *Freshman English News*, 17(2), 19-25.

28. Rothenberg, A. (1990). *Creativity and madness*. Baltimore: Johns Hopkins University Press.

29. Seligman, M.E.P. (1991). *Learned optimism*. New York: Alfred A. Knopf.

30. Schulman, P., Castellon, C. & Seligman, M.E.P. (1989). Assessing explanatory style: The content analysis of verbatim explanations and the attributional style questionnaire. *Behaviour Research & Therapy*, 27, 505-512.

31. Flower, L. & Hayes, J.R. (1981). Plans that guide the composing process.   In C.H. Frederiksen & J.F. Dominic (eds.), *Writing: Process, development and communication*, pp. 39-58. Hillsdale, NJ: Erlbaum.

32. Stein, V. (1990). Elaboration: Using what you know. In L. Flower, V. Stein, J. Ackerman, M.J. Kantz, K. McCormick & W.C. Peck (Eds.), *Reading-to-write*, pp. 144-155. New York: Oxford University Press.

33. Brufee, K.A. (1984). Collaborative learning and the "conversation of mankind." *College English*, 46(7), 635-652.

34. Durant & Durant (1965). *The age of Voltaire*, p. 573.

3

Fluency

First there is the difficulty of writing *at all*. The full, abundant flow that must be established if the writer is to be heard from will not begin. . . . It may be that the root of the problem . . . is self-consciousness that stems the flow. Often it is the result of misapprehensions about writing. . . . Often it is the result of such ideals of perfectionism as can hardly bear the light of day. . .

Dorothea Brande, *Becoming a Writer* [1]

Dorothea Brande's little book, still beloved after a half century, cast the die for manuals of advice about writing problems. Its two main themes, both visible in the excerpt above, set a course for this third chapter: the first is about the general struggle to put things in writing, and the second theme deals with the misbeliefs and misbehaviors that block our writing. Here, at last, we get on with the issues of fluency and dysfluency. It is one thing to motivate and plan; it is another to write.

I like to start discussions about fluency with a perusal of Dorothea Brande's work because she helped popularize the common cure for dysfluency, free writing [2]. Her clarification of writing blocks, even though she did not use that label, remains as useful today as it was in 1934. She concluded that the fearsomeness of writing causes an imbalance between our artistic and critical sides; when fear and self-criticism dominate, we write haltingly or not at all. Her method of combatting fear and criticism is to push self-consciousness aside:

Write anything that comes into your head: last night's dream, if you are able to remember it; the activities of the day before; a conversation, real or imaginary; an examination of conscience. Write any sort of reverie, rapidly and uncritically. The excellence or ultimate worth of what you write is of no importance yet . . . your primary purpose is not to bring forth deathless words, but to write any words at all which are not pure nonsense. [3]

This method, writers assure me, helps deliver what Brande calls the "full, abundant flow." I call it fluency.

As my writers and I read Brande's old book (reprinted in paperback), we make broader plans for understanding fluency. Sixty years have produced additional information about ways to overcome blocking. We begin with questions about (1) what makes writing so difficult and why so many writers block, (2) how well usual treatments for writing blocks, including free writing, work in everyday practice, and (3) whether we can profit in reframing the traditional concept of writing blocks. Then, writing groups assume a familiar stance. We team up for brief reports about the literature on blocking. But here, because I have spent a couple of decades sorting this information [4], I provide most of the material. Despite my long experience I am often sent scurrying back to the library for sources that my writers have gotten wind of. In the pages ahead I portray what I typically discuss with groups and how they react. Here, as there, I summarize what I have read and what data I have collected on fluency. We share and we all coach each other; perhaps that give-and-take will even affect readers.

We begin this third leg of our journey with the question most common among writers.

WHAT CAUSES WRITING BLOCKS?

Actually, this question has two parts. In one part we ask, as did Dorothea Brande, what makes writing so difficult. In the other part we ask, what disposes some of us, more than others, to block. There is even a third query implicit here: What, exactly, happens during blocking? These are not idle explorations, certainly not for writers who wonder when they will block again. There is enjoyment in this patient discussion of problems; this literature makes for stimulating conversation.

What Makes Writing Inherently Difficult?

Even for the best-prepared of writers, writing imposes uncommon demands. One reason owes to a peculiarity in usual patterns of intellectual development: our productive abilities grow much more slowly than do our critical abilities. So it is that we can all too readily demand a standard of writing for others that we cannot muster for ourselves [5]. And, so it is that we often set unreasonable standards for the quantity and quality of our own productivity. The solution to this dilemma combines patience (of course) and regular practice. Too many of us find it easier to be meticulous critics than disciplined writers.

Another reason for usual difficulties with writing is more familiar. The problem is a matter of timing and it occurs during the commonly awkward passage between planning and writing. This is a moment of shifting demands, one that often brings hesitation, dysfluency, confusion. It is, by broad consensus, the point at which writers most often block. Linda Flower and John Hayes, contemporary leaders in the field of composition, put it this way: blocking is likely in front of a keyboard, unlikely while planning in the shower [6]. For one thing, the transition from planning to writing introduces a whole new set of constraints. Suddenly, it seems, the text must be fully explicit. Abruptly, the writer must account for plans, goals, audiences, conventions of prose, and more. Where planning seemed to demand little more than inspiration, writing demands control and logical focus.

For another thing, this boundary makes writing seem especially messy and mysterious. The usual ambiguity about how to begin writing prose encourages writers to believe they can leave composing up to blind chance and inborn talents. Thus, writers may rush ahead while struggling to find what they have to say, without the benefit of planful prewriting. Or, writers may wait passively for clarity and purpose before writing. The longer writers actively struggle or passively wait, the greater the impatience, the more the self-consciousness, and the greater the forgetting of plans. When writers rely on blind chance or passive waiting they remain unlikely to learn better means of vaulting the chasm between planning and prose [7].

Linda Flower explains the difficulty of managing fluency without prewriting and planning: Our real struggle in starting to write lies in finding words. We can, all too easily, suppose that the words and images we need lie at the ready in our memories, available for immediate use. In fact, though, the networks and linkages for calling up fluency rely on thoughtful practice and preparation. What makes words and ideas directly accessible are notes, plans, drafts, schematic representations, and imagined readers (Chapters 1 and 2).

Reflections on what makes writing difficult. Writers in the program grant that writing is mysterious and difficult; why shouldn't it be? But they linger over a related question: If writing occasionally does work, amid all the difficulties, why not leave well enough alone? Writers generally dislike the idea of replacing mindless acts with conscious planning and self-discipline:

I'm wondering if we aren't missing something critical here. Sometimes it is, absolutely is, quite possible to draft great copy completely from old and new memories without a bit of obeisance to prewriting. That could be what good writing should be about--about something that happens spontaneously and beautifully, just like a work of art . . . like grace under pressure.

All of us share this romantic opinion, from time to time. But we know, full well, the reasons why most of us cannot count on unplanned spontaneity for our writing: It hasn't worked well or often enough. Without prewriting and discipline, writers too often block at this very junction. A custom of writing that works only sporadically is not sufficient to optimize potentials; those of us most likely to remain blocked deserve a chance to be read.

Nonetheless we struggle over plans that threaten to take the spontaneity out of writing. Perhaps because the topic is too close for comfort, we start with examples of order and discipline from elsewhere:

I had thought much the same thing once before, with a lot of negativity and indignity, when my company instituted a new executive training program that included the explicit learning and practice of countless subtleties. To my surprise it worked . . . . I found myself working out my social interactions in advance, rehearsing my presentations with something like a sense of audience, and I knew what I wanted to say, more or less, in critical negotiations. What's more, and Bob will like this, what we all thought would add an overload of extra work eventually saved time and made our days much easier.

With our indecision still at the fore, we pause to look for confirmations that we need better, more planful ways of finding fluency as writers. We continue with ideas we have just read or overviewed: In particular, we share insights about what makes planful writing so difficult. Example: Few things encourage procrastination more than tasks that demand simultaneous acts of conscious searching and planning [8]; but when, on the other hand, we proceed with ambiguous and ambivalent intentions, we encourage confusion [9].

Next comes the realization that the very nature of writing demands planfulness and preparedness. Writing can overload us with requirements to keep a whole array of simultaneous considerations in mind [7]. While we juggle words and sentences and larger plans, there are other things to do: think of audiences, ward away distractions, and pay attention to constraints. Writing is as much a struggle of noticing what we should not say as of finding what we can say. With these competing demands at hand, we might easily see more possibilities for failure than for success.

A related observation nearly completes this preliminary picture of what makes writing difficult. Writing, like other public performances including dancing, is susceptible to excessive self-consciousness. When we begin to attend too closely to our every move, two problems commonly arise. For one thing, we can lose the calm and breadth of perception essential to momentum and problem solving. For another, we may notice a fatal flaw in the sequence of acts that make up a performance: The closer we scrutinize it, the more we suspect it may not have been well-learned and well-rehearsed, and the more we are unsure of some of the steps. With uncertainty and missteps, we hesitate and even back away in embarrassment. We block.

Then, just as we conclude that we have completed our coverage of what makes writing difficult, we come to a belated insight about our preference for entering into writing with vaguely formed skills and plans. We realize that this willingness to proceed without careful preparation reflects an assumption that we are already expert at writing. Curiously, we launch into writing as though we will need little more than a modicum of learning and practice to thrive. How come? We already know at least one reason why we bring an unrealistic and impatient expectation of expertise and perfection to writing. The ability to write with spontaneity and without obvious help or effort is a supposed sign of genius. The other reason may be less apparent: Most of us undertake writing with a minimum of useful instruction. We learned how to think and write largely on our own.

I like to note the parallel in both these answers to a seemingly different activity, teaching. It is a task whose practitioners customarily receive the sparest of training and practice. Yet, most new teachers imagine themselves already masterful, needing only the right conditions to bring their talents and philosophies into bloom [10]. While their expectations of success are high, their plans about how to teach are blurry and unformed. The customary mindlessness of many teachers resembles what the writer Joanna Field discovered in her classic self-study:

All I can see as I look back is a picture of myself going about my daily affairs in a half-dream state, sometimes discontented but never trying to find out why, vaguely making the best of things, rarely looking ahead except casually, almost as a game dreaming of what I would like to happen, but never seriously thinking how I could set about to make it happen. [11]

What makes teaching (or, for that matter, writing) so mysterious and difficult? In reality, new teachers have not been coached in the skills they will need most: (1) the ability to pace themselves and avoid stress; (2) the resilience to face less than perfect performances and the disappointment that accompanies them; (3) realistic expectations about the lack of ready appreciation of what they do from colleagues, students, and the general public; and (4), most important, habits of planning and of studying their own performance in ways that encourage mindfulness and improvement. New teachers (and inexperienced writers) are, all too often, unprepared for the hard work, the time-use demands, the disinterest, and the self-education that underlie excellence [12].

What Other Hindrances Do Writers Bring to Writing?

Most writers laughingly admit that they bring to writing a lot of what therapists call baggage. But, as was true for Joanna Field, our initial understanding of how we block ourselves seems vague and unhelpful. What helps get us past that ambiguity is the kind of self-study that Field prescribed as a first step in gaining self-control. (It is the procedure we first saw in Chapter 1, retrospective-thinking-aloud exercises.) The usual pattern of recollecting holds true. At first, when asked to recall times of difficulty in writing, writers provide superficial accounts:

Oh, who knows? I've always been kind of neurotic. Why should writing be an exception? I make much of my life painful and I make writing a misery. What more can I say?

With practice and coaching, the exercises produce revealing accounts of how writers block:

When I really re-create the situation, when I fully imagine myself there, I can just feel the press for perfectionism, almost like a maddening urge. I thought: "You can't be satisfied with the usual run-of-the-mill palaver. You *have* to do something outstanding, something that will bowl people over." At the same time, though, another voice is saying, "So what makes you think that you, with your nothing record, could do such a thing?" The perfectionist and the pessimist debate and I wait. And fret.

What comes to life when I transport myself back there is painful. This is real pain. I am thinking about my writing being rejected again. I'm saying it over and over again, like a broken record: "They'll just reject this. They weren't fair before and they won't be fair this time." I feel down . . . , like a failure struggling for a chance in an unjust world. I say to myself: "No wonder; I have nothing original or clever to say. I am a fraud who should be thankful for not yet having been found out."

It isn't the thoughts that dominate at that moment of blocking. I seem to have almost none at those times when I absolutely cannot write. What is there is mostly mood, infiltrating, darkening everything like a heavy fog. I am depressed, de-energized, never more so than when I try to write. This is what it is like at that moment of blocking: I am slowed down, just dragging myself along, not feeling like doing anything except maybe escaping from the pressure to write. I just look at a blank screen and shuffle papers around and look at the wall and suffer.

There is more, much more, in our discoveries gleaned from sessions of thinking aloud. Despite all the discussions we have had in the prior four months, the time is ripe for an unprecedented outpouring about blocking experiences. See if your own experience resembles that of writers who find special relief in clarifying their discomfiting experiences and in discovering that few of them are unique:

I feel good about having gotten in touch with what has happened to me. I think that I usually put such things out of my mind. Repression . . . . I feel much better about sharing my experiences and in seeing that other people have similar experiences. I don't know that I feel any less stupid but I feel less lonely in my stupidity.

The time is ripe for one more thing, another assessment of our blocking tendencies. This time, instead of talking aloud old memories, we employ a standardized test format. It answers questions in more explicit ways: How do each of us compare to larger samples of writers? Have we, in our re-creations of thoughts and feelings of blocking experiences, overlooked any blocking tendencies?

A self-assessment exercise. The Blocking Questionnaire (BQ) is a self-test based on many years of development with a diverse group of writers [13]. It can provide a broad appreciation of the common ways we block. It suggests patterns of blocking in a profile of severity and in comparison to general norms for problem tendencies. And, it helps writers become better observers of their problematic tendencies as they occur. The BQ does one more thing that reminds many writers of the collecting and imagining exercises we have been carrying out (Chapter 2). It helps organize a plethora of information about writing blocks into a manageable list of distinctive problems, each accompanied by suggestions for change.

There is, as we use and discuss the BQ, an interest in how it grew to include its unique list of blocking tendencies. I keep my explanation brief. Originally, I constructed a catalogue of possible blocking factors from an analysis of about 100 of the most informative sources I could find on the topic--articles, books, and dissertations [14]. Then, in a decade of sorting the most telling categories, I pared the list down to the following seven blocking tendencies that writers bring to writing:

1. Work aversion and laziness (e.g.,, the writer would rate herself or himself strongly on an item like "Others hear me complain about how difficult and fatiguing writing is").
2. Procrastination (I would say to myself, " I need to wait until the last minute to get work done").
3. Writing apprehension ("I often feel nervous about writing").
4. Dysphoria/depression ("I tend to see criticism or rejection of any single piece of my writing as proof that all my writing will fail").
5. Impatience ("Others hear me express disappointment when I cannot write easily, quickly").
6. Perfectionism ("I often suppose that others, even friends, think less of me if they see my unformed or erroneous writing").
7. Rigid rules ("I rarely need outlines; my best writing occurs without extensive planning").

Related points: There are patterns in how most writers score on these BQ items. Work aversion (i.e., a distaste for the hard work of writing) is the most common problem. Some blocking factors, like impatience and procrastination, tend to go together. And, most significant, the common outcome is a configuration of moderately problematic tendencies. Most writers score surprisingly high across the list, including all but one to three factors. Blocking is, apparently, a complexity of influences working together in discord. Some of the factors are well known from informal study (e.g., writing anxiety); some are not (work aversion, impatience, rigid rules). Most writers who take the BQ uncover more problems than they might have anticipated.

Other Considerations of Blocking and Fluency

No one in the writing groups, least of all me, assumes that I have the last word on blocking. Nor should you. We have already encountered too many disarmingly observant people such as Dorothea Brande, Peter Elbow, Joanna Field, Linda Flower, C. Wright Mills, and Donald Murray to surmise that. We are learning, slowly but surely, about the value of staying in touch with broad conversations. Of the collected notes and schemes about blocking that I share with groups, these are judged as favorites:

Old accounts of automatic writers on fluency. Spiritualists, especially at the zenith of their popularity more than a century ago, made the public aware of strategies for inducing both fluency and novelty in writing [2]. As they trained their "mediums" to take "dictation" from spirits in the nether world, spiritists invoked an early version of free writing. They called it automatic writing. Their "mediums," some of whom became famous for their prolific outbursts of imaginative poetry and prose, wrote in trance states, without the self-consciousness that impedes writing.

The main points for us in this fascinating literature on automaticity are these: First, when stuck, writers can most easily establish momentum by writing without paying close attention to content or correctness. Perfectionism is better put off until much later, in proof editing. Second, by minimizing self-conscious perfectionism, writers are better able to discover what they can say. Third, in assuming that they will have something interesting to write, writers proceed with confidence. And fourth, in moving away from thinking to doing, writers find fluency.

Modern researchers on hypnosis. Ernest Hilgard and his students, in addition to bringing some respectability to hypnosis, specify many advantages of unresistant, trusting immersion in writing--what they call hypnotic susceptibility [15]. Writers who score highest on tests of this susceptibility fare best at writing because they work with less immediate concern for exact wording, with more initial freedom from internal editors, with more awareness of their emotions, and with less reliance on suppressive and repressive defenses. Writers who resist hypnosis, on the other hand, generally focus on a word or a sentence at a time. They work with the nagging presence of a background editor. They proceed without the security of glancing at the larger picture and its guiding images. In short, they do few of the things that could lure them into easier, more fluent writing.

Our review of hypnosis makes an important point about the value of a trusting involvement in writing: hypnotic susceptibility makes us more open to join and learn from conversations. It lends the confidence we need, as writers, to stand up and say "this is who I am."

The literature about regular, disciplined writing. These oft-overlooked readings remind us that fluency awaits regular practice at writing [16]. They also cue us about what blocks: irrational beliefs and irregular habits. One memorable example comes from Issac Asimov, an exemplar of fluency:

Alas, there's no such thing, no magic formula, no secret tricks, no hidden shortcuts. I'm sorry to tell you that it's a matter of hard work over a long period of time. If you know of any exceptions to this, that's exactly what they are--exceptions. [17]

Another example of rational thinking about writing comes from a leading researcher, Mary Frank Fox, about the common excuse for nonproductivity:

Such scarcity of time is the proverbial lament of scientists and scholars, and lack of time can certainly be an impediment to intellectual activity. Yet research data indicate that simple availability of time is not the critical determinant of productivity. [18]

If lack of time is not the real problem in fluency, what is? The more crucial agents of blocking are failures to establish motivation, imagination, and habitual practice--at least according to this book.

Exponents of free writing. Free writers are inheritors of traditions of hypnotically induced, automatic writing. Contemporary free writers offer the best-known and most reliably immediate treatment for dysfluency. The influential exponent of free writing nowadays is Peter Elbow. He, like Dorothea Brande, offers an unpretentious and realistic view of what blocks writers:

. . . schooling makes us obsessed with the "mistakes" we make in writing. Many people are constantly thinking about spelling or grammar as they try to write. I am always thinking about the awkwardness, wordiness, and general mushiness of natural verbal products as I try to write down words. But it's not just "mistakes" or "bad writing" we edit as we write. We also edit unacceptable thoughts and feelings, as we do in speaking.

In writing there is more time to do it so the editing is heavier. . . . It's an unnecessary burden to try to think of words and also worry at the same time whether they're the right words. [19]

Elbow, like others in the tradition of automaticity, offers a practical solution for premature, compulsive editing: his own version of free writing. The Elbow method frees writers to find what their meaning can be as they think, unself-consciously, on paper or screen and then, later, to clarify what they produce via rewriting. Stated another way, free writing externalizes our often blurry consciousness onto paper or screen. Once we have it there, we can more readily reorganize what we want to say and plan what we want to do next [20].

But Elbow doesn't just repackage old strategies. He helps us understand what can dissuade us from free writing, despite its obvious value in unblocking. There is, after all, a frightening aspect to free writing--the chaos and disorientation experienced as our thoughts flow, essentially uncontrolled, onto paper or screen. Free writing offers both the surprise of discovery and the risk of feeling out of control. The solution for this discomfort is already familiar: As writers learn to be patient, to delay closure, and to relax, they become more tolerant of ambiguity and chaos; we must, as the old saying goes, give up control to get control. When writers tolerate temporary confusion they are better able to carry out the all-important alternation between planning and writing.

Tolerance of change, in Elbow's view, promotes more than just a single switch. Writing done well demands a constant alternating between planning and writing because "Working in ideas gives you perspective, structure, and clarity; working in words gives you fecundity, novelty, richness." [21]

The literature on playfulness and fluency. A major theme in this obscure writing about play is that traditional, on-task attitudes of our schools discourage it [22]. Some of the best books of advice for stymied writers promote forgotten or unlearned childlike postures of play, usually while putting aside the sobering messages we have learned from teachers. Joan Minninger's book *Free Yourself to Write*, has a loyal following because she integrates play with writing. Here is a sample:

Many people avoid writing because former teachers have overwhelmed them with strictures and even constructive criticism before they have had a chance to "play around": with writing, with being carefree children with words, pencils, and paper. [23]

Predictably, perhaps, Minninger proposes a kind of free writing as the means of liberating oneself to write. She prescribes assignments that build imagination, in stepwise fashion, at a relaxed pace, and during a scheduled time to write (e.g., work regularly and begin by writing about the excitement of a coming summer vacation from your vantage when you were in grammar school). She does all these helpful things, some of my writers note delightedly, without sounding the least bit like me.

Research on fear of failure. Esther Rothblum summarizes the consistent themes in these inquiries, many of which she researched [24]: Women, more than men, generally behave in ways that manifest fear of failure. Their real fears in fear of failure pertain to expected interpersonal consequences such as rejection; individuals with a high fear of failure avoid situations that demand risks of publicly poor performance. And, it follows, this sort of fear inclines its sufferers to shun feedback about how they are doing.

Fear of failure also helps explain a part of procrastination: One major factor of procrastination consists of fearful components (evaluation anxiety, low self-esteem, and perfectionism). The other factor revolves around laziness and aversion to the hard work of the task being delayed.

Fear of failure provides a special insight about the psychological side of blocking: To find fluency, we must quell our anxieties about public embarrassment, build our self-confidence about having something to say, and generate more involvement and motivation for difficult tasks.

Cognitive research. Recent work in this burgeoning field suggests that unblocking requires an act that begins and continues with cognitive controls, effective self-management. For example, a good daily schedule is the key to quality work [25]. Working regularly at writing and at keeping projects fresh in mind builds some of the most essential parts of fluency--noticing, accumulating stores of ideas and solutions to problems, and rehearsing [6,16]. This kind of cognitive self-management comes by way of what Ellen Langer calls mindfulness:

A true process orientation [i.e., mindfulness] also means being aware that every outcome is preceded by a process. Graduate students forget this all the time. They begin their dissertations with inordinate anxiety because they have seen other people's completed and polished work and mistakenly compare it to their own first tentative steps.

Mindfulness, in contrast to usual impatience and self-focus, gives writers the chance to develop their writing in realistic, gradual fashion. It can also, Langer adds, expose irrational notions about genius:

. . . my students and I asked people to evaluate scientists who had achieved an "impressive" intellectual outcome . . . When the achievement was described as a series of steps (and virtually all achievements can be broken down this way), they judged the scientists as less smart. [26]

There is more to cognitive research on writing and writing blocks. Contemporary approaches to helping writers understand the causes of their blocking commonly include thinking-aloud procedures to identify maladaptive thought patterns [14]; in this book I include a variety of samples of cognitive study in excerpts of writer's recollections. And most modern therapies for writing blocks include a component of cognitive therapy, usually an intervention to reduce or replace negative thinking. Still, evidence for its effectiveness is limited [4], for reasons we will see down the road.

Procrastination. Jane Burka and Lenore Yuen [27], pioneer researchers on procrastination, provide some especially useful insights into blocking. Procrastinators are, for instance, uniquely incapable of enjoying free time; they have trouble relaxing because they customarily rush from one immediate task to another as a way to avoid other, less pleasant activities such as writing. That is, instead of using free time wisely as writers (e.g., relaxing, noticing, and putting ideas into writing), they spend it on busywork (e.g., reading and responding to unnecessary memos) or distractions (e.g., office cleaning to the point of obsessiveness). When they cannot stay busy, they worry.

Procrastinators also, because they approach tasks blindly and try to complete them hurriedly, do not learn to make realistic estimates of how much time major tasks like writing will take. First, they underestimate the time needed for prewriting, rewriting, and editing. Then, they fail to appreciate that large projects can be completed in an accumulation of brief, regular bits of work.

Other researchers make similar points about procrastinators. For one thing, procrastinators stand out for their use of negative emotions (anger, anxiety, guilt) as both motivators and as excuses; writers who rely on pressure to work may then feel too tense to write [28]. For another thing, procrastinators rush to submit what is clearly less than their best effort; they impatiently and recklessly shortchange the proofreading and other minimal safeguards against misunderstanding and rejection [4].

An interim summary on the literature on blocking. I could overview much more here; this literature has grown to enormity over the past century [29]. But too much of it is as fanciful as claims that blocking owes to maternal rejection and that unblocking requires little more than sharpening lots of pencils. Too much of it is redundant; writers on writing blocks rarely take the trouble to check for precedents or evidence. And, too much of it has not proven helpful to stymied writers [4].

WHAT ACTUALLY FOSTERS FLUENCY?

This is a point at which I ask writers to reflect on where they are in the program. Most have just moved from prewriting to writing; most are working in bds (brief, daily sessions); most are beginning to establish fluency. No juncture is more crucial than this for combatting old inclinations to dysfluency.

Still, as we learn more about blocking, we work with the confidence of new habits that help control it. There is an air of optimism amongst writers:

Well, I don't mind the regular sessions any more [the bds]. I just do them every morning as an ordinary activity. What I like is that this little time often turns out to be the best part of my day, the most satisfying. I'm a long way removed from my old discomforts with writing and I'm beginning to see that I'm getting much more done.

Yet, there is still cause for concern:

Listen, I know myself. All this planning and discipline will probably flutter away once I'm well into the writing. That's what has always happened before; even when I have started projects I usually quit them at some stage when they are about two-thirds done.

OK, here is what I think will happen, all right? Planning is not really writing. I know that. Everyday writing is not natural, not for a naturally disorganized and traumatized woman like me. I haven't failed yet because I haven't been given a good chance. Once I'm more on my own, facing the hard parts of writing, I'll revert to old ways. You'll see.

How do we counter these lingering fears? We agree that we are already doing one thing that helps: the regular practice of writing and reflection combined with the continuing exercise of patience and planning. Then we more hesitantly embrace the strategy that is becoming more explicit in this third phase of the program: self-study.

A scheme that works well for managing self-study, I note, combines a re-listing of what we have already learned with notes on how it relates to our everyday experience. The key addition to our already existing schedules (mainly a bds for writing and for reflection on each weekday) is a more serious plan for making journal entries about personal incidents as writers. Much like Joanna Field, then, we assign ourselves the task of observing what helps, of noticing what brings happiness and fluency, and of recording them.

Evaluations of Common Methods for Unblocking

To bring some order to our inquiries into blocking strategies, I ask participants (including you, the reader) to spend a few minutes of daily journal writing by responding to questions posed beforehand, in reference to traditional curatives for blocking. These are the usual queries we use to stimulate brief journal entries:

What about free writing as an unblocking strategy? Writers in the program note an ongoing investment in free writing; most of them practice a daily combination of Brande and Elbow's prescriptions as part of generating momentum, of prewriting, of reflecting, and of journaling. Daily journal entries attest to their utility:

What about free writing? I like it. It uncovers a part of me I hadn't quite known or suspected. I can be creative. It is, in a way, unfocused and freeing and brings out my creative impulses. It surely gives me momentum to write, at a moment's notice. It can also be focused. Anything that I choose to free-write about can be developed in new and unforeseen directions, just by picking one of the thoughts lying on the edge of my awareness. It makes me feel much more in control of my creativity.

If there is a reservation about free writing, it resembles what Joanna Field noticed when she began to find better ways: What if we simply forget to do it, or get distracted from doing it?

I don't want, ever, to abandon free writing, and its fun. But what is it that will keep me from doing so?   Other good things I have done in the past--dieting, exercising, meditating--have gone by the way and I don't even know why. This is what we, the group and I, need to work on--hanging on to what is good.

What about dream therapies? We continue, some of us, to try the hypnotic technique of implanting suggestions for motivation and inspiration into our dreams (see Chapter 1). There is, on the one hand, no resentment about the task:

It's quite pleasant, the relaxing sessions where we induct suggestions for getting past my fears of failure, the prospect of making my dreams more positive.

But dream therapies continue to produce dubious results:

Does it make much difference? I can't tell and I doubt it, after months of patient execution (a strange choice of words). I have had a few dreams about me as a writer, some good and some not so good and some confusing. But never in the dreams am I writing or doing anything definite. Never is it the scenario we rehearse, about me putting aside my irrational fears and sitting down to write with poise or me managing the success and acceptance I deserve. . . . I have to think that other, waking, things like free writing are much more effective. . . .   Maybe the dreams get better after the writing gets better.

Nonetheless, almost no one decides to drop dream work permanently. We optimistically assume that we will find ways to use it more effectively later.

What about contingency management? Consensus is clearest here. Making ourselves write by way of rewards and punishment works to help push aside blocking ("It makes me write, just as I should, whether I feel like it or not"). Nonetheless, some of us do not like it.

I know what I dislike so about it. It is a sort of forcing different from and worse even than writing under a major deadline. It is like forcing under a deadline every day and I'm tired of it. . . . I want to be writing because I want to.

And yet, we see a legitimate place for contingency management. There are times when we may want to be pressured to write on a schedule, when waiting until the last minute will be too costly, when daily forcing is necessary. Moreover, we notice, more and more of us are growing to like the enforced discipline. Or at least we tolerate it:

So what's so bad about not getting to read the newspaper until I do my writing first? I have to go to work every day to get paid. That's not so bad. Or if it is, I don't see the payoff in fighting it, of making myself suffer over it. I don't mind having to write every day. There is something wholesome in doing it right, like a professional.

What about insight therapies? A near majority of the literature on writing blocks has a Freudian bent. Zachary Leader's book, *Writer's Block*, is a recent favorite. Leader, like many psychoanalysts these days, teaches literature from an analytic perspective; while he offers little in the way of specific therapies, he presents intriguing twists on how blocking affects famous authors. Examples: He uses Mark Twain's metaphor for blocking, of a tank running dry. He distinguishes blocking from, say, Keats' diligent indolence. He assumes literal truth in the speculations of analysts such as Hannah Segal who supposed that using words distances us from our world and brings a sense of loss. And, he adds his own inferences about what caused the blocking of writers such as Wordsworth: "at any moment, the impulse to write can be false . . . . the flatness here [referring to a passage of Wordsworth's writing] is a species of blockage . . . rigidity and its consequences are everywhere evident" [30]. Leader sees what the untrained observer might miss.

And Leader provokes us to new thinking about blocking. But how do psychoanalytic ideas such as his translate into practical use for writers fighting off their own blocks? To provide a fair test of this question, I sampled only the journal entries made by patients already congenial to psychoanalytic notions. The norm for these participants is represented in these two samples:

What does it do for me? It interests me. It educates me. I want to be literate and a more literate writer. . . . I'd like to have the command and confidence of a Zachary Leader or even the outlandishness of an Edmund Bergler [31]. . . . But that's about all it does, make me feel literate.

All the stuff about normal cycles of agitation and its blocking being natural is just that, stuff. The stuff about needing to be blocked to gain insight is just stuff, stuff unrelated to real, disabling writing blocks. . . . To my surprise and chagrin, the things that work best for me are the behavioral things. The scheduling and planning work, not my hard work on uncovering my anger toward my father or guessing about where dead authors' flatness of writing might have been blocking.

Nonanalytically oriented writers in the groups, including me, are tougher critics of the notions of Leader and his compatriots. We sense there an annoying vagueness or secrecy about what writers can do to unblock. And we see in Leader's book an especially off-putting, elitist attitude: his assumption that only already successful writers, those who have proven their talent, have real writing blocks (and, somehow, that they grow via blocking).

What about emulating the most productive writers? Generally, the most fluent writers disappoint: they display little interest in the topic of blocking. Instead, like the most successful people in a variety of endeavors, they mention procrastination and other kinds of blocking, if at all, as acts they simply don't indulge [32].

So can productive, successful authors yield useful hints for writers in the program? We begin our inquiry by looking to see what successful writers model that we could emulate. The most common clue is about habits; writers like Anthony Trollope relied on regular practice of writing for their fluency [33]. Trollope makes a point echoed by later writers: even those of us who do nothing but write for a living need no more than three hours a day to achieve our best, most prolific work. Bds have a long but inconspicuous history.

Over time, our journal entries confirm this advice and add an important reassurance. Models of fluency are most helpful as reminders of what we already know and practice:

What comes of posting quotes from famous writers, including the infamous "Wait," of rotating them of them in and out of my drawer, of seeing them on the cork board daily? How do I use them? As goads, prompts, I suppose. They carry more weight than my own admonitions would if written and posted. I like them for their familiarity. Not one of them includes any surprises. . . . Have I picked only the quotes that reinforce my new beliefs or do they capture most of the best advice? It's probably a combination of both.

What haven't we considered as models that nonetheless prove influential? As a rule, my writers tell me, the examples that come to mind are the writers like Ayn Rand [34] who worked in binges, to the point of undermining their health and mood. While negative prototypes rarely get listed among the Post-Its around our writing sites, they come to mind as opposites of writers whose examples do surround writing sites.

What about patience and involvement in bds? This is a major theme of the program; it shows up everywhere. Even so, we discuss this familiar strategy for unblocking just as patiently as we do the others listed above. The following example of a writer's private musings about patience and involvement typifies the ambivalence that surrounds involvement in bds:

What about it? A big IT. It. it. Does it work, do I want it to work, can I do it? Maybe. Maybe not. Easier said than done. I may always be prone to rushing, to bingeing. Maybe what will work for me is to be able to haul up patience and bds, etc., when I most need them. The rest of the time I can be me. Imperfect but getting by.

There is consensus here, especially in group discussions, that strategies of regular involvement may work best in the long run. After several months of practice, bds show something that other methods of fluency have not:

This is why bds seems to work . . . . It has become part of my daily routines. I don't have to struggle or feel in the mood. I just put in my time and it works. It works and I like it. Why? Because the more I do it, the easier it gets and the faster my writing moves along and the better I feel about myself as a real writer. . . . Nothing else has come close to working this well.

The question could be what helps the most. Time will tell, but for now I cast my vote for the bds ticket. It has me writing just about every day and enjoying it. I can't think of a better way, only why I didn't think of it before.

What about self-study? We can learn something surprising while examining our habits as writers. We might sense, most of us, that what will work best to keep us on track amid all the strategies we are trying will be regular self-study as writers. The familiar custom of putting our thoughts about writing on paper and clarifying them may hold the key to understanding the self-statements, moods, and habits that get in the way of our writing:

This is the lesson: Field says it [in her book--11] and it shows up here. If it can't be put down on paper, I can't really understand it and deal with it--if I can't be as explicit and calm and confident in facing my fears as I am in facing my writing, I won't make much progress. This is the irony: these little seances, these moments for reflections about myself as a writer, may be more important than my writing project. This may be the most important thing I'm doing.

Each day that I make notes about fluency, even a word or two, I don't lose touch with what I want to do and change. . . . It's the way to keep it all from slipping away by not thinking about it for a few days. I need to put it outside my consciousness where I can see and hear it.

Two other things typically emerge as self-studies move along. One is the desire to share and sharpen ideas with other writers. The second is the desire to see how strategies for fluency actually stand up to systematic testing.

Tests of Methods for Unblocking

There is, I remind you, evidence for the effectiveness for the methods we have been trying [35]. In the main, systematic tests of unblocking make two points. First, no single therapy for blocking, say free writing, works well in isolation, especially in the long run. Second, a gradual combination of treatments works best in terms of inducing a lasting and comfortable level of fluency.

A related finding suggests why singular interventions work with but limited scope. Each addresses a separate but crucial part of fluency. Consider some examples: Free writing, first of all, allows us to generate thinking on paper with few inhibitions. It works best in the short run to induce momentum and imagination, and in the long run to promote the kind of reflection essential to self-study. Contingency management, second, also works best in the short run. On the one hand, it forces us to experience regular habits of writing that can later become self-sustaining. But contingency management, on the other hand, carries the risk of turning writers away from writing; its forcing, if carried too far, associates unpleasantness with daily sessions and can generate the desire to escape its aversive discipline.

A third category of methods for unblocking, cognitive therapies, proved equally specific. Its focus on moderating negative thinking helped promote comfort and patience in writing--by making writing more self-motivated and less reliant on external forcing. But when cognitive therapies were not accompanied by free writing and contingency management, writers did little regular writing over the long run. Patience works best in concert with involvement.

The next category, making writing a socially skilled act (procuring support and feedback, writing with a sense of audience, writing with public acceptance), had similar limitations. It, like cognitive therapies, worked best once writers were already fluent. Without the precedents, writers developed a sociable sense of writing but not reliable outputs. And without the social skills training as an addition to fluency, writing too often did not become public and publicly acceptable. Involvement works best when it moves beyond self-focus.

I ask groups at this point, by now somewhat immersed in their new habits of self-study, to reflect on what they have learned from this literature. One thing seems obvious, the need for moving beyond traditional methods of treating writing blocks which rely on a single intervention. The other lesson emerges more gradually: the optimal sequence for interventions. Free writing and forced scheduling appear to work best to initiate fluency. Cognitive therapies and social skills training seem essential to making fluency a self-sustaining and acceptable act.

At this point, we clarify what these lessons mean for each of us:

For the first time here, things are finally fitting together in an understandable pattern. I'm relieved to know that treating writing blocks can be more than a hit-or-miss proposition. . . . It makes me optimistic.

You know what I like? The catholicity. Great word, eh? Any one approach, including Bob's, is limited and narrow. No one individual has all the answers. Isn't that great, encouraging? I mean, we can learn from all kinds of sources, including ourselves.

I don't know. We're only talking about one series of tests. They may not be the final word. We may be overreacting. There may be a lot more, whole lot more to undoing writing blocks than we know yet. I'm keeping an open mind, a skeptical outlook.

If you want to know what I think, I think it's still far too complicated. . . . This combination takes a long time. A whole year. Why isn't there a quicker way?

No, no, I can see why this will work. It makes good sense. It combines all the best aspects of traditional methods. It is based on careful testing to winnow out what worked from what didn't. It . . . put the things that work into a workable chain. I'll put it to the skeptic in the group: What else would work better?

The next step seems inevitable. We agree, with little prompting from me, to begin to formalize fluency exercises in our program.

FORMAL INTERVENTIONS FOR FLUENCY

What we add at this point complements the regular practices already put in place. The methods for finding motivation remain in force; we continue with regular pauses to maintain comfort (e.g., does your writing posture need readjustment?) and patience (e.g., does your rate of errors suggest that you are rushing and tiring?). We retain a moderate emphasis on staying in conversations; there is always the danger, once working on fluency, of resuming old habits of reclusive writing. And we stick with habits of noticing, collecting, and planning--also at moderated levels. We continue to look out for new angles, new materials that could be incorporated into revisions. We, of necessity, reflect each day on what we have accomplished and how it fits in with overall plans. And we persist in free writing. We use it to get unstuck when writing or planning and we use it as the principle means of self-study in our journal entries.

With these practices in place, fluency comes easily, almost painlessly. By this time, most writers are already practicing the fundamentals of initiating fluency in a general way. What remains is making the practices more systematic. Experience has taught me to insert a caution in the midst of this enthusiasm: keep daily sessions brief, to as little as half an hour, to no more than two or three hours. Fluency, once flowing, can become runaway: as Samuel Johnson said, "one of the laws of composition is that a pen in motion, like matter in Newton's first law, continues in motion unless it is compelled to change that state by forces impressed on it from without" [36]. And, fluency, once runaway, brings fatigue and inefficient work more quickly than we realize [37]. A good way to see if daily sessions are too long is whether you maintain their practice, day after day.

This is how we program fluency:

Step 1. Preparing for Daily Sessions

The step comes in addition to the planning already in place--the conceptual outlining, the tentative schedule for moving through parts of the project, the prompts for pauses and reflections. It is a preparatory moment to instil an optimal frame of mind for writing. With practice, this moment prompts an optimistic mood, a focus on the right problems, and a sense of audience. Free writing works nicely for this task, as demonstrated by its master, Peter Elbow, in such an anticipation of his own writing:

Let me think for a minute about audience. . . . So how do I talk to professionals and academics. I can't be too missionary and preachy. That's a tone I fall into; and I feel missionary about it. . . . What is their situation? Like mine: having lots of things to write; always being behind; being skilled at words and even at writing--but (here this differs from how I now feel) being skittish and even scared about writing. Having mostly unpleasant experiences at writing. [38]

What can come of this exercise? As Peter Elbow proceeded with his own preparations, he made better sense of what he wanted and needed to say and how to say it. As he achieved greater clarity about what he could do to best serve his message and his audience, he apparently became more confident. The more formal prose that followed probably came more easily and clearly. For writers in the program (and I trust, for readers), these things actually happen.

How long does this exercise take? For most of us, it lasts for only a minute or two; even writers working with bds as brief as ten to fifteen minutes have time for it. When there is confusion about how to say things, the extra time is better spent preparing than on prose that is off-target. But a warning applies here. We need to watch out for successive sessions where this kind of prewriting disrupts the flow of prose. The point of free-writing-to-plan is to supplement, not supplant daily writing.

Step 2. Making bds a Regular Habit

Fluency demands a regular habit that persists in the midst of already busy days. Without this regularity and habituality, all the other things that need to be a customary part of writing--the motivation, the imagination, the skills, and the satisfaction--may founder. So, to begin to make bds a habit, most writers rely on contingency management, at least for a month or two (and later, whenever they drift away from regular practice).

There are three reasons, all familiar, for making writing a daily habit. First, habit pushes aside the usual struggle to write. Second, habit makes writers more productive than do its usual alternatives (e.g., bingeing); regular practice at bds produces remarkable, reliable fluency without disrupting daily necessities. Third, habit disciplines writers to surmount laziness and sloppiness about writing. Writers consistently tell me that this act of self-discipline instills more confidence and pride than any other in the program. This is a turning point.

In my experience, the habit of bds is optimally established in a sequence of exercises like this:

1. *Limit bds to weekdays, to daytimes, to early times.* Begin with this resolve: Even the busiest people can find time for writing during weekdays and so can you. Find times, as brief as ten minutes to begin with; insert them into your normal daily schedule, during a small part of your lunch hour if necessary. Do not, though, suppose that you should get up earlier than usual for your writing time; most writers simply do not persist in arising when they are tired; as a rule, writing perseveres best where discomforts and inconveniences are minimal. Still, you may have early morning time available in your existing routines (especially if you install the unusual practice, for writers, of going to bed early and getting enough sleep). I, for example, use the early morning time when I might prefer to read newspapers for a writing time. Almost anyone of us can claim a brief period for writing from our week days: It might be the first

half-hour in an office. It could be a morning coffee break.
Whenever, there are productive openings in the days of every writer
I have known.

If possible insert your primary writing time in the A.M.; almost all
writers work best in the morning when they are most alert (the
exceptions are just that, as Asimov might have said, exceptions). Try
to avoid writing times (but not times for reflection or journal writing)
in evenings. Writers who imagine they can think clearly after a long
day and a heavy dinner kid themselves. Writers who manage prose
in the late evening not only work amid fatigue but they also risk
insomnia and even greater tiredness.

Another caution about finding writing times: Don't fall prey to usual
advice of making writing a high-priority activity, something around
which you will schedule the rest of your days. It won't work, for a
good reason. Unrealistically high priorities, just like New Year's
resolutions, fail sooner or later because they demand too much change
from customary activities. Consider the reasons why. They force us
into routines that become aversive through their excessiveness. Most
people who take up exercise regimens overdo them; most newcomers
I see at the gym start with long, demanding regimens. They rarely
last for more than a month or two. The writers who begin by
resolving to take large chunks out of their days for writing suffer a
similar fate. They not only overdo writing but they schedule it so
that it conflicts with more important activities such as social life,
exercise, and sleep. My advice here, based on long experience, is to
make writing a moderate priority, nothing more. That's all it ever
needs to be.

After all, bds that grow to sixty minute sessions typically suffice to
produce some 200-300 pages of prose per year, sufficient output for
all but some full-time writers.

The basic principle here is sometimes called Minsky's Law (after
Marvin Minsky, a pioneer in the study of artificial intelligence).
When we make an activity like writing an artificially high priority,
we undermine its chances for success. The point proves important
enough to merit listing:

RULE # 9: Writing, at least in the short run, need be nothing more than a
moderate daily priority, something that ranks below more important activities

such as social life and health-inducing activity. Unrealistic priorities and goals, like New Year's resolutions, usually fail.

2. *Limit bds to ordinary workdays.* Because most writers can manage more than enough productivity in bds inserted amid usual workdays, they need not do serious prewriting or composition during evenings, weekends, or vacations. (Major revisions and proofings may be the exception.) The majority of "graduates" from my programs join me in eschewing writing at times when we deserve to be doing other things. By limiting primary prewriting and writing times to workdays, we not only encourage more restful lives; we also experience the special pleasure of entering evenings, weekends, and vacations knowing that we "have done enough" as writers for the time being. The usual pressure of living, day in and day out, with the sense of never having done enough, of never being caught up with one's writing is a high-powered form of stress, one that, among other things, drives many academics into nonacademic careers [39].
Here too there is an imperative crucial enough to merit a rule:

RULE #10: Learn to accept the planned outputs of brief, daily sessions as all the writing you need or want to do for the day; being able to enjoy evenings, weekends, and vacations without supposing you should be writing is an essential pleasure.

There are other reasons for limiting writing to the interstices of workdays. One concerns hypomania. When we leave large, undisrupted periods of time open for writing, we tend to extremes. We may use part of the open time for small errands and then suppose that we no longer have sufficient time for writing. (This pattern brings procrastination and disappointment.) Or when we manage to begin writing, we may lapse into bingeing. We already know the perils ofbingeing, specifically the impatience, grandiosity, fatigue, and eventual inertia and depression that come with hypomania (Chapter 1). All this bears the constant reminding and talking-aloud of a rule:

RULE #11: Avoid writing at times when you might better be getting rest or recreation; writing in large, undisrupted blocks of time invites hypomania and procrastination.

Restated, the rule reads: Keep writing in its rightful place, as something that doesn't fatigue, as something not to be done under fatigue; make room for it in the midst of other routine daily patterns.

3. *Limit bds to clearly defined goals.* This point is implicit in the foregoing advice but it bears repeating. Use trial and error to discover what constitutes a reasonable daily goal for output (most writers, in my experience, aim for 1.0-2.5 pages of prose per hourly session, including rewrites). Use good sense to make goals flexible when encountering unusual circumstances such as sticking points, complex material, or illness. And, use your imagination in setting useful goals for prewriting (e.g., completing a revision of your conceptual outline; reading and annotating four resources in a bds).

This essential goal in practicing bds finds a related expression in yet another rule:

RULE #12: At a minimum, stay in touch with your ongoing writing projects on a daily basis. At the least, peruse what you have been doing and contemplate what lies ahead, so that your project remains fresh in mind.

Advantages of daily contact include more noticing of things that relate to the writing, noticing that adds ideas and connections because the writing stays fresh in mind each day. Daily contact with writing projects helps in a related way by eliminating most or all the need for warm-up in each new session.

Another goal has almost equal consequence, that of setting limits for session lengths. Recall what rule #5 (Chapter 1) said: that learning to stop writing is as important as learning to start writing. Without clear, reasonable limits, writing displaces necessary daily activities and turns into bingeing.

4. *Establish moderately undisrupting conditions at your writing site.* The essentials of making writing a high probability act (to use behavioral language) revolve around stimulus control procedures. While these precautions for productive conditions may sound annoyingly behavioristic, they in fact predate any systematic psychologies. These rules for productivity persist because they work, regardless of writers' general philosophies:

a. Arrange a regular site where you do writing and little else. Situate it in a pleasant, fairly quiet surround with an outlet for resting your eyes (preferably a window through which you can distance focus). Clear the site of distractions such as magazines, newspapers, and correspondence unrelated to your project. When you are at your writing site but cannot write, make a pact with yourself to sit there quietly for some minimum time such as five minutes. It is important not to do other, nonwriting, things (e.g., phone calls, errands) during writing times. At the least glance over materials (see rule #12); if you can't write, you can think about and make notes about your project. A final thing often helps: plan to end each bds with freewriting about what you will write the next time. (This act helps maintain momentum).

b. Keep interruptions at a minimum by posting a sign on your *closed* door (e.g., "This is my sacred writing time; please do not disturb me except for dire emergencies and even then for only one minute; thank you for your cooperation"), by turning off your phone or by switching your incoming calls to an answering machine, and by informing appropriate people of your regularly scheduled writing times. Other people will look for clear, unambiguous signals from you about how important your writing is to you.

c. Remind yourself that all but life-threatening emergencies can wait the fifteen to sixty minutes until you are finished with your writing session. Fluency depends, in a way, on tolerating uncertainty (even not knowing who might have called).

d. Prepare yourself to immediately return to work after interruptions; if you find yourself off-track, reimmerse yourself with the help of free writing and practice calming exercises.

5. *Ensure a moderate, comfortable pace of working*. Reinstitute the habits of stopping every fifteen to twenty minutes to relax (e.g., stretch your arms, neck, back, and legs; lower your tongue to the bottom of your mouth; track your breathing in and out of your nose), to check for postural comfort, and to curb rushing/fatigue (e.g., by monitoring your work for a high rate of errors and by noticing an impatience about taking breaks). Taken together, these admonitions for arranging optimal writing conditions make up a notable rule:

RULE #13:   Make a habit of writing amid comfortable, moderately uninterrupted conditions where all you do is writing (or things closely supportive of it).

If possible, add a final component of stability. Write at the same time of day on most days. The habit of writing, like any other, grows stronger when we it expect it to occur at predictable times.

Step 3. Begin with contingency management.

An obvious essential in establishing a regular habit of writing is involvement. Talk and good intentions, in themselves, rarely build strong habits of writing. To ensure regular practice of the habit of writing in bds and in optimal surrounds, institute moderate external pressures to stay on schedule and on location. There are several workable variations on contingency management (another Skinnerian term that has found wide currency; it simply means making an activity that you would prefer to writing, say reading a newspaper or taking a morning shower, contingent on first doing a modicum of writing for the day). The admonitions that follow array contingencies from least to most aversive; always work with the least pressure sufficient to keep you at your schedule of bds:

First, motivate yourself with a chart of your daily compliance and productivity (e.g., a bar graph that shows time spent per bds and that depicts output per bds). Post the chart of your compliance in a public place and encourage other people to attend to it. (The novelist Irving Wallace found such graphs a strong motivator to continue writing [40]).

Second, pressure yourself to stick to scheduled times for writing with the help of a social contract. In one arrangement, ask someone to call you at the time just before your bds begins, to provide a brief, friendly reminder of your obligation. In another, more powerful variation, meet with another writer for mutually quiet, separate bds--in a neutral setting such as a library table. In the most compelling variation, collaborate with another writer and meet for regular work on your joint manuscripts.

Third, push yourself to write by making other, more desirable things such as watching television contingent (for the day) on first completing the moderate goals of your bds. Resist the temptation of making essential activities your contingencies (e.g., valued social interactions; eating). Never add to the costs of not writing penalties that will further undermine your day-to-day welfare.

Fourth, force yourself to write, under dire circumstances, by writing in order to avoid punishments. A common version has writers prepare a series of signed checks, place them in addressed and stamped envelopes, and leave them with neutral persons who agree to mail one check each day that goals for a bds are not met [41]. To make this punishment maximally effective, write the checks to a hated organization (e.g., the NRA; ACLU; or whatever offends you). But use avoidance strategies only as a last resort, temporarily; with longer use, their aversiveness can generalize to the act of writing itself. That is:

RULE #14: Use external contingencies to instil (or to reinstall) a regular habit of writing, at least in the short run. Employ minimally effective forcing to ensure fluency and aim to replace it with internally generated motivations such as habit and enjoyment.

The limitation of this fourteenth rule is that most writers at this stage are, as yet, prepared to appreciate only its first part, using contingency management as a short-term measure. Later, with regular bds for at least six to twelve months, the force of habit will become apparent. In the meanwhile, the usual caution applies: patience.

I usually present this list about optimizing fluency to my writing groups in written form, much as I have here. There is little in it that is new; as usual, every new step is already in practice, more or less. And there is nothing here that we haven't already doubted and debated. Still, this is an occasion for expressing seasoned reservations, for dispelling some old doubts. To proceed in our journey without addressing this turbulence, I have learned, is to invite unnecessary trouble.

INITIAL REACTIONS TO THE RULES FOR FLUENCY

You might anticipate the two, usually conflicting thrusts at work here for writers I have known. Writers are committed, by this point, to trying and mastering each new strategy. But, at each step, they question the addition of yet another rule and obligation to an enterprise that once seemed spontaneous. So while they generally welcome the lists of advice just above as convenient knowledge, writers understandably resent the additional assignments:

Oh, I don't know, does it have to be so hard?

Is there no end to this? It's so much more complicated than I had hoped.

But at this point in the program, resistances appear to be more easily placated than early on. When we hear grumbling that signals impatience, we dismiss it, with due reverence, as such. When apprehension about complexity is spoken, we reply with reminders that we have already started practicing most of the things being demanded:

This is what I see. Nothing, absolutely nothing new to do. The only real change will be doing a few things more regularly, especially the contingency thing. I haven't really done it yet, but I can't see it as a problem, not beyond my deeply held philosophical beliefs about free will and my even deeper hostility for behaviorism (laughs).

As these usual hesitancies fade, concerns about practical problems of implementation come to the fore. Some prescriptions, especially about closing office doors or not answering phones dominate worries:

I can't just close my door. I'm the chairman and people are used to being able to come in whenever they have a problem. . . . I don't think my colleagues and secretaries and students would like it.

Not answer my phone? Oh come on! What if an important call came in? How could I concentrate on writing if I'm worrying about missing important calls?

My kids and husband are used to popping in when I'm writing. After all, its the morning, and they're running around getting ready and they need me.

These concerns are so crucial to our progress that I reflect patiently on each point. More important, I take the time to get groups involved in problem solving that underlies good answers.

To keep us on track, though, in this unusually emotional discussion, I begin with a caution. I ask groups to recall a point made quietly in the first stage of the program (Chapter 1 in this book): the most consistently fluent, efficient writers welcome a modicum of disruptions while writing. Without these distractions, writers might get too narrowly involved in the task. Without them, they could neglect needed pauses for relaxation and comfort. My point in restating that old observation is this: None of us needs to make the rule about closing the door or not answering the phone iron-clad. Instead, the goal should be to preserve a fair amount of undisturbed concentration for bds.

That reminder provides a bit of relief for our discussions and we agree on some compromises. Really important calls, we decide, can be monitored on an answering machine and picked up, when necessary, briefly. Desired visits, we happily agree, can be welcomed, at least for an essential moment. The key to staying fluent, we concur, will be this: keeping most disruptions brief and undisturbing. We will know if we have succeeded by noting two things: (1) the readiness with which we can return to our writing (perhaps with a bit of free writing to help reinstate ideas and momentum); and, (2) the extent to which we still meet daily goals (perhaps with a bit of flexibility).

When we have clarified these permissions to be practical and sociable about establishing undisrupted conditions, my writers take over the ensuing discussions. They provide the assurances:

You know, this is what we should keep in mind. We're only talking about not answering the phone or getting up and going to the door for a half an hour or so. That's not so unreasonable. That's not so bloody awful.

I've been doing this for over a month and I can tell you that most of your worries are unfounded. When I told people in my office that I would be working alone at my writing for the half-hour before I start, they didn't look at me disapprovingly at all. . . . What several people said was reassuring: They said, "I should be doing something like that. I need to find times to write." . . . In fact, some of them have.

I can't say for sure how this works over time, but when I asked my husband and my daughter if I could have a half-hour of quiet time in the mornings, they agreed right away. My husband not only thought it would be nice for me to have my own time, but he began extrapolating all kinds of things that he could be during that time for himself. He would like to exercise then. My little girl thinks she will be content watching TV or doing her homework. . . . At least no one objected.

Then, as we deal with matters of practicality during the next several weeks, group members share increasingly more practical accounts of putting fluency measures in place:

There is no way I can get privacy at my desk. My secretary doesn't want to have to decide which calls are important, who should and should not be allowed in. People are used to popping in anytime. I had to find some place else to go. I found an ideal spot where I can take my portable computer. It's a bench inside an empty conference room. It's perfect. I'd be happy there even if I weren't doing anything, which is sometimes just what I do. . . . It's also been good for me to take a break from my office.

I have been trying out your suggestion of finding a writing partner. I have a colleague who wants to write, so we are experimenting with fifteen minute sessions together. We tried a few at her house. That didn't work because she felt compelled to entertain, to get tea and that sort of thing. It seemed rude not to talk. We tried to meet at my office. She didn't feel comfortable there because of the constant hallway noises and the occasional knocking at my door. We're now trying the periodicals room at the library, a big table where each of us can spread out our things. I'm still having trouble getting settled down, if you know what I mean, but I think this will work. . . . For sure, I have gone to my writing sessions on days when I wouldn't have written on my own. I don't want to let down my partner.

Well, I've been doing contingencies, seeing what works. I asked my wife what I should make contingent and she suggested going without lunch when I didn't write. That way, if I didn't write I wouldn't get any fatter (laughs). . . . I tried doing writing to earn newspapers, but I found I could do without them. . . . But I had a clue on days when I couldn't read my newspapers. I was even more attentive to the evening news on TV. So I had the idea of not allowing myself any news for the day, magazines, newspapers, or TV, unless I did my writing and met my goals. I've missed only one bds since and I did not like missing it.

I hope no one else had this problem. I found out, when I tried to find times for writing, that my lover doesn't really approve of my writing. . . . When I set up an 8:00 A.M. time, she put up a real clatter with house cleaning. Loud noises from vacuuming, banging around, you know. Other times, other disruptions. We had a creative battle going. . . . I decided to keep my writing, the notes and the word processor and the time, all at work, all elsewhere. I do it all there and on the train and I say very little about it at home. I think that this is the best strategy for us because it shows _____ that my writing isn't a lover competing for her affection at home.

As each variation of these problems comes up, we are better and better able to generate problem solutions. We agree, almost without exception, that we all can find reasonable times and optimal locations for bds. We discover, to a person, that working in comfort and with moderated temptations to do other things leads to remarkable increases in our daily productivity. And we have proof, in our charts and graphs, of accomplishing far more as writers than we would otherwise have managed.

Three special insights dominated these conversations. The first is about working without unnecessary delays:

The truly amazing thing is no warmups. No more time wasted on futzing around, figuring out what to do, getting myself going.

The second insight is related, about working without bingeing:

I honestly did not believe I could do my good writing without one of my marathons, or even without at least a couple of hours at a time. . . . But, here I am, doing better without them because I can pick it up again right away in the daily schedule and I can do even better writing when I've been thinking about it in between. . . . No more weekends whiled away, I should say frazzled away, on exhausting binges.

The third realization also relates to an outcome of giving up bingeing for bds:

I can say what is best of all. It's the steady accumulation of writing by working every day. Like a water torture, a drop at a time, but better. I'm pleasantly surprised at how easy it is every day and how much it all adds up to after only a month. At my present rate, even without pushing, I figure to finish my whole book manuscript in the rest of this year. I didn't get that much done in the past three years combined.

A fourth realization comes more gradually for participants (and probably for you, the reader). We begin to notice, as our strategies for ensuring fluency work slowly and steadily, that we are, at the same time, dealing with our old bugaboos, writing blocks. What had seemed insurmountable when we spoke of problems such as perfectionism and fears of failure now seems to be under control by simple means of regular work. But not surprisingly, this cognizance brings an unsettled feeling. We wonder: Have we, in putting aside our direct consideration of blocking, left its underlying components dangerously disregarded?

I can't be the only one to feel funny about the conspicuousness of its absence, eh? One minute we're steeped in talk of blocking, this collection of old, unsolved mysteries. The next minute we've settled for fluency exercises. Are we putting the cart before the horse by dealing with mechanics first and leaving our real blocks untended?

BACK TO BLOCKING

With fluency becoming a regular habit, we feel even better prepared to deal with writing blocks. Earlier in our journey, it now seems, we managed little more than a superficial acquaintance with blocking. All groups at this point have decided to spend a session or two readdressing blocks. At my encouragement, we begin by asking two questions. The first is about timing: are we now, having begun to master some unblocking strategies by way of establishing fluency exercises, better able to understand traditional notions of blocking? The second question is about perspective: has the concept of blocking been posed in a useful way?

Revisiting the Literature

When we look over our annotations of what has been written about writing blocks, we agree, even the romantics among us, that they disillusion. The entertainment value of this scattered literature far exceeds its practical worth. To that conclusion we add some specifics: First, much of the literature on writing blocks relies on speculation, on untested and dubious assumptions such as putting work away, in a drawer and out of mind, until inspiration strikes [42]. For how many people and how often does this advice prove optimal? Second, too much of this literature borders on the spectacular. Consider Edmund Bergler's claim that writers block as a symbolic gesture of rejecting their mothers' milk [31]. Did Bergler ever check to see if any other accounts of blockers include confirmations of his predicted acts of regurgitated food among writers? (None do.) Do fantastic explanations of blocking turn serious people away from the topic? Third, even where strategies work, as with free writing, their scope is narrow. Why don't accounts of unblocking, even the best known of them [42], include checks for their effectiveness in assisting writers through the long-term act of completing, revising, publishing, and writing again?

With those doubts expressed about usual approaches, we ask the inevitable. Would we fare better with a new conceptualization of blocking?

Reconceptualizing Writing Blocks

As a rule, I encourage the growing skepticism about writing blocks with this observation and query: Writers are unique in labeling their dysfluencies as blocks. Why do writers persist with a unique concept, one that has produced little help, one that encourages no links with knowledge about similar maladies in other activities? Consider a few parallels to blocking. We don't label public speaking anxiety as speaking blocks. Instead, we see this dysfunction for what it is (e.g., excessive self-consciousness, tension, and underpreparation) and treat the symptoms with interventions that work for a variety of anxieties [43]. Nor, for another example, do we call phobias about leaving home (e.g., for crowded spaces like shopping malls) traveling blocks. Instead, we observe what inhibits the desired acts (e.g., spouses who encourage reclusiveness, unrealistic fears of public embarrassment) and treat them with marital counseling and exposure therapy [44]. People with speaking anxiety or agoraphobia have wide access to well-publicized treatment programs. Hundreds of respected therapists treat patients with documented success, often with support from large federal research grants. (In contrast, I know of only a handful of writing block therapists, including me.)

Why do writing blocks remain largely untreated? Why are most accounts of blocking and its treatment amateurish and less than credible? Where else can we find similarly unimpressive results? The answer to the last question is easy and illuminating--in traditional programs for weight loss in obese people. Put simply, dieting generally leads to failed plans and even greater weight gains in the long run [4]. The reasons for this expensive failure are becoming more and more apparent. For one thing, diets typically rely on external forcing. For another, weight loss programs ignore the problematic patterns behind diet failures, particularly binge eating. They even, as a rule, overlook the deficits that dieters suffer in areas such as relaxation, self-focus, and self-esteem.

Not only does this example sound familiar to groups. It also primes writers to suggest a reason why treatments of writing blocks have been even less successful than dieting. At least part of the problem lies in the usual conception of writing blocks. There is, again, the unique label and connotation of blocking. Furthermore, there is the tradition of seeing writing as mysterious, as enigmatic. Group members have a wealth of examples to amplify this point:

Think about it! Where else do you talk about a well running dry? Or about Muses who desert us, that paralyze our writing arms or our souls?

Yeah, there are lots of these oddities. Writers who imagined they could write only with the smell of rotting apples . . . or with the smell of cork-lined walls, or with their clothes taken away until they finished. Interesting foolishness, wouldn't you say?

Yes, imagine going for treatment of a fear of flying in planes and being told to go home, to put your fear in a drawer, and to wait until you felt inspired to fly. It could be a long wait, right?

An old thought of ours comes to mind. Most writers don't want rational, sensible explanations of writing and fluency. They want magic.

You know what else? I'll bet that a lot of writers, once they are writing, don't necessarily want other writers to know how to find fluency. No wonder there are so few writing block therapists; once people discover how to write, they feel disinclined to share the secrets.

Sooner or later, we return to our original question. Would we fare better with a replacement for the concept of blocking? We agree, my groups and I, to seek only a tentative answer; there is no hurry for a decision given our current success in managing prewriting and writing. To find clues, we return to our habit of looking at relevant literature. This time, though, we search outside the area of writing and writing blocks. Clinical psychology, for example, produces promising clues about how to reconceptualize writing dysfluencies. My two most recent groups independently came up with the same favorite, a scheme for making sense of self-defeating behavior.

Writing Dysfluencies Considered as Self-Defeating Behaviors

We rely mostly on the work of a psychologist, Roy Baumeister [45]. In his view, self-defeating behaviors are everyday, normal (but dysfunctional) acts such as:

1. Self-handicapping (e.g., discounting our abilities and prospects for success due to a combination of insecurity about future performance and unrealistic ideas about the requirements for success).
2. Substance abuse (because it replaces immediate pressures with pleasant sensations and with lowered self-awareness).
3. Face work (e.g., where we save face by retaliating in the face of embarrassment).
4. Shyness (e.g., when we try to promote a favorable public image by remaining quiet, and, at the same time, avoid both the anxiety and rejection of public performance).

Both times that groups have generated summaries of Baumeister's conclusions like the one above, the same question has come up: "But does he talk about writing?" Other group members have answered it in much the same way: "He doesn't need to. Writing applies just the same as anything else." Thereby, in seeing hope for conceptualizing writing problems in more general terms such as self-defeating behaviors, we begin to foresee some of the things we still need to work on--as writers and as everyday people. With that prospect in mind, we take a few minutes to apply some of the notions of self-defeating tendencies to writing.

You may be like writers in my groups who see another ready application, in Baumeister's conclusion that self-defeating behaviors don't typically block us from getting things done; instead they slow our progress and make us generally miserable. Thus, we concur, we needn't wait until completely stymied before we work on getting rid of maladaptive behaviors. We might better, contrary to traditional conceptions of blocking, work at them until we are uninhibited and happy as writers.

Then we move on to similar discussions about other observations of self-defeating styles of behaving: First, we note, writers often persevere in short-term solutions that undermine larger goals:

I know. When I settle for forcing my articles under deadlines, I'm just making it harder to get to where I want to be--to real excellence as a writer that I now know is going to require everyday practice and patience.

This reminds me of my procrastinations. When I put off my writing to run errands, or because I feel tired, I put off my big goals.

Second, writers choke under pressure when they excessively self-monitor a performance and then notice that they lack conscious knowledge about how to execute the response:

No arguing with that. That's just what I do. And the more I do it, the more I do it. The more I do it, the more nervous I get and the more nervous I get, the more I watch what I do with an eagle eye. I think it's a vicious circle and I'm just getting an idea how to break it.

Where that happens to me is when I start editing too soon. Just like Peter Elbow warns me not to. . . . When I see how incomplete and how imperfect my story is in the beginning, I tense up and I generate those critical voices of my old composition teachers.

Third, writers become helpless in the face of adversity because their past efforts have not helped:

That's me. . . . As soon as I stumble, I dwell on how I failed before. And then all I want to do is to quit, to get away from writing and even the thought of it.

Sometimes I give up before I start. I think of the difficulties and the rejections awaiting and I can't see any way around them . . . at least I couldn't in the past.

Fourth, writers use counterproductive bargaining strategies such as making excessive demands or aiming too low:

The poor bargaining strategy that hits home for me is the zero-sum game. I am all too quick to suppose that any gain for an editor is a loss for me, to imagine that his gain is my loss. Rationally I know that is not necessarily so, but in practice, when I'm feeling defensive in the face of criticism, I tend to overreact, to antagonize editors unnecessarily. I fight over every change, no matter how small, as a personal loss for me.

The bargaining strategy of aiming too low is all too familiar now that I think about it. I have a history of taking the first suggestion of settling for a lesser publication instead of sticking to my original goals. . . . For instance, twice I let journal editors talk me into condensing really significant articles (I now realize) into brief articles. You know, that acquiescence made my work look less significant and it didn't do much for my self-esteem. What would it have hurt to have made my case and to have asked for a chance to revise, or for another opinion? When I see other anthropologists making my same points in more prominent articles, I cringe.

And, fifth, we tend to use ineffective ingratiation procedures, notably in making our approval-seeking actions too obvious:

Ah, this doesn't feel so splendid to admit. I do this and when I've finished, I know I have made things worse than if I hadn't tried to compliment someone like an editor or a luminary. . . . I once sent a submission letter in which I went on and on about how much I admired this editor's work. Really laid it on. Then a day or two later, I realized how it must look to him. Like cheap manipulation. . . . He rejected my manuscript briskly, without mention of my groveling. What was I thinking? Or I should say, why wasn't I thinking more clearly?

With this list completed, one other thing occurs to us: When we chronically act in self-defeating ways, when we stumble over stupidities that are only partially visible, we cannot improve our confidence and self-esteem. The realization that follows is another point made by Baumeister. Self-defeating behaviors also produce strong negative emotions. This is important because negative feelings--of fear, anxiety, embarrassment, and uncomfortable self-awareness--demand rapid solutions in the form of short-term relief. So it is, we note, that writers turn to avoidance, substance abuse, and deadlines that force them to write.

Then we check to make sure that we can apply the principles for understanding self-defeating behavior to usual writing problems. What, for instance, does it have to do with perfectionism? The answer, we concur, is that perfectionism is a short-term answer to fears of being rejected, of being judged as mediocre, of being publicly exposed as a fraud. When faced with the discomfort of not knowing whether we can do something perfectly, we put it off. To assuage our fears of being seen as less than a genius, we do work at the last minute, when no one can expect our best efforts.

Or, for another, what does Baumeister's point about the demands of negative affect for quick relief have to do with the laziness we often show in regard to writing? Laziness, we decide, can reflect indecision and uncertainty as much as anything else. If we are faced with a difficult task for which we have no convenient solutions, laziness may be the immediate answer. When we say we are too tired or busy to write, we can avoid the more troubling reasons for not wanting to write.

You might imagine that with so useful a set of ideas in hand for making sense of what we usually call blocking, writers work at capsulizing them into a rule. Formulating this one requires some hard thinking and many revisions, but both of my recent groups settled on this version of applying notions of self-defeating behavior to writing dysfluencies:

RULE #15: The dysfluencies we ordinarily call blocking could just as well be labeled self-defeating patterns (such as self-handicapping, face work, shyness, choking under pressure, helplessness, and ineffective bargaining strategies).

There are understandable dilemmas in adding this perspective to what we are already considering. Self-defeating behaviors are much broader than writing problems; they even suggest that many of our writing difficulties derive from more general problems of life style. So writers ask: "Are we really prepared to deal with all this? Aren't we talking here about changing our whole selves?" I agree that we may not yet be prepared to manage broad life changes. We are still struggling with relatively small changes as writers. For the moment, we agree to notice self-defeating behaviors most obviously connected to writing. Over time, I add, we may see ways of letting our new habits as writers influence our overall lives. Group members make a related point that provides comfort, almost as though our discomfort demanded some immediate, short-term attention (though here the response is not self-defeating): The essences of self-defeating behaviors are simple and, in most cases, we are already combatting them. There is nothing new in looking for self-handicapping, shyness, helplessness, choking, or poor problem-solving strategies. And, there is much to be gained by noticing these tendencies in terms of common, everyday acts that slow and discourage us in many ways.

This discussion also proves a timely point, about two months after we began systematic work on fluency, for sharing information about how well our exercises are working.

OUTCOMES

To give a sense of how well writers generally do by this juncture, I present more of the results from the study group of fifty-two writers who have completed the program. These data provide a sense of how our individual progress compares with norms. The results also help provide important confirmation that the program continues to work. It is a moment for reasserting the long-term payoffs of a wise passiveness.

Reflections on Prior Steps for Comfort and Planning

There are, even in the most compliant participants, still problems in following directives for regular pauses while writing:

It works least well when I get most excited about my writing. Even so, I know the benefits of stopping for comfort checks and relaxation and reseating and all that, even when I'm rolling.

It isn't that I don't intend to keep on doing these things. I do. They just aren't like old habits yet, I guess. They don't come naturally; they just fade away if I don't make myself notes and reminders. . . . I'm still not sure they will work for me.

When I sort out the some thirty writers who managed this plan best by this point, I can see some commonalities: These writers, most distinctively, made conscious plans to ensure regular breaks and maintain patient prewriting. They also, as suggested above, added cues such as notes to remind themselves to maintain these still formative habits. One more thing stands out. These were the writers who reported the breaks and the prewriting as most enjoyable.

Problems lingered for the other writers who were still trying to master regular pauses and "writing before writing" (as some composition teachers such as Donald Murray call prewriting):

Control, that's my problem. Once I have a train of thought, I don't want to take the time for comfort pauses or to prewrite. Why? I think it's because I still fear losing the pure thought and never again finding another. Still, there's a good side. I am still working at patience--it works some of the time, and that's a change. I'm still plugging away at the imagination exercises and I can see that they work. It's just a matter of bringing things--my, what?, old fears and my new habits--together.

Could something in the nature of writing be contributing to the often slow and imperfect progress evidenced at this stage? Ratings of patience had dropped from the time of the outset for this set of exercises in fluent writing, from a mean of 7.1 (where 10 = maximum) to 6.2. These fifty-two writers noticed their growing impatience and mentioned it frequently:

There is something about getting underway that makes me want to go even faster. I find I have lots and lots of ideas for new projects and I want to get finished with this and move on to them. I'm realizing, more than ever before, what my potentials are and it's hard not to want to experience them right now.

I was better at slowing [down] and appearing to be a patient person in the planning and outlining. Writing just speeds ahead on its own, or so it seems. . . . I know what you're going to ask. Am I pausing, and so on. No, I need to do more of it . . . or maybe I need to believe more in it.

So two of the things that discouraged the practice of comfort and planning were the inertia of the familiar (e.g., sticking with old fears and habits) and the exhilaration of not limiting momentum. Still, even the most troubled of writers (some one-fourth of writers at this stage) managed far more comfort, slowed pacing, and prewriting than ever before. And all of us could look to the more advanced patterns of the most successful writers in the program to find hope in persisting with these preliminary exercises.

Results of Fluency Exercises

Probably because the program went to lengths to ensure that most writers did at least a modicum of prewriting, 80 percent of participants met the criterion for "easing the transition" (i.e., a conceptual outline where every point and paragraph was accompanied by at least one descriptive sentence), and nearly 90 percent reported the actual transition as painless or almost so. Some writers' comments about this experience spoke to its newness:

This has been a novel experience, for certain. Never before has the first page, the first chapter come off so effortlessly, so pleasurably.

And some were testimonials about the effectiveness of prewriting:

Sure, we had been told all this. But not until you do it--you can't see the advantage. You move right along and you know where you are going and you can tell you are doing better writing.

The thing I like best is the controlled and steady speed of writing. With the prewriting standing beside the screen, I can concentrate on putting the ideas into a clear wording, without having all the struggle with what to say and where. . . .   I can tell that prewriting will actually save time by the end.

Later analyses of writers' progress, I like to add, confirm the impression that this is a crucial turning point in enhancing the fluency (and comfort) of writers. In the midst of this brief discussion, related insights are shared by group members. For example:

In a way, I think, translating the filled outlines into prose makes prose writing an even freer kind of free writing. I found that when I knew what I wanted to say, I could say it again and see how it came out and often say it better. Little struggle and lots of creativity.

Writing in bds. This exercise was harder, because it demanded compliance day in and day out. Satisfactory performance (writing in the bds format for at least half of scheduled sessions over the last two weeks) was still mediocre (66 percent of participants at this point) but growing; only a handful of writers refused to try bds in most weeks of this phase. Normative lengths for bds ranged from twenty to forty minutes per work day; only six writers relied on periods as brief as ten to fifteen minutes on most week days and they were looking for longer openings in their especially busy days.

What characterized the sixteen writers who carried out bds while meeting daily goals for output during at least three-quarters of the planned sessions in the last two weeks of this stage? One thing, again, was a strong involvement and success in comfort and planning that had continued here. A second thing follows from the first. These exemplary writers were most likely to report bringing a well-formed set of ideas for writing to fluency exercises. As a result, they worked steadily and seemed to welcome bds. Their mean daily output in typed page equivalents (including rewrites) was 1.5 pages per weekday, compared to an average of 0.6 pages for other participants. Patterns of self-ratings for comfort, confidence, and patience showed a similar contrast: exemplars self-rated near 8.0 (10 = maximum) on all three rating scales; other writers were below 6.0.

What kept some of the fifty-two writers from regular practice of bds? Reasons fell into some general types. The first, and most common, reflects temptations to do other things:

Oh, something often comes up. Do you know what I mean? This morning I had to make three separate trips to take members of my family either to or from the train station. Right during my writing time. [In response to my question about what she might do to avoid a recurrence:] Well, I don't know, I can't control the trains. But, wait, I know, I know: I could stop being chauffeur to anyone and everyone who needs a ride. I have more important things to do (although they don't seem to know it) and *I* find my way to the train by catching a ride with a neighbor. When I'm gone to a conference, they do manage on their own.

The second reason reflects a common resistance and doubts that may never go entirely away:

Does it have to be every day? I don't like that, the grueling regularity, the discipline and the schedule. It is too reminiscent of my parochial schooling. . . . Why can't I just write on the days when I have time? [In response to my suggestion of finding a compromise such as settling for two or three bds in most weeks:] Yeah, that might work. I don't know. I'll see. [It did.]

I just don't believe that I can do good writing in such brief periods.

And third is the lure of binge writing. Revered old habit that it is, bingeing persisted in the reports and observations of ten writers. For half of this subgroup, it was only an occasional lapse that did not interfere with overall fluency measures. A binge here and there seemed essential for special tasks that demanded more "wholistic" contact with writing (e.g., proofreading and revising a long manuscript). These occasional lapses exacted no apparent price. But for five writers, one lapse led to others and then to periodic silences. In these two months of fluency exercises, writers whose binge time outweighed their bds time managed only an average of 0.2 pages per week.

Why, then, did even these writers persevere with binges? What, if anything, were these seeming malingerers learning in seeing their results compared to nonbingers? Most binge writers offered encouraging answers:

No, don't worry, I'm getting to it. I just move a tad more slowly than most people. I just need more time. I just need more proof than do other, more trusting sorts. I've done enough of the bds to see that they can be better. I'm just working out my own stubborn compromise at my own stubborn pace, all right?

I think I grasp the problem here. I've never had training, none that took, at discipline in writing. My humanities background didn't only leave me suspicious of schedules and rewards but it let me unpracticed at self-discipline. I'm coming around. You'll have to be patient, all of you.

When we examined the records of bingers, we learned even more: For one other thing, binge writers, more than anyone else, made no strong efforts to set limits on session lengths (rule #5: Learning to stop writing is just as important as learning to start writing). For another, bingers were uniquely resistant to working in more pleasant surrounds (advice from Chapter 1):

That's true. I still believe, somehow, that if I have something else to look at, I wouldn't write. . . . I've always thought that good writers deliberately find bleak circumstances. My dissertation adviser told me that one of the great advantages of living in Iowa City was that it left him untempted to do anything but his research and writing. I guess that comment had a strong effect on me. Too strong, do you think?

With these things reviewed, we slow down to draw some preliminary conclusions. One is that we can learn from both the least and most productive writers at this point. Exemplars suggest that bds and their precedents work. Problematic writers demonstrate that both slow involvement in the exercises and slow disengagement from old habits such as bingeing inhibit progress. The other conclusion is less readily apparent. Writers agree that crucial involvement includes both regular practice and having a small group with whom they can share experiences and learning in a variety of terms. One participant said it best:

This is what I think it is. At first it isn't enough to just say or hear or read it. You have to do it. And you have to do it day after day. But then, to get the most from it, you have to say it and get it straight with others who are trying to do it, to get it clear about what works and why.

CONCLUSIONS

The third stage of the program, represented here as Chapter 3, marks the crucial transition in writing, the shift from planning to prose. Its importance in the scheme of things is represented by the unusual number of rules generated in this chapter, seven new admonitions for optimal fluency. But fluency, in many ways, reinvokes the rules we saw in preceding chapters as well. Consider the second rule, from Chapter 1: Involvement almost always precedes optimal, reliable motivation. Here too. The same goes for patience. New pressures in this third program stage, born of new demands and opportunities for unfettered momentum, caused many writers to struggle again with impatience.

The fourth rule carried equal weight in this potentially difficult period: Nothing substitutes for a regular habit of writing (although here we became more aware of the value of sharing the experience with a study/support group). The old adage with the most relevance grew originally from our work on imagination (rule #6): here, as much as there, the most fluent and comfortable writers spent as much time at prewriting as at writing. Clearly, the writers who entered the transition from planning to prose with well-developed conceptual outlines were also the best prepared to demonstrate consistent fluency. Moreover, they evidenced the most satisfaction, confidence, and productivity as writers over the two months of fluency exercises.

Once in this third part of the program, though, we began to clarify other useful strategies. We started organizing our time and our priorities by making writing a moderate priority, one that needs no more than the brief openings already available in usual workdays (rule #9). In an extension of the ninth rule, we reapplied an earlier caution (rule #5: Learning to stop).

We saw rules reflected in the patterns of study group members. Writers who remain fluent do so in part by learning to accept the output of a bds as sufficient for the day (rule #10); anything less adds to the weighty burden of never feeling we have done enough as writers.

A third new rule (#11) completed the directives for time management. It said, in essence, that we may never escape bingeing and procrastination until we stop seeing large, open blocks of time as ideal for writing: Whole days, weekends, vacations. Such times, the most successful writers demonstrate, are better used for rest and relaxation.

The next three rules (#12-14) dealt with ways of making bds most effective. The first sets a compromise for days and weeks when we cannot or will not write. Then, at the least, we profit in perusing the materials of a project to keep it fresh in mind. This simple act, manageable even during illness or other, more pressing projects, suffices to (1) reduce warm-up time when writing resumes, (2) encourage noticing and imagination for the semi-abandoned project in the meanwhile, and (3) hasten the return to fluency. The second canon about brief daily sessions (rule #13) helped moderate the distractions that writers too often tolerate, notably excessive interruptions of callers and visitors and temptations to read or deal with other things in the writing locale. The third rule in this series (#14) made the regular practice of all the others realistic in the short run. It is the device, sometimes called contingency management, of finding just enough external force to make us write on schedule. These kick-starters for momentum work to initiate and reinitiate momentum so well that few writers can in fact manage in the short run without them (or a facsimile such as waiting for deadlines).

Toward the end of this third stage, when we had managed a fair start at fluency, an initial concern reemerged. What about traditional notions of blocking and their implications of deeper, underlying causes of dysfluencies? Another look at the literature on blocking proved disappointing; most accounts of blocking seemed fanciful and most claims of cures unsubstantiated. When we looked elsewhere, to the clinical literature on everyday problems that provide a more useful account of stymied writing, we found the basis for the last of the rules (#15) in this chapter: Most of what we have called writing blocks can be explained more parsimoniously in terms of common self-defeating behaviors including self-handicapping, choking under pressure, helplessness, and poor problem-solving strategies. Blocking can be seen as ordinary misbehaviors of normal people.

As we journey through all these rules, two outcomes stood paramount in this third stage. First, when writers prewrote with care, the usually difficult transition from planning to prose became painless and efficient; prewriting made a large contribution to fluency. Second, when writers practiced prose in brief, daily sessions (bds), fluency reached its highest and most consistent state in this stage. The most planful and habitual writers wrote nearly two pages a day, even with writing sessions of less than an hour extracted from busy schedules. More spontaneous writers, those who stayed with strategies of indifferent prewriting and of bingeing prose, produced little more than nothing over the same period.

At this transition point in our travels together, then, the program gives every appearance of working. We can add bds to our store of effective strategies for finding comfort and fluency as writers; Dorothea Brande would have approved, I believe. Yet, writers looking ahead know that we have a distance to go. Not only that, we are still not out of troubled waters. An undercurrent in Stage 3 was the sense that even the most compliant of writers were struggling with new, formative habits (and that they relied on unfamiliar crutches such as notes and reminders while coping). The related concern was that our old blocks, even if we called them self-defeating patterns, remained more or less unresolved.

Nonetheless, most participants appreciated the challenges lying ahead: the need to make motivation more internal, to quiet maladaptive attitudes and habits, and to make their writing more skillful, more acceptable. All these and more make up the three chapters that remain.

The nearest thing to writing a novel is traveling in a strange country. Travel is a creative act--not simply loafing and inviting your soul, but feeding the imagination, accounting for each fresh wonder, memorizing and moving on. . . . And the best landscapes, apparently dense or featureless, hold surprises if they are studied patiently, in the kind of discomfort one can savor afterward.

Paul Theroux, *Discovering Dingle*, 1976

REFERENCES

1. Brande, D. (1934). *Becoming a writer*. New York: Harcourt, Brace, pp. 28-31.

2. Boice, R. & Myers, P. (1986). Two parallel traditions: Automatic writing and free writing. *Written Communication*, 3, 471-490.

3. Brande, D. (1981). *Becoming a writer*. Los Angeles: J.P. Tarcher, pp. 72-73. (Originally published 1934.)

4. Boice, R. (1993). Writing blocks and tacit knowledge. *Journal of Higher Education*, 64, 19-54.

5. Perkins, D.N. (1981). *The mind's best work*. Cambridge, MA: Harvard University Press.

6. Flower, L. & Hayes, J.R. (1984). Images, plans, and prose: The representation of meaning in writing. *Written Communication*, 1, 120-160.

7. Flower, L. & Hayes, J.R. (1980). The cognition of discovery: Defining a rhetorical problem. *College Composition and Composition*, 31, 21-31.

8. Puffer, S. (1989). Task-completion schedules: Determinants and consequences for performance. *Human Relations*, 42, 937-955.

9. Vallacher, R.R. & Wegner, D.M. (1987). What do people think they're doing? Action identification and human behavior. *Psychological Review*, 94, 3-15.

10. Bullough, R.V., Knowles, J.G. & Crow, N.A. (1991). *Emerging as a teacher*. London: Routledge.

11. Field, J. (1981). *A life of one's own*. Los Angeles: Jeremy P. Tarcher, p. 19. (Originally published 1936.)

12. Boice, R. (1992). *The new faculty member*. San Francisco: Jossey-Bass.

13. Boice, R. (1990). *Professors as writers*. Stillwater, OK: New Forums Press, pp. 129-149.

14. Boice, R. (1985). Cognitive components of blocking. *Written Communication*, 2, 91-104.

15. Hilgard, E.R. (1977). *Divided consciousness: Multiple controls in human thought and action*. New York: Wiley.

16. Tremmel, R. (1989). Investigating productivity and other factors in the writer's practice. *Freshman English News*, 17(2), 19-25.

17. Asimov, I. (1981). *Asimov on science fiction*. Garden City, NY: Doubleday, p. 40.

18. Fox, M.F. (1985). The transition from dissertation student to publishing scholar and professional. In M.F. Fox (ed.), *Scholarly writing and publishing*, pp. 6-16. Boulder: Westview Press, p. 8.

19. Elbow, P. (1973). *Writing without teachers*. New York: Oxford University Press, p. 5.

20. Brufee, K.A. (1984). Collaborative learning and the "conversation of mankind." *College English*, 46(7), 635-652.

21. Elbow, P. (1973), *Writing without teachers* p. 52.

22. Scardamalia, M. (1981). How children cope with the demands of writing. In C.F. Frederiksen & J.F. Dominic (eds.), *Writing: Process, development and communication*, pp. 81-103. Hillsdale, NJ: Erlbaum.

23. Minninger, J. (1980). *Free yourself to write*. San Francisco: Workshops for Innovative Teaching, p. 52.

24. Rothblum, E.D. (1990). Fear of failure. In H. Leitenberg (ed.), *Handbook of social and evaluation anxiety*, pp. 497-553. New York: Plenum.

25. Flower, L. (1990). Introduction: Studying cognition in context. In L. Flower, V. Stein, J. Ackerman, M.J. Kantz, K. McCormick & W.C. Peck eds.), *Reading-to-write*, p. 27.

26. Langer, E.J. (1989). *Mindfulness*. Reading, MA: Addison-Wesley, pp. 75-76.

27. Burka, J.B. & Yuen, L.M. (1984). A procrastinator's guide to telling time. *Working Woman*, September, 78-81.

28. Ottens, A.J. (1982). A Guaranteed scheduling technique to manage students' procrastination. *College Student Journal*, 16(4), 371-376.

29. Boice, R. (1986). An annotated bibliography on blocking and other hindrances to writing. *Social and Behavioral Sciences Documents*, 16(2), 37-38.

30. Leader, Z. (1991). *Writer's block*. Baltimore: Johns Hopkins University Press, pp. 171, 179.

31. Bergler, E. (1950). *The writer and psychoanalysis*. Garden City, NY: Doubleday. (See the review by G. McGrath, *British Journal of Psychiatry*, 1993, 162, p. 142, about later editions.)

32. Wagner, R.K. & Sternberg, R.J. (1986). Tacit knowledge and intelligence in the everyday world. In R.J. Sternberg & R.K. Wagner (eds.), *Practical Intelligence*, pp. 51-83. New York: Cambridge University Press.

33. Trollope, A. (1953). In the *Oxford Dictionary of Quotations*, p. 549.

34. Brandon, B. (1986). *The passion of Ayn Rand*. Garden City, NY: Doubleday.

35. Boice, R. (1992). Combining writing block treatments: Theory and research. *Behaviour Research and Therapy*, 30, 107-116.

36. Johnson, S. (1967). In W. Durant & A. Durant, *Rousseau and revolution*, p. 36. New York: Simon & Schuster.

37. Rabinbach, A. (1990). *The human motor*. New York: Basic Books.

38. Elbow, P. (1992). Freewriting and the problem of wheat and tares. In J.M. Moxley (ed.), *Writing and publishing for academic authors*, pp. 33-47. Lanham, NY: University Press of America, pp. 42-43.

39. Boice, R. & Myers, P.E. (1987). Which setting is healthier and happier, academe or private practice? *Professional Psychology*, 18, 526-529.

40. Wallace, I. (1968). *The writing of one novel*. New York: Simon and Schuster.

41. Nurnberger, J.T. & Zimmerman, J. (1970). Applied analysis of human behavior. *Behavior Therapy*, 1, 59-60.

42. Mack, K. & Skjei, E. (1979). *Overcoming writing blocks*. Los Angeles: J.P. Tarcher.

43. Paulman, R.G. & Kennelly, K.J. (1984). Test anxiety and ineffective test taking: Different names, same construct? *Journal of Educational Psychology*, 279-288.

44. Himadi, W.G., Boice, R. & Barlow, D.H. (1986). Assessment of agoraphobia-- II: Measurement of clinical change. *Behaviour Research and Therapy*, 24, 321-332.

45. Baumeister, R.F. & Scher, S.J. (1988). Self-defeating behavior patterns among normal individuals: Review and analysis of common self-destructive tendencies. *Psychological Review*, 104, 3-22.

4

Control

Poetry is the spontaneous overflow of powerful feelings; it takes its origin from emotion recollected in tranquility.

William Wordsworth [1]

What Wordsworth meant was that effective writing depends on emotional sensitivity and emotional control [2]. What he implied was that failures of self-control are defaults at writing. Consider, for instance, how different Jean-Jacques Rousseau was from this ideal. He constantly struggled with exhaustion and temptations to quit writing; finally he did, before reaching his potential. In the view of historians, he lacked the ordered mind, patient will, and quiet temper to enjoy writing. When he had to reason and feel at once, the necessary self-denial was beyond his reach [3].

This fourth stage of the program helps combat emotional excesses in writing. Chapter 4 extends our journey beyond its three initial stages--of motivation, inspiration, and fluency. Those steps, essential as they have proven, are not always enough in the long run. To this point, I would argue, we have just begun to find durability as writers.

Here's why. Where Chapters 1-3 focused on "initiators [4]," this fourth chapter deals more with what I have come to call "maintainers." Acts of maintenance and self-control work mainly by helping writers become their own therapists. Even so, my role is no less important, I think. Guiding writers to moderate the excessive moods and cognitions that can derail writing is one of the most difficult of my tasks (and yours).

How does this move, usually starting at about nine months into the program, correspond to the progress of most writers? Some participants are into the first drafts of one or two manuscripts (some writers prefer the novelty and cross-fertilization of simultaneous projects). Some are finishing conceptual outlines; some are revising complete drafts of manuscripts. The important thing is that everyone is working with at least a modicum of fluency.

Other things have commonly occurred. All but a handful of writers express surprise over their success so far. Some of the celebrants had not believed they would actually finish a particular manuscript:

You can't imagine how many false starts and unfinished efforts I have gone through in the last 10 years. I could always do my other writing, my technical reports and my newsletters, but I have never before finished an essay. I had, I now realize, neither the beliefs nor the proper habits to do it.

Even more writers express delight in writing in bds (brief, daily sessions) and in not having to struggle at starting each new session:

It's the nicest thing to be writing during my writing time every day and to feel like a real writer, someone who is serious and productive about writing. No more excuses, no more battles, just fun and progress. I do something every day and I like what I'm doing. I'm proud of myself.

But, in their newfound fluency and confidence, many writers see less need for continuing participation in the program:

What more do we need? We're doing all the exercises, we're writing regularly, and we're cranking out the very stuff we had, many of us, dreamed of. I'm ready to go off on my own.

This is where I once terminated programs. All but a few writers seemed headed in the right direction, and there were always waiting groups of newcomers with writing problems. Now, I'm more patient; I wait. To test the assumption of participants that they need no more programmatic help, I encourage writers to work without the program for a few weeks. At the end of that brief hiatus, we all report back. The ensuing accounts demonstrate the need for maintainers.

FIRST SIGNS OF MAINTENANCE PROBLEMS

What happens during vacations from the program? Without the support and coaching of program sessions, writers almost immediately record occasional lapses in motivation and discipline. Nothing drastic, just a bit of undoing of the progress we had made toward consistent pleasure and productivity. Specifically, the usual orderliness and calm of bds are disrupted by unanticipated or underestimated emotions of everyday living. Writing is waylaid, at first for a day here and there, and then for days at a time. The following events are cited as common interrupters in retrospective reports:

1. Calamities of health and relationships (e.g., prolonged head colds; discord in spousal relationships);
2. new responsibilities at work (e.g., cluttered work days; promotions ortransfers; even layoffs) and at home (e.g., remodeling);
3. rejections, criticisms, and discouragements of writing ("you know, you might fare better at one of the newer publishing houses; they're harder up for manuscripts");
4. reemerging doubts about abilities to imagine and write; and,
5. reinstatement of feelings of busyness ("I'm too busy too write").

As distractions grow, so does impatience; writers typically turn to longer, more irregular sessions and they write when they have nothing urgent to do. Bingeing reenters the picture and coincides with decreases in motivation and productivity. Progress that took months of hard work and discipline can dissemble in days.

As writers experience this "regression," they generally see things in a new way. They wonder: has the writing program been too insular, too isolated from the reality of other pressures and responsibilities facing writers?

There is so much else to do, so many problems. . . . I'm not just a writer. I have to organize a whole new program at work . . . hiring and training and evaluating new managers, supervising and editing the writing of training manuals. I don't even know when I can return to the really small bds, the ten to fifteen [lengths of] times I began with, or if I want to write if it is going to be so impractical.

I've gotten married and the writing doesn't seem so important some days. I have responsibilities that I didn't have before. I'm not so sure my wife approves of my spending time at home on my book. She likes us to go for walks in the morning and I find it hard to say no to such a decent request.

The old me is coming to the surface now that I'm more on my own. There are, I guess, more and more stretches where I still hate writing, where, you know, my stomach churns, where I want it to be easy. There are times where I hate the daily schedules with a vengeance, where it feels regimented and oppressive. . . . At the bottom of it all, I'm noticing, are the same old insecurities: Am I clever and smart enough? Will my shortcomings be all the more apparent in my writing? Will my college professor prove right in predicting no future for me as a novelist? . . . These things don't just go away because I've cajoled myself into writing for a few months.

I imagined I had things going my way until I got a poor reception to a manuscript two days ago. My entire consciousness was dominated by the editor's reserved comments and cool tone. It ran through my mind over and over again, punctuated only by my feelings of embarrassment and anger and revenge, and lots of other things. With that going on, there was no thought, no inspiration to sit down and write at the usual time. More likely, I was thinking about whether I would *ever* write again. . . . This surprises me because I thought, with my new habits of comfort and productivity, that this sort of reaction would be a thing of the past.

Simple. When I'm upset, I don't write.

Something else happens at this point of relative independence: motivations wane and everyday distractions take on larger and larger proportions:

I think I consciously realized it only today, as I watched the sun filtering though the oaks outside my office window. Today it produced the unsettling feeling that perhaps I should be doing something more pleasant than the hard work of forcing words onto a screen. I said to myself, "Why am I doing this when I could be out doing gardening on this beautiful day? What compels me to do this, this hard work? My roses need me." Naturally, I had some well-rehearsed rebuttals--about having something worthwhile to say, about enjoying what we have been calling the "conversation," about seeing my writing in print . . . so I've perhaps made some progress. But I wondered, "Tell me, why am I still so ambivalent? So why isn't my hard work and conscientiousness in the writing program working better?"

How do we deal with these doubts? The writing groups, as usual, provide the most effective answer. Each group, independently, paused to review what we had learned that could be most valuable in helping writers maintain new habits. Writers hoped that by reteaching each other the essential principles of motivation, inspiration, and fluency (with minimal involvement from me), their ideas would become more their own property. It worked.

A STOCK TAKING

There is an immediate benefit in this reviewing and reconceptualizing. Participants take pride in explaining what they have learned and how principles apply to their specific situations. Just hearing ideas and solutions expressed in individualized terms brings new appreciations:

Here's something that helps me. Nothing complicated. I couldn't stick with the comfort breaks; sooner or later, I forgot. . . . [Name of group member] mentioned the trick that works. The idea of stopping every time my word processor automatically saves my entries (you know it says, what, at the bottom of the screen, "Please wait"). I have to pause then anyway, so I use it as a reminder to stretch out, rest my eyes and wrists, check out postural things, and relax. [Another writer who writes mostly by hand and on a typewriter accomplished much the same result by installing a timer that chimed every ten minutes.]

Similarly, the expressions of what each writer had done well in the first three phases of the program offer a satisfaction that builds resolve:

My greatest pride came in getting organized and excited in the prewriting--so that I knew what I would need to do and I didn't struggle at all to do it.

Without question, my breakthrough came in regular sessions, in discovering that I could be so productive without the binges over weekends.

. . . the other things are nice but I value the newfound comfort, the surprisingly pleasant mood that I have been able to bring to my writing, most of it at least.

With generalities stated, we move to the more demanding revelations of retrospective thinking aloud exercises. We ask each other to re-create the thoughts and feelings that accompanied turning points in the program. The most common experiences of progress and control are typified here:

My first real turning point is something I think about often. It came while I was doing the exercises in patience, in slowing down and listening and joining the conversation before I tried to write. I had gone to the library to look up some of the things I admired. I was sitting surrounded by a stack of books, almost like a group of old friends. I looked at one, and left a page open, then another, and so on as I took a note here and there. . . . For once, I knew, I was being unhurried about writing and enjoying it. I thought, "I feel serene, that's what it is." I thought, "This is nice. I'm enjoying this and I'm learning something. I'm listening and watching these other authors doing their best things, and I'm soaking it all in, thinking of ways I can do similar things." . . . I left with a calm sense of charge.

My big breakthrough came from the exercise I hated the most, taking all those notes and playing with them until I generated new ideas and plans. There was one moment when it began to work, when I began to like it. I had dug out the plots of eight books somewhat like mine and added thoughts on the wing as I plodded along. For awhile, I felt like a tired scribe with another tedious job of copying. But then, when I made a new set of notes about the themes in the plots and how they compared to mine, things changed. I saw some surprising things. I had overlooked some interesting alternatives and twists that now seemed obviously essential to my story. I can recall two things: I suddenly felt more confident that I knew what I was doing--or that at least that I would know. And I said, "You could learn to like these preliminaries."

Someone has to tout the bds experience, and I can give a glowing testimonial. When I first set the schedule, for thirty minutes in my office at midmorning, I couldn't imagine it working. And I don't think it would have if other people hadn't agreed to act as enforcers (to keep me in and intruders away). Anyway, the turning-point experience came one day about two weeks after I had written on schedule. Something came up, a call from a secretary trying to schedule a meeting during my writing time. I immediately said "No, that's a time that is always booked for the half-hour; could you move it back to 11 o'clock?" She could. . . . Then I had a reverie of sorts. I sat and thought, "You know, in the past, you would have put aside your writing for something like that, something that could have been moved for your convenience." I thought, "You did this without sounding like a fanatic, no one got upset, and you will stay on schedule." I sat there for a minute or two . . . just enjoying the glow of my small step of progress.

With each of these accounts of turning points came reassurances that something substantial and lasting had been learned in the first half of the program. But for all the confidence reestablished in this stocktaking of what worked, we needed to deal with that other experience, the recent disappointment of working more independently of the program in the past few weeks. Here too we relied on the thinking-aloud protocol to get at the essential experiences behind the lapses from programmatic habits. The following excerpts typify the most common accounts; in the final analysis, most "slips" from newly established habits fell into two categories, either disturbing thoughts or distracting emotions:

The politics at my place of work are a big, big problem. Last Tuesday, when I sat down to write, I found myself thinking about a kind of a slight. I was thinking, "Why didn't I get invited to go with the crew that went to lunch together? What have I done to offend them? What should I do to get back in their good graces?" And so on, ad nauseam. I felt too low, too unloved to write. I thought to myself, much as though my mother might have said, "You don't have to go to school today,"--"You don't have to write today." And I didn't. I just sat there and luxuriated in my depression.

This was a turning point for me. By last weekend, I thought that I needed to finish an overdue project, a commissioned piece that I had wanted to get in two weeks ago. I set aside Saturday and Sunday to catch up. At first I congratulated myself on finding enough time for writing. I said to myself: "This is the way to get things done and get them out of the way so that you can get on to other things and not have this hanging over your head." Later, late Saturday, I was maybe halfway finished but I vaguely noticed something else. I was speeding. I wasn't stopping to eat or rest. My body ached but I ignored it. And, something I might not have noticed in the old days: I was making lots of keyboard errors. But I really couldn't get myself to slow down to make changes or rest. The writing had taken on a life of its own and I was just along for the ride. On Sunday, feeling hungover and old, I resumed. By Sunday evening I had finished and mailed the manuscript. I spent an irritable evening at a party, thinking what jerks the people were. I haven't written since.

When my groups and I looked over these collections of negative turning points, we came to a consensus. What was really involved was not so much a problem of not knowing what to do. It was more a failure of control. We would do better, we agreed, by devising more self-reliant methods for controlling a) the negative thoughts that block writing and b) the impatience that leads to bingeing. We began with discussions about the nature of negative thinking and disruptive emotions in writing.

UNCONTROLLED THINKING AND EMOTING

Most of what we know about negative thinking owes to the revolution in cognitive psychology; until recently only a few brave psychotherapists like Albert Ellis dealt with the self-talk that underlies negativity [5]. Even as I preview Ellis' campaign to subdue irrational thinking, I like to put the topic into more familiar terms.

Depression

Depression at its simplest is negativity and hopelessness. It builds on pessimistic expectations and explanations that are internal, stable, and global [6]. *Internal* means that we attribute the cause for a negative event to ourselves, and not to something external; in other words, a depressed person habitually accepts the blame whether it is rationally justified or not. *Stable* means a pessimistic assumption that the negative experience will persist or recur. (If, for instance, our current writing is rejected, we could depressively project the same fate for our future efforts.) And *global* refers to an unfortunate tendency to generalize, to imagine that criticism or rejection from one or a few individuals portends the same sort of reaction from almost everyone. When depression about writing contains all three aspects of pessimism (the internal, stable, and global assumptions), writers are unlikely to remain fluent in the face of even occasional frustrations. Yet this kind of "depressogenic attributional style" is common for many writers, especially in the midst of high stress, rapid change, and disappointment.

Stated another way, writers anxious about the likelihood of failing and suffering will opt for escape and other self-defeating moves. Some people make themselves even busier, perhaps by impulsively joining a board of directors for a charity (self-handicapping, Chapter 3). They may then conclude that writing can only be accomplished at the expense of their social lives (the zero-sum game). They may even engage in a bit of face work (another self-defeating act, this one in response to embarrassment) by reporting imaginary descriptions of progress to friends ("I'm nearly finished with it"). And, once well-immersed in self-defeat and its excessive self-consciousness, a return to writing can easily bring choking and panic. Thus, without ever abandoning the overarching goal of writing, writers can fall into self-defeating behaviors that not only displace their writing but add to their depression as well.

Depression also has a gentler side, one not so readily appreciated because of its modest behavioral effects. With mild sadness comes lessened energy; our faces, our postures, and our productivities sag a bit without our notice. A keen observer might see that we have less fun than usual at tasks like writing; that we are less fun to be around; that we are increasingly isolated and inefficient, seeming to work with only a vague awareness and mindfulness. But we, ourselves, might overlook the whole sequence and wonder what has happened to our fluency and comfort.

Contemporary psychological treatments for depression. Even in this usual vagueness we can find hope of controlling depression and its negativity in writing. The briefest of glances through the cloud can break the spell. When we become habitual monitors of our self-talk, we can discover what is producing our languor and pessimism. One of the pioneers of therapy for depression, Aaron Beck, identifies its causes in terms of the problematic cognitive styles of depressed patients [7]. These are the most common:

1. Indecisiveness.
2. Seeing problems as overwhelming.
3. Self-criticism in a recurrent, stereotyped fashion.
4. Absolutist thinking.
5. Difficulties in concentration and memory.

When we follow these cognitive bents, we become more passive. And we tend to give up too soon at complex tasks. Both these tendencies (passivity and giving up too soon) undermine our motivation and endurance as writers; they are a kind of blocking.

Customary treatments for depression resemble those for writing blocks. Therapists commonly coax depressed patients out of their passivity and hopelessness by scheduling them into regular, outgoing activities. And to enhance compliance, therapists assign new activities in gradual fashion, in so-called "graded task assignments" that start with easy chores and move to more difficult activities. Ideally, the moderate pace keeps patients from quitting the program. This usual approach to depression resembles the interventions for dysfluent writers in our own program.

But given the longstanding sophistication of therapies for depression, we can expect more than kick-starting. Beck and his colleagues coach patients in a kind of mindfulness that diminishes the excessive self-consciousness of self-defeating behaviors [7]. To manage this, they might turn the attention of their patients to the essential acts of writing. When patients practice this "concentration on process," they replace a wandering self-focused attention with a forward-looking consciousness that identifies both roadblocks and solutions. Much as in the approach we have been pursuing in our writing program, my groups and I notice, Beck involves his depressive patients in a series of demanding exercises that recruits them as observers and recorders of their self-talk.

Beck's patients are taught to categorize their negative thinking into major categories such as inferiority, self-blame, and victimization. They are coached to identify the root causes of their depressive thinking (e.g., feelings of inferiority). And, they are guided in correcting their negative thinking. First they learn to notice and stop negative thoughts; the simple, self-spoken command to "STOP" is helpful. Then patients work at supplanting negative thought patterns with more positive varieties such as saying, "Once I get involved in this thing, I will enjoy it, so I might as well get started."

This, then, is what Beck does beyond initiating (i.e., merely forcing patients out of their inactivity): First, he helps them identify the rigid, self-defeating patterns of thinking that occasion depression; this "exteriorization" of irrational thoughts onto paper helps patients distance themselves from their depressive self-talk. Then he immerses patients in problem-solving activities to reduce the likelihood that they will continue to misinterpret disappointing events.

Another influential pioneer in cognitive treatments for depression is Donald Meichenbaum [8]. He has popularized three steps designed to take treatment beyond initiating interventions:

1. Education about the causes of depression and related phenomena in maladaptive thinking.
2. Rehearsal in anticipating disappointments (by way of practicing self-talk that "inoculates" patients against misinterpretations and overreactions).
3. Application of these new cognitive coping strategies to real life situations.

Meichenbaum's prescription, not surprisingly, works nicely with dysfluent writers. In one treatment study, blocked writers identified negative self-statements about writing and then displaced them:

In the educational phase, subjects were provided a rationale that interpreted their writing anxiety as a function of their self-statements. Subjects learned that their anxiety could best be understood by considering different aspects of the writing task such as preparing for, confronting, feeling overwhelmed by, and evaluating their writing. In the rehearsal stage, subjects were encouraged to identify, elaborate on, and articulate their negative self-statements. . . . The therapist used modeling to demonstrate coping self-statements and behaviors. . . . Emphasis was placed on positive statements about the self (e.g., "I know I can do this"). [9]

Cognitive therapies help maintain motivation and fluency. My own systematic studies of single versus combined treatments for blocked writers, indicate a special role for interventions that moderate negative thinking [10]. While identification and displacement of negative self-talk do little to initiate motivation, inspiration, or fluency, these cognitive strategies help maintain them. As negativism and depression decline, so do overreactions to disruptions, distractions, and disappointments. What might have been interpreted as overwhelming can be seen as surmountable. The difference is depicted in this before-and-after sampling from the journal of a writer:

[before] A note about why I'm not writing today. My neighbor stopped by to drop off some vegetables and we talked for about an hour. Now it's 10:45 and I'm disgusted with myself for wasting the whole morning. I'm hopeless.
[after] A note as I start my bds: A disruption as always, but a welcome one. I like getting free veggies and flowers from _____. She took some time but I was able to send her away nicely. I said, "enough fun, now work," and she smiled. I can still do some good writing this morning, in the best of both worlds. . . . I can be a writer and have friends too.

Another thing that moderation of negative thinking accomplished was a steadying of mood for writing. When writers scan their self-talk to spot and dismiss their negative and irrational chatter, they are better able to generate more positive and relaxed moods. Here again we can see the difference between ignoring or confronting negative self-talk at writing times:

[before] Entry for start of bds: Tense and not inclined to write. Writing doesn't seem appealing and I feel like getting the shopping for tonight's party finished now.
[after] Entry for start of bds: I want to do other things that seem to be on my mind. Errands, calls, cleaning, just resting. Feeling tired and out of sorts. What I have been thinking during this subdued mood (I have to force this inquisition . . . it's hard to get past the thoughts about how tired and overworked I am): First, I am thinking in absolutist fashion, [to use Beck's terminology]. I'm supposing that if I take the time and energy for writing, there won't be enough left for me and the things I want to do, like playing tennis this afternoon. Having written this down, having exposed the vampire to daylight, I know what to do. I tell myself that I know how to write in ways that manufacture both relaxation and enthusiasm, that can, if I take care of myself, make me less tired. I realize that I can take care of myself as a writer and as a tennis partner. I'm feeling better--the tired, self pitying mood has slipped away.

Anxieties

Nervousness and fright often accompany negative thinking and depression in writing. Anxious, negative thinking includes anticipations of failures lying ahead, repetitive messages from internal critics about likely occasions for embarrassment, and impatience about not achieving success and appreciation soon enough. Our mounting fears can make us want to avoid the activity that brings the anticipation of fear; we might even come to avoid the fear of having the fear (to paraphrase Winston Churchill). Thus, when we try to write amid depression, we may feel too sad and unenergetic to write; when we add anxiety, we ensure escape or panic.

Why bother to make the distinction between depression and anxiety? Because, within limits, the two states of negative thinking demand different kinds of correctives. In psychotherapy, treatments for affective disorders (e.g., depression) and anxiety disorders (e.g., social phobia) are generally quite different. The former aim more at moderating pessimistic thinking, the latter more at reducing irrational fears. (In many ways the two categories overlap.)

Therapies for anxiety also begin with kick-starting. Phobic patients are routinely exposed, usually in gradual fashion, to the very activity they fear irrationally--they are escorted (supportively, slowly) onto high bridges, on airplane flights, into glass elevators, in crowded lines of people, and so on. At the same time, patients are coached to practice relaxation techniques which reduce the usual anxiety that can be consciously associated with the situation. Because these initiating interventions work imperfectly, therapists add maintenance interventions. Phobics are helped to consciously confront the fears most deeply underlying their phobias (e.g., fear of public embarrassment by fainting, falling, and exposing their undergarments). They are taught to accept and ignore the symptoms of anxiety such as a rapid heart rate in situations that they had previously avoided (much as bomb-defusing squad members learn to work amid distress). And they are coached to notice cues in their physical and social environments that contribute to their anxieties (e.g., having a spouse who acts as an "enabler of agoraphobia"--the anxiety about leaving the house for public encounters--because the spouse prefers a mate who is always available to look after needs at home [11]).

Usual treatments for writing anxieties. Most treatments for writing anxiety include many of the same components as for phobias. First steps typically include exposure (gradually increased reimmersions in writing) and relaxation (doing muscle relaxation exercises before and after writing). Our own interventions come close on both accounts. We have involved ourselves in prewriting (exposure) and in brief, comfortable sessions that invoke only a modicum of the anxiety that might be felt with more usual attempts to write ("I only have to write for fifteen minutes, including pauses to stretch").

But we can learn something important in studies of test anxiety, the most commonly studied variation of anxiety disorders. Test anxiety appears to be only partly the result of failures to relax; its occurrence, evidently, depends as much on a lack of careful, mindful preparation [12]. Students who are least prepared for tests or for public speaking (in terms of carefully compiled, organized, rehearsed materials and anticipated audience reactions) commonly perform amid the most anxiety. Inducing these same test-takers or public speakers to relax can help, but not unless they are also induced to prepare and plan more thoroughly. Some of the application of this well-known finding in research and treatment on anxiety is already familiar to program participants.

The more patiently and mindfully they prewrite and write, the less anxiety they report experiencing. (That is precisely what my analysis of the fifty-two writers used as the reference group for this book indicate.)

There is still more, a clue in what Albert Bandura [13] and other researchers on self-esteem and self-efficacy prescribe: with graduated experiences at success (i.e., beginning with assured accomplishments and working from those successes toward more challenging goals), writers can build the store of information and skills necessary to displace insecurity. While preparation and relaxation help, the capstone of anxiety reduction is success.

So it is that I routinely advise writers, especially those struggling with anxiety and depression, to build-in periodic opportunities for easy acceptance and approval of their writing. All of us can find such outlets by volunteering reviews, reports, and brief essays for newsletters, local newspapers, and abstracting services (e.g., academics can submit summaries of convention presentations to ERIC, an online storage system that can be accessed and read by scholars with similar interests). The point, just as with any therapeutic activity, is to use these crutches sparingly but sufficiently.

We can, if necessary, arrange even simpler successes. At the least, when we are stymied by anxiety or depression, we can profit in writing for ourselves. Peter Elbow [14], once more, offers comforting, helpful explanations of how free writing helps: It is an easy method for putting the confusion of interior thinking on paper where it can be reconsidered and reordered. On paper or screen, our irrationalities and obscurities can be seen for what they are. And, free writing is a satisfying means of transforming our direct thoughts into more positive bits of intelligence, creativity, and lively language for writing. In other words, the simple act of exteriorizing our thinking enables us to begin to see what we have to say and how we can arrange it in more rational, calm, and productive ways. Then, as we grow better prepared, we become more confident and less vulnerable to anxiety and depression.

Hypomania

When writers work without having learned to reduce their vulnerabilities to depression and anxiety, they commonly experience emotions that interfere with writing. Consider how emotion interacts with depression and anxiety: The sad discouragement of depression disinclines us to activity as writers; anything proactive can seem too distant and painful for contemplation. But when we are pressed to write anyway, the discomfort of anxiety and the painful anticipation of fears of rejection incline us to short-term solutions. We may, for instance, escape into less threatening activities (e.g., beautifully or vengefully crafted memos when we could be doing our projects). Or, with deadlines looming, we may turn to impulse. Hypomania and its euphoria and rushing promise a more pleasant state that actually immerses us in writing--at least in the short run.

Here we summon up what we have learned about hypomania in earlier program segments: It comes of bingeing in an activity like writing and, once in motion, carries a ready appeal for supplanting struggles with momentum, ideas, or confidence. In particular, bingeing offers the promise of projects completed quickly. But in reality, as we have seen, bingeing generally produces more problems than advantages. Its unpleasant aftereffects include fatigue, depression, and suspiciousness (all help make writing more aversive). Its rushed and unreflective mode of working result in writing that could have been clearer and more publishable if written and revised in more patient fashion.

Writers usually take a while to share my interest in learning more details about hypomania. We begin with a broader inquiry, the literature on emotions just reemerging about a century after William James had once made its study fashionable [15]. Our collaborative accounts of research on emotions confirm what we have experienced first hand: Negative and irrational thoughts induce heightened states of physiological arousal and of self-awareness that would almost necessarily block writing. Much the same result would be expected with excessively positive emotions--as in hypomania.

Given this, we wonder. Are emotions nothing more than nuisances that must be eliminated if we are to write consistently? The answer, it seems, is less pessimistic that we had imagined. Emotions do have eminently reasonable uses, including a role in signaling action readiness (i.e., motivation). As emotions alert us of our readiness, they give us clues about the events that caused them, and they forewarn us about the possible consequences of action [16]. When we translate this academese into language that applies to our writing, the messages are these:

1. Strong emotions of depression motivate us to passivity or avoidance, offer reasons (often irrational) about why these unproductive courses of action are suitable, or, at best, prod us to reconsider our usual actions.

2. Mild emotions motivate a serene approach to a kind of noticing that broadens the range of associations available and the flexibility in using them [16].

3. Positive emotions, if left unchecked by mindful attention to patience and rationality, may become rushed and irrational; as they intensify, they push for impulsive, unthinking solutions as a way of dealing with the underlying sense that we have insufficient resources, skills, and time to do a proper job [17].

4. Strong emotions, when maintained, not only make writing tiresome and risky; they also impair our ability to see the conversational, social side of writing objectively; with prolonged depression or hypomania comes a tendency to grandiosity and to suspicion (e.g., overattributing hostile intentions to reviewers). Nothing, not even

incompetent writing, damages a writer's potential for social support more than suspiciousness. Nothing hurts the feelings of writers or editors more than being told, directly or indirectly, that a writer finds them untrustworthy.

So where, in this discouraging picture, do we find hope of managing our emotions without unduly suppressing them? The answer lies, somewhat unobtrusively, above. When we can generate and maintain moderate levels of happiness, we fare best. Fortuitously, my groups and I have already been practicing some of the methods for ensuring that sort of moderation: comfort pauses and relaxation exercises while writing; rewriting and planning that build patience and lessen anxiety; bds that limit fatigue and enhance productivity, and so on.

In group discussions of emotionality, we add a few new considerations from our literature searches. One is a matter of individual predispositions to emotionality. People whose right frontal brains are dominant tend to be temperamentally shy, wary, and reticent [18]; in other words, they are especially vulnerable to depression. An inevitable question follows this report. Does this fact mean that difficult tasks in writing prose, like rewriting for clarity, rely more on "left-brained" actions like planfulness than on "right-brained" mechanisms of spontaneity? Those of us who have reviewed the scant and mostly speculative proof for notions of left- and right-brained styles of behaving can only waffle. We say, "perhaps."

Instead, we wonder if we might learn more in looking at reasons why emotion has been neglected for most of recent history. For example: Darwinian notions and a Victorian society cast emotions as shameful vestiges of our animal heritage [16]. Even in the twentieth century, save a couple of libertine eras, emotions were not to be seen or heard in the Western world. Not surprisingly, most of us have learned only a few, inefficient methods for the self-control of emotions. Consider the best known method, sighing and deep breathing [19]. It typically fails badly, as those of us know who have tried to use it to quell onrushing emotions of stage fright, injury, or anger. It is too little too late.

But there, in the realization that we commonly try to intervene in emotions when they are past practical control, lies a pair of clues for improved interventions. They are prevention and moderation.

Customary treatments for hypomania. Hypomania provides an ideal ground for testing prevention and moderation. But hypomania has garnered only a small, scattered literature related to writing. Where we had hoped to find treatments, we uncovered little more than explanations. Even these, however, prove fascinating.

The bulk of writing in this area comes from romantics who see the mania of manic-depressive illness as the fount of creative genius [20]. Somehow, these accounts proclaim, the most original artists and writers are visited by sporadic states of creative madness, almost as if by Muses. Well-publicized fund raisers are held with the naive goal of honoring manic-depressives, much as though preserving an endangered species [21]; well-known inquiries into mania repeat the misinformed worry that its cure might drain our society of creativity. What the romantics miss seeing, though, is the real horror of mania as a chaotic, delusional, terrifying condition [22]. Truly manic states do not permit coherent writing. Instead, manias often necessitate hospitalization and drug therapies (typically with lithium); without these moderating influences manics may go on shopping binges, sign regrettable contracts, take sexual risks, and even attempt suicide.

What about *hypo*mania, the more common and less destructive form of mania? It too has the appeal of euphoria, speeded thinking, and heightened imagination--especially in its moderate phases. Hypomanics give the appearance of being more gregarious and poised. They show unusual levels of ambition and self-esteem. And, when in a hypomanic phase, they perceive themselves as more individualistic and artistic than when not [23]. Hypomania presents an alluring prospect to writers: it brings an increase in alertness and sensitivity, in productivity and creativity, even in sexual prowess [24]. Periods of speeded thought, euphoria, creativity, and conquest are commonly reported as enjoyable and valuable [23]. No wonder we might prefer to wait for binges and the hypomania that comes from sustained, intense work:

I know the feeling as well as any. It can feel as good as any drug-induced high. It can push aside all my usual hang-ups and inhibitions, all my self-doubts. It turns me from a person devoid of clever ideas to someone teeming with them. It allows me to use time I have available, like holiday weekends, to catch up on writing. While it lasts, it makes me feel powerful, unassailable. It makes me a writer.

Having reaffirmed our oft-stated fondness for hypomania, a state that all but a few of us have utilized many times, we return to its downside. Left unchecked, without relaxation to reduce tension and without bds to limit euphoria, hypomania carries many of the same risks as mania. In its strong form, hypomania becomes associated with gloominess, diminished leisure, and inner conflicts [25]. As it grows even stronger, it produces irritability [26] and chaotic thinking [22]; its invariable impatience discourages planning or proofing. Hypomanic writing tends to be confused and mystical [27].

Our new literature search also reminds us of other, now familiar costs of hypomania. Strong episodes tend to be followed by periods of enervating depression; when writing binges are finished, disinterest in writing keeps writers away from projects far longer than otherwise [28]. Moreover, binges and hypomania work inefficiently and exacerbate writers' doubts about their lack of creativity and fluency in comparison with more successful writers. "If," as one writer put it, "I have to rely on binges for my creativity, how creative am I? How much in control am I?" We add other cautions about excesses in hypomania: Hypomanics are, for instance, more likely to abuse alcohol and other drugs [23]. And, perhaps because writers so often employ hypomania to induce motivation, imagination, and fluency, they apparently suffer depression at uncommonly high levels. In my own analysis of the fifty-two writers over the long-term, those individuals who most often binged at writing scored highest on a standard index of dysphoria, the Beck Depression Inventory (BDI). In fact, the highest BDI scores came in the wake of binges lasting at least ten hours (sufficient to induce the usual symptoms of strong hypomania). Even successive writing sessions of at least six hours per day sufficed to induce moderately high BDI grades among writers who otherwise scored as nondepressed.

Clearly, it seems, hypomania provides a common entryway to depression among writers who otherwise show little tendency to negativity. And depression, as we will see, occasions a kind of irrational overreactivity that makes us vulnerable to more bingeing.

How writing gets associated with mental illness. As my groups and I discuss the literature and my analyses about hypomania, we begin to make sense of a related literature. This is the insight:

You know, if you suppose that there is a creative madness, that writers have no other reliable or unreliable means of creativity, then you make no attempt to discourage hypomania or to encourage discipline. You just romanticize hypomania, even its costs. And you do little of the prewriting things we are practicing. You wait for big blocks of time and then work in a kind of mindlessness, planlessness.

The discussion continues like this: There is, after all, an ever-popular literature on creative madness, one that casts writers in an unfavorable light. Its most common theme is the link between depression and writing [29]. One oft-cited study reported that over a third of the writers sampled (all of them winners of one or more specified prizes) had been treated for an affective illness, usually depression [24]. Of these, a third reported histories of intense mood swings, many of them extended and elated. Virtually all the writers in this study recounted intense, highly productive and creative episodes of writing that lasted for about two weeks. The picture of creative madness usually turns darker: Most accounts of creative writing and depression emphasize their coincidence with suicide [30, 31]. While this impression about writers and writing is almost certainly biased [29], it has had a curious effect on writers--and on writing about writing.

On the one hand, claims about the potential of writing as a depressant have helped confirm its reputation as an inherently unhealthy activity [31]. (Incidentally, as this link is mentioned and rementioned in the media, no one pays much attention to the fact that most such effects are exclusive to small samples of poets and playwrights [29]). So what? I have known many would-be prose writers who use this widely but vaguely known information as an excuse to avoid writing. Some, as we saw earlier, fear the price to be paid in madness and suffering. Some imagine they lack the madness requisite to creativity because they are rarely depressed. The most important problem with this portrayal is that it misses the heart of the problem. Writers may be so often given to depression because they work in binges and under excessive hypomania, not because writing itself is inherently unhealthy. When we look to other activities that demand concentration and encourage bingeing, we can see the same general pattern of resulting tension and depression. For example, W.C. Fields set a lasting pattern in his young career as a juggler by practicing his craft in binges of perfectionism; after strenuous sessions, he became more and more tense, depressed, and alcoholic [32].

On the other hand, this literature baffles by providing no direct suggestions about how to moderate the depression that can accompany writing (other than by not writing). Usual characterizations of hypomania provide few useful clues about its control. As a rule, both depression and hypomania are made to sound like inherited and stable traits, things that preexist and that seep out in predetermined cycles of dysphoric passivity and euphoric productivity [23]. No mention is made of the role that writers can play in inducing hypomania by way of writing habits including impatience, intensity, and bingeing. Instead, tradition perpetuates notions that only lucky (or are they unlucky?) writers can rely on madness for fluent, creative writing [20].

Hypomania and balance/moderation. There is, upon a closer look, evidence that hypomania functions better in moderation. Where, for example, researchers have examined long-term patterns of fluency in relation to affective cycles, writers' best work seems to occur during periods of relative normality and mild hypomania [24]. The journals of writers and artists who chart their cycles of productivity and moods make the same point. In contrast, highly elevated moods coincide with distractibility, dysphoria, and stimulus seeking (i.e., restlessness and recklessness), all of which interfere with productivity [22].

In our discussions of this little-understood topic, my groups pay particular attention to what at first seems an aside. Episodes of hypomania, depression, and mania usually peak during summers. Our own experience suggests a reason. Summers offer the most free time (long days and vacations) to binge at writing.

We also seek out obscure accounts where hypomania is somehow kept in bounds. In one researcher's opinion, the ideal pattern begins with hypomania underlying a useful cycle: It starts with enthusiasm, imagination, and fluency--albeit in excess. Then, presumably, the ensuing dysphoria (i.e., a mild depression or bad mood) helps cast a critical, obsessive, but helpful eye on the material generated in the grandiosity and recklessness of hypomania. In other words, our hypomanic sides generate writing and our depressive selves judge it [24]. Therein may lie the germ of a more workable solution. Perhaps, we suppose, hypomania and its companion, depression, can be moderated, reigned in, during their usual cycles. Thereby, we might enhance our writing without imperilling or even taxing our mental health. But how? As usual, the literature mostly frustrates; where control of mania is mentioned at all, the solution is almost always lithium [33], not an appropriate therapy for hypomania. What we do find in accounts of lithium therapy, however, is another confirmation of the benefits in tempering the excesses of mania: as the emotional state is moderated, consciousness moves away from a misty and indistinct state to one of more definition and information; what had seemed valueless becomes less gray, unpleasing, and tiring.

From all this new scenery in our travels, we reach a useful consensus about what we are seeing:

Maybe we are better informed about the nature of hypomania. I think so. But I think we are pretty much on our own in figuring out how to control it, how to moderate it. That's exciting in a good way, I think, because I came into this with the expectation that this sort of thing about writers would have been figured out. . . . I didn't expect that we would contribute so much to our solutions.

And we share a common skepticism about accepting even the most promising suggestion uncovered, the notion of alternating between moderate episodes of hypomania and depression:

No, I don't think so. I've been doing that, more or less, for a long time and I don't recommend it all. It doesn't stay so neat and clean. Sometimes the episodes are exaggerated and the writing and the writer suffer. Believe me, . . . depression has to be a poor means for doing decent judgement and editing. (Although maybe that explains the personality of some editors I know.) . . . I especially don't like the idea of giving up control to some cycle that has me alternating between excessive ecstacy and sadness. It's not healthful. I want to be more in control and I want writing to be a pretty much consistently enjoyable, stable experience.

See if you anticipated the next consensus: The better alternative may be to keep hypomania and depression at such modest levels that neither one dominates any bds or its wake. Several writing groups have found the clue for this moderation and balance in a source that offers unusually sensible advice, the pioneering book on creativity by Frank Barron [34]. One of his best-known ideas has lasting appeal for its insistence on making priorities of stability and discipline. We make it a rule before we are entirely sure how to use it:

RULE #16: Frank Barron reminds us why the chaos and spontaneity of hypomania act in self-defeating ways: "Without knowledge, no creation; without stability, no flexibility; without discipline, no freedom." [35].

Then, by restating Barron's rule for specific problems such as finding moderation, we find more comfort with it. Here are examples of derivative rules that occur immediately, imperfectly: Without moderated levels of depression, anxiety, and hypomania, what comes next?--no consistent fluency or comfort. Without checks for passivity, negativity, distractedness, and speeding, what next?--excesses and inefficiencies. Without moderation in unproductiveness--suspiciousness, and irritability, lost audiences. Without prewriting and planfulness--less creativity.

With these working rules in hand, we feel primed to set out on systematic procedures for controlling our tendencies to excesses of negativity, anxiety, and hurry.

FORMAL INTERVENTIONS FOR CONTROL

As usual, groups help generate plans for interventions; each new group of writers suggests important alternatives and variations. We work though the three categories of excessive habits in the same order as before: depression, anxiety, and hypomania.

Depression

Most writers I have known, after reviewing the array of cognitive therapies for self-control of depression, come to share my preference for the oldest and most practical method: I have had particularly durable success with Albert Ellis' Rational-Emotive Therapy (RET). It is credible and easy; its directives for writers can be divined from a brief, readable paperback like *Overcoming Procrastination*. [5] Moreover, writers can find follow-up support with RET therapists almost everywhere. Ellis and RET are well-known from his many publications and public appearances; his no-nonsense New York City style leaves an indelible impression. (So do his disciples at local workshops around the United States [36]).

Review. RET condenses the usual notions about negative thinking in terms of a few, memorable cautions about irrational thinking. There are, in Ellis' view, three main causes of depression in activities like writing:

1. One cause is self-downing. It begins with irrational self-talk in which we tell ourselves that we must perform all meaningful tasks well and/or that we should expect the approval or love of others. Self-downing reaches problematic levels when we turn these beliefs into dire necessities, usually by way of shoulds, oughts, and musts.
2. Another cause of irrational thinking is low frustration tolerance (LFT), sometimes known as laziness. LFT stems, at least in part, from the realization that we must experience present pain to manage future gain, and from exaggerations of that pain as intolerable. In LFT, we convince ourselves that we *must* not experience unpleasantness, that we deserve only easy and enjoyable experiences, that anything else would be intolerable.
3. A third cause is hostility. Its roots resemble those of LFT because it stems from the unrealistic belief that other people *should* treat us considerately and fairly. When they do not, we grow angry and difficult.

Just as RET (Rational-Emotive Therapy) depends on only a few explanations of negative thinking, it also requires only a handful of easy curatives. It begins with ABCs: locating the activating event; winnowing out the irrational beliefs that occur in reaction to the event; and, noting the consequences, such as depression. There is also a D, as in disputing the irrationality, and there is an E, a new cognitive-emotive-behavioral effect. It's almost as simple as it sounds.

Exercises. RET requires only a minute or two, once we practice it regularly. I usually ask writers to rehearse RET throughout their days--by pausing to check out negative affect (by backtracking to an activating event, and by looking for the irrational belief that might have been elicited). Where do we find the time? My writers and I contract to spend some of the few minutes of free writing used to warm up for bds (brief, daily sessions) as the regular time for RET. We use those moments to audit, record, and dispute irrational thinking.

The ABCs generally take only a few weeks of practice to become habitual and effective. In the exercise of checking at the beginning of bds, writers usually find a clear A, the activating event of another writing session. That alone, for most of us, suffices to reveal some well-rehearsed irrationalities. The most common irrationalities (the Bs--beliefs--of ABCs) that occur in this context have been reliably documented [37]:

1. "writing will be too fatiguing, too stressful for me;
2. it is okay for me to do something less anxiety provoking than writing before getting down to writing;
3. I am not in the mood to write; I need to feel inspired and ready;
4. I must hurry my writing because my progress is far behind where it should be, and I don't have time for patience;
5. my writing must be of a superior sort, not the common stuff that most writers produce;
6. my writing will be judged harshly and unfairly and I will once again be victimized; and,
7. my writing works best when I follow the same old rules, such as, for example, working without an outline or in a single draft."

With a daily habit of noticing and recording irrational thoughts like these, writers become deft observers of what prior had seemed nearly inaudible and invisible:

Astonishing what goes on in my head. All sorts of unbidden little horrors. No wonder, on closer examination, that I often loathed writing. . . . Way back there, in the dark antechambers of my mind are these voices, all mine really, trying to talk me out of writing. . . . Protect me from not just my friends, as the famous saying sort of goes, but more from myself.

Goodness!. . . I would, I saw, be saying things such as "Oh you don't have to write today, not today when you're tired. It's such hard work. You really don't have time and you have so much to do." My god, what a baby I must think I am, deep down. . . . The mystery is how this could have going on all these years without my doing anything to get rid of these ridiculous, unhelpful, intruding, unwelcome thoughts.

When I first realized what was going on, I felt much as I once did when I once discovered a family squatting in my summer cottage. Indignant, angry, and swift to act-- just as I now react to these irrational beliefs.

We are, by now, almost always a step ahead of ourselves as we get to the Cs of ABCs; the consequences of our irrational beliefs have already leapt into view as we recorded our thoughts at writing times:

Well, now that I have spotted these things, I can tell all too clearly what the consequence is. When I repeatedly tell myself that my writing is not first rate, that it will be roundly rejected, and that I will be exposed and embarrassed and worse, I get discouraged and depressed. On seeing the connection, I might ask, what else could anyone expect?

I had a harder time seeing what the consequence of LFT [low frustration tolerance] was. I could spot the statements about why writing was too hard and too unreasonable but I couldn't, honestly, see the problem. I truly believed these things [that writing is too hard and unreasonable] and I didn't, I thought, show any signs of the anger that can come from such thoughts. . . . Then it hit me like a broadside. These thoughts kept me from getting much writing done or, at the least, made the beginning of each writing day more miserable than it had to be. The more I listened to this chatter about how hard writing would be, the more I saw its overstatements and counterproductivity. I found myself listening as though I were a fair-minded judge hearing my pleas for not wanting to write--in a kind of imagined court of appeals for writers--and then I finally found myself responding incredulously: "Oh come on now, writing isn't that painful. You sound like a child whining about swallowing some cough medicine. Just get on with it."

With the ABCs in place, we turn to D, disputation. This too is underway; notice that the writer's comments excerpted just above include a disputation of the irrationality of LFT. But disputation, more than the other steps, requires role-played rehearsals, group support, and repeated refinement; disputations of old, firmly held beliefs and expectations do not always work well at first. New scripts must be learned and rehearsed with more diligence than lines for the theater. Here, unlike the earlier stages of RET, each new occasion for disputation demands unexpected shifts in scenery and events.

Take the instance of disputing the irrational beliefs behind LFT. To tip the balance toward rationality, we begin with questions that simply ask if writing is indeed so awful. I model the process for writers and then I have them re-create the same procedure, in their own words and in the imagined variations of their own situations. So, for instance, when I take on the role of a troubled writer, I ask, "What is it that is so awful, what is it that I suppose that I can't stand?" At first, I note, it seems a foreign inquiry, one that elicits little more than puzzlement or indignation. Until it becomes familiar, this question can be dismissed as trivial and stupid. The parts of our minds that spew out the irrationalities hang on to their old scripts with remarkable tenacity and ingenuity.

But once such questions are underway, all of the writers not only generate answers; they also come up with more questions. These new queries and their answers become the basis for an effective habit of disputation. For example:

All right, writing isn't easy. So it does take time and it doesn't guarantee success. But what's so horrible about that? What would it do to me that is worse than what I am enduring now? Don't I put up with unpleasantness to get other things I want? Yes, I do. Like dating [laughs]. Aren't you maybe overrating the terribleness of writing a bit? Why do you insist on making something you want to do so difficult, more difficult than it needs to be?

And, with D in place, E (effect) is soon taken care of:

Sure, it works. When I dispute the unreasonableness of my self-talk, it fades away like the vapid stuff it really is. It has little substance in the light of day, written out on paper. And when I do that, I can feel the, what should I call it, the laziness and the hesitancies, vanish as well. . . . Nowadays I can generally do the whole thing, going from sad to glad, in a few minutes. When that discouragement pops up, I get rid of it with just a few disputations.

Then, we repeat the same process for other major causes of depression in writing, including self-downing. We begin, again, by noting the antecedent:

It doesn't take much, just the merest prospect that I will be judged or evaluated, to set off the chain of self-downing. Nothing works better to bring it out than getting set to write, unfortunately. Somehow, reflexively, the whole array of critics I have known, teachers, editors, my ex-husband, whole legions, leap into action . . . with my generous help, of course.

As a rule, awareness of the B (belief) precedes the A (activator); the chorus of irrational voices gives us a clue about the activities that cause them (continuing to quote the same writer):

My internal critics make quite a clamor. They remind me of my greatest embarrassments, and not just in writing, perhaps to point out my vulnerability when trying anything risky. They like to talk about how terrible it will be to be criticized. But now as I listen to them, more carefully and more objectively than ever before, I literally shake my head. I know what foolishness it is.

The C (consequence), D (disputation), and E (the new cognitive-emotional effect) come reliably for another determined writer; he is by now well-practiced at RET:

The first thing I say is, "Wait a minute, this isn't fair to me. This is all too negative and exaggerated." And as I say it, I notice that it has been making me feel like putting my writing off, that it is making me sad and depressed over what a loser I am. So I ask myself, "Why am I doing this cruel and unfair thing to myself?" I may be at a loss for good answers for the moment. I can say (and have said), "Well, maybe I'm protecting myself from disappointment and hurt." But just as fast, I have a disputation: "That isn't helping and it isn't protecting. It is making every day that I try to write a living hell. I'm suffering hurt and disappointment every day, not just when my writing is rejected, and that, come to think of it, is something that doesn't happen so often." . . . What I decide to do is to calm down, push the negativity out of mind, and do some good work and show myself that all my pessimism need not come true. Then, you know, without those negative thoughts, there is no real struggle to get started.

We also practice RET in response to a broader variety of common and uncommon irrationalities. One of the most common themes resembles the one just overviewed:

So I have to ask myself what it is that I think I can't stand about criticism. With my irrational brain still speaking, the answer is interesting. It says, "Well, I can't stand it because it makes me feel awful." Then the disputer in me asks, "So what is so awful about that? Don't you get criticized about other things and don't you survive that?" I get no answer. My disputer chuckles and says, "Just as I thought, you can't defend it." But just as it says that, another irrationality pops up. It says, "I'll tell you what I really hate, I hate it when I don't look smart." That silences my disputer for a minute. This isn't an easy battle. But I remind my disputer to reply with the stock question: "So what's so awful about not being seen as smart every moment of every day? What difference does it really make?" And then I add even better questions like "So how do you feel about someone you like and respect when he does something stupid? Don't you just dismiss it as something out of the ordinary? Why do you place pressures on yourself that you wouldn't on your friends?"

The special value of rehearsing and reviewing our ABCDEs in our groups is that we use each other's dilemmas and solutions to build a richer store of experience. For instance, one group member listening to the writer just quoted reacted with this comment:

Yes, that's a good example. That was a good way to dispute, I think. I've had much the same debate, I'd say, and something else occurred to me. I disputed what may be an even more fundamental assumption--that being criticized is tantamount to being unsmart. I said, "Why do you assume that a criticism or a rejection means that you will be seen as unintelligent? Why do you think that you have to be different than other writers? Don't you remember the things you've read about how even the most successful and brilliant writers have long records of rejection?" . . . I even dispute my need to be seen as smart: "Why worry about being smart when you're not even sure what it means and who should be the judge? Why not pay attention to having a good time at writing and at impressing just some people? Why would everyone have to think you are smart?"

In this sequence of events, as we practice RET, one more thing happens. As a rule, our fluency in noticing and disputing irrational thoughts grows more and more into skill at prevention. We don't just notice and dispute, we also think about ways to reduce the occasions for negative self-talk and its noisome consequences. We anticipate our usual irrationalities:

Now, in effect, I expect my whining voices to be there and I just brush them out of the way. "I don't want to hear any whining or excuses," I say, quietly but firmly to myself-- even before they emerge. I might say, "This is just a half-hour of writing and you can damn well get though it and maybe even enjoy it. Let's get going and use your energies for something worthwhile."

We even, as part of our move toward prevention, look back to what we have read from editors who recount the usual failings of writers; if some of the common mistakes can be avoided, so too can some of the frustrations that incline us to irrationalities and depression. The commonplace list of writers' failings includes: a lack of careful proofreading, an absence of clear themes or theories, a shortage of rich descriptions, a dearth of signposts such as lead sentences that tell readers where the writing is headed, and too few indications about what makes the story or article worth the reader's while.

There is, we notice, another benefit in anticipating mistakes: With these cautions in mind, we can turn from irrational worries to rational worries:

Oh yeah, these are better things to worry about than things that are untrue or that I can't control. I can do a better job of putting more descriptive things into my fiction. Editors have told me so and I can see the need. If I'm worrying about doing that, about making notes when I walk to my office, and not about managing to become instantly rich and famous, I think I'll do better.

Finally our practice at RET takes us to the point where we can reliably reappraise our problems, foresee the usual outcomes of sticking with irrationalities, and replace our customary struggle with more positive feelings and plans. We become better and better at conjuring upbeat moods and actions to temper depression; active, on-task writers working with moderate pacing and ongoing checks for relaxation are not, in my experience, seriously depressed.

A natural outcome of mastering RET is building a set of rational rules that we can carry with us, like amulets, to ward off irrational thinking. The most central of those is a rule about the value of RET:

RULE #17: Albert Ellis and Rational-Emotive Therapy point out the irrational thinking that commonly inhibits and depresses writers: the shoulds, oughts, and musts that cause self-downing and low frustration tolerance. Writers who spot such irrationalities and supplant them with rational self-talk can replace depression with more economical, productive thinking.

With Albert Ellis and RET now in our repertoire, we look for more of the same; there is a special pleasure in bringing rationality to some parts of our days. We easily find additional maxims to encourage rationality and discourage pain.

Heuristics for preventing depression. Over the years, groups have uncovered a compelling collection of maxims that work to help writers with depression. The best of these aphorisms have commonalities: they often help writers develop more felt control over their work and they speak to economies and simplicities in the midst of a complex task. A favorite source is a generally forgotten book on advice on finding personal freedom by Harry Browne [38]. While some of his notions are too extreme for everyone in the writing groups, most of his advice strikes us as a logical and useful extension to our RET exercises. The efforts of several writing groups have produced the following list of Harry Browne's maxims that we post near our writing sites for daily reminders. Each is a translation of his admonitions as we imagine he might have worded them for writers:

1. When you feel vulnerable, recognize your own contribution. Vulnerability often comes from associating with people and situations that upset you and encourage irrational self-talk and action.
2. Appreciate what you cannot control: your own nature and the nature (i.e., dislikes and personalities) of others. Discover what you can control: The who you interact with and how you react to interactions.
3. Don't waste energy expecting people to like your writing, no matter how well done the manuscript. Not everyone shares your knowledge, perspectives, and objectives--or wants to.
4. To find kindred people, advertise the kind of person you are in your writing.
5. Just as critics evaluate you, evaluate your critics. Dismiss critics who suppose you should have written their manuscript, and listen to those who have your best interests at heart.
6. Never focus on weaknesses--in other people, in writing, or in yourself--as subjects of interest in their own right. Instead, attend to how you can best deal with them.
7. Never lie or try to be something other than what you really are; instead, get to know yourself better and how to better please yourself as a writer.
8. Acknowledge that time is the most limited resource for a writer. Identify the prices you pay for your choices and make certain that what you are getting from associations and projects is more valuable than what you are foregoing.

My writers come to some quick agreements about Browne's maxims; you might do the same. For one thing, it will take some time and practice to get used to their meanings and uses. We agree to revisit them from time to time. For another thing, we may not agree with all his notions; he sounds like a hard-hearted objectivist whose advice sometimes misses the necessary irrationalities of everyday life:

I'll have to think about Browne before I decide. In some ways I'm sure he is right on. He pushes me to put aside the foolish reactions, the attempts to please everyone, my neglect of my own best interests. His stuff is a breath of fresh air in that regard. But he is also off-putting in some ways that I can't quite get a handle on yet. It may be a little too pat, too oversimplified. . . . Still, I think I will try to use it, in moderation.

In spite of this ambivalence, more than we expressed with Albert Ellis, we concur in wanting to state Browne's ideas in a single rule:

RULE #18: Harry Browne's maxims for finding freedom from depression remind us that while we cannot control dislikes and personalities, including our own, we can control our reactions to irrationalities by more carefully choosing our interactions. In so doing we can better please ourselves and the minority of people predisposed to like what we have to say.

The immediate worth in Browne's maxims, we acknowledge, lies in the relief from pressures and anxieties that we bring to writing. It reminds us that depression has both a cognitive and an emotional side.

Anxiety

We have a head start on controlling anxiety in our routine checks and exercises for comfort, relaxation, and moderate pacing. We have even foreseen the value of careful preparation as a means of diminishing anxiety. And now, with the addition of daily work at RET, we have instituted actions that reduce irrational anxiety (this is indicated reliably in the self-ratings of participants). Clearly, writers are helped by disputing anxiety-producing thoughts and by replacing them with calm, rational thought that put risks and discomforts into realistic perspective. Rational thinking helps control both the cognitive and emotional components of depression.

What else, then, could you or any other writer want? Many program participants, nearly half those I have studied, want more; they still worry, even with all the program's exercises in regular practice, about being able to handle large doses of anxiety. This writer voiced the most extreme kind of concern:

What we've done is nice, don't misunderstand me, and it helps make me a less anxious writer. I worry less. I'm less tense and I'm enjoying sessions more. But this experience hasn't included having to cope with a big set of pressures (when, for example, I have to write an important speech at the last minute). It hasn't really, as far as I can tell, prepared me to cope with the most frightening instance--anxiety attacks . . . . If you've ever had a panic attack, you'll know what I mean. You don't worry about writing, you struggle to keep breathing and you hope against hope that your heart will bear up through all its wild pounding.

Here too, my groups and I look for answers in the literature. In the main, we bring little of it back for abstracting and sharing. The most demonstrably successful approaches for preventing strong anxieties involve drug therapies, usually with tranquilizers. (These we reject for their addictive and soporific properties; drug therapies are not advocated for activities like writing that demand concentration.) The other promising solutions for anxiety revolve around relaxation exercises (usually elaborate routines of muscle relaxation) and cognitive therapies that lessen anxiety-inducing thought. We have already, my groups invariably tell me, included as much relaxation and cognitive modification as we are likely to want.

What we apparently need, then, is an approach that builds on the calm, unrushed writing we have practiced to avoid impatience and hypomania. What might help even more is attention to calm and patience that precedes writing sessions. To distinguish it from exercises limited to writing sessions, we call it pacing, the moderation of tempo and mood that permits euphoria without fatigue, one that ideally precedes and follows writing.

We begin by elaborating on what pacing offers writers. Pacing can, for instance, pull us back from rushing; it can also help mitigate the anxiety that arises, often without accompanying irrational thoughts, once we are speeding:

I can see why pacing can do things to really help avoid strong anxieties, even
panic. . . . If you can apply it, not only to writing, but also to the things you do before you write, then you wouldn't be so disposed to manickiness and panic. Once I began monitoring my bingeing, I noticed that I did a lot of other things in binges. . . . I was constantly rushing, feeling busy, feeling rushed, feeling out of control, with my jaw tensed. When it came time to write, I not only felt I was too busy. I was also a nervous wreck about writing. When I start my days in calmer fashion, pacing myself and doing most things a bit at a time, I become a lot less anxious about my writing . . . even about my insomnia.

Hypomania

Pacing also does something more unusual, for most writers I have known. It moderates enthusiasm. Here, it seems, lies a hope for making real progress with hypomania. Once again, because we are having to invent our solutions, we look to the literature on hypomania for hints, this time from a more practical and approximate vantage.

Background. In one group meeting, now, we might share and discuss seven summaries of the literature. Then, in the next meetings, by way of quick review, we might concur on a briefer list (like the one that follows) as having made the essential points that we need to moderate but not eliminate hypomania. Most of what we abstract seems only marginally relevant at first but proves useful:

1. We review E.B. White's [39] well-known admiration of writers who worked in ways that would leave them feeling unsatisfied and gloomy, and we wonder why writers so often suppose that good

writing must involve misery. We puzzle about whether White was inordinately influenced by the dour, Puritanical culture in which he did much of his work. Was he justifiably afraid of the strong positive emotions that can accompany writing?

2. We look again at Broyard's claim [40] that madness makes writing warm and intuitive, we wonder how he could picture either depressed or manic people as warm, and we speculate that he, like E.B. White, equated good writing with strong suffering.

3. We revisit Perkins' [41] observation of poets who want it understood that they "compose by a fine species of frenzy," and not by dint of hard work and slowly emerging insights. Perhaps, we suppose, writers like to excuse their usual bad and painful habits of rushing and worrying as the madness that makes for creativity.

In every group, this sort of discussion leads to a listing of the emotional states we think we want to foster as writers. Three states seem optimal. The first is a condition of mild happiness because it not only brings comfort but it also broadens the range and flexibility of our associations in thinking [16]. The second state is moderate hypomania--for its power to impel and sustain writing. The third is a condition of calm, reflective pacing punctuated by breaks, a gait that permits quality work and moderates fatigue.

Exercises for moderating hypomania. Each writing group schedules much the same series of exercises for controlling hypomania and incorporates them into existing bds, usually with a checklist to monitor compliance and progress. These are some suggested steps for everyday use:

1. Beginning days with a calm, unhurried pace by sitting on the side of the bed after awakening, and relaxing/meditating for a few minutes while reviewing a plan for moderation and efficiency. One group settled on a common admonition to be repeated throughout days, the advice of John Wooden to his basketball players, "Be quick but don't hurry."

2. Maintaining that calm, unhurried pace until the morning writing time.

3. Beginning writing sessions with a patient, observant scan for negative thoughts *and* feelings--then making notes and disputations of either, by practicing RET. Writers learn to check for more than negativity; impatience or irrational happiness bear just as much watching and challenging.

4. Settling into writing sessions with one or two brief, preliminary acts aimed at inducing a state of mild pleasantness (e.g., via a visualization of floating in warm, shockingly blue Caribbean waters)

and mild enthusiasm (e.g., by anticipating how enjoyable the flow of ideas and words will be, once underway).

5. Relying on carefully prepared plans and prewriting that leave the writer with little more to do than translating and elaborating already practiced ideas into prose. (This allows writers to be quick without hurrying.) When practiced this way, without struggle and with calm quickness, writing generates a ready sense of mild euphoria. To know when happiness and enthusiasm become excessive, writers monitor for the sense that "it feels too good to be true," more specifically for a lack of interest in pausing to rest.

6. Recommitting to regular pauses for comfort, relaxation, and pacing during bds (especially during longer writing sessions).

7. Setting firm limits for the length of most sessions.

What makes this approach different from usual means of dealing with hypomania? As a rule, writers conjure it by way of hours of intense, uninterrupted writing; when hypomania comes as the result of bingeing, so do its unfortunate qualities (e.g., impatience, fatigue, grandiosity) and the increased likelihood of not writing regularly thereafter. Here, in contrast, we induce it in mild and stable fashion by working from prewriting and without a background of impatience or negativity. Excessive hypomania, the kind commonly borne of binges, is harder to induce and harder to stop.

Because I aim to encourage an uncommonly moderate state of hypomania, I urge you to add unique exercises to this routine. Two additions are already in practice: one is pacing of activities that precede and follow writing sessions; the other makes a more explicit point of associating sessions with mild happiness. Why is pleasurability so important? Among other things, it associates writing with feelings and experiences that take away much of its usual aversiveness. People who make usually distasteful tasks (e.g., exercising) something they eagerly anticipate have linked them to secondary rewards [42]. Exercisers who persist and enjoy demanding routines have something in common; they manage to emphasize secondary rewards such as (1) the release from daily worries, (2) the exhilaration of finishing, (3) the satisfaction of sticking with a difficult task, and (4) the slowly accumulating benefits for health and physique. Persistent and enthusiastic writers, similarly, manage this "conditioned pleasantness" by associating their sessions with mild happiness, comfort, discovery, and accomplishment.

Experiences in controlling hypomania. Some parts of this regimen come easily to writers in the program. Almost no one resists ideas of extending a moderate, unhurried pace to the beginning of days:

Now you've got me doing things that may make a big difference in my daily life, not just in writing. I'm sitting meditatively on the side of my bed, taking a moment to be calm, and I'm putting aside my usual habit of rushing around from the moment I get up. I'm not leaping out of bed. I'm thinking coolly about what I want to do that will be most important. And my days feel less hectic. They feel less overwhelming. I'm more in control, I think, and I can tell that I will be able to get more done with less effort than before. . . . This definitely makes writing easier, less of a struggle. I'm not as rushed, not as tense, not so caught up in feeling that I don't have time for writing. Of course, I've begun to approach other things the same way, the things I value and want to do well and enjoy. Like making a good meal.

Some aspects of routines are more difficult. One of the hardest, among writers I have studied, is the assignment of deliberately bringing an air of mild pleasantness to writing sessions. The problem isn't, as groups often imagine at first, simply a matter of reversing traditional beliefs that equate suffering with excellent work. Instead, most writers suppose that attending to emotions of mild happiness would be too distracting from the fierce concentration they usually practice in writing.

Even as my writers begin to see the contradictions in this irrational thought (by, for example, practicing the disputations of RET), they look back to an old scene in our journey together. The notion first came up in our discussions of writers who could not stand disruptions that might set aside a current flow of thought (Chapters 1 and 2). At that time we found an applicable idea from the composition literature that provided an effective disputation: The worse the writer, the greater the attachment to the writing [43]. And we agreed on another way of stating it: healthy writers welcome interruptions (at least of the moderate variety) for their potential in disrupting a narrow, rushed train of thought, among other things. The same rule now translated into a disputation to combat the irrational belief that we cannot attend to thoughts *and* emotions while writing:

RULE #19: The worse the writer, the greater the inattention to emotions while writing.

This rule brings to mind the well-known consequences of neglecting emotions while writing (e.g., an absence of mild happiness inhibits problem solving; an absence of euphoria lessens motivation). And it suggests some new ones. Writers attuned to emotions have available a wealth of information about how well they are doing in domains such as clarity of expression and likely audience reactions. They have access to a whole array of feelings and moods that can be translated into interesting prose: the passions of characters being depicted, the joys felt in making discoveries, and the struggles experienced in the writing. They can even, by momentarily assuming a different emotional stance, better represent the actions of a character and better anticipate the responses of readers [44].

When groups share experiences about moderating hypomania, they make a communal effort to refine the strategies for effective control.   Reflections usually start with notes of moderation and sarcasm:

Yes, yes, there is, after all, plenty of time for subtle, fine adjustments in a set of practices that will accompany us for the rest of our lives.

Oh come on now! I'm still looking for something to get my writing career launched. When I'm famous and revered I'll revert to my old ways and write the way I really want to. This is all just a pose.

Then we come up with a more detailed, but still practical plan for moderating hypomania like this:

1. Not just beginning days by slowing down and planning calmly, but writing with relaxed, softly smiling faces and relaxed, open postures. (Even native New Yorkers manage these unnatural acts.) The key here seems to lie in moderation: we increasingly take more time to notice and savor the things we really enjoy, but we try to maintain aneven keel emotionally.

2. Not just practicing RET to rid ourselves of negative thinking, but to replace pessimistic, fearful self-talk with optimistic and helpful thoughts (e.g., "I can find real pleasure in coming up with new ideas and associations, in crafting clear prose, in feeling competent").

3. Not just beginning bds with associations to pleasantness but reproducing the same sorts of mildly happy moods at each pause during sessions.

4. Not only relying on prewriting to make writing easy and quick but previewing and enjoying these preparations in a revisit to the material during the preceding afternoon or evening; here, at last, we may find a useful role for traditional notions of incubation of creativity and enthusiasm.

5. Not just making a stronger habit of sticking to limits for session lengths but adding self-congratulations (e.g., a "well done" for stopping in the middle of a roll; even for the mere act of maintaining contact and continuity with the material during busy days).   One important self-assurance lies in accepting a session's output as enough writing for the day. When writers chronically imagine they have not done enough, they make themselves vulnerable to stress and impatience.

6. And, not just managing our emotions and thoughts but also paying more attention to writing in pleasant, comfortable surrounds.

The last of these additions brings a sigh of relief to those writers who have found many of these plans too idealistic and ambitious for comfort, at least for the moment:

I'm glad we finally included something I can really see myself doing that isn't so quixotic. I can't see myself smiling or looking pleasant for a whole day. My face would break. I would feel like a beauty contestant. I can, though, see myself attending to my writing site. . . . I write in a room that has all the charm of a storage closet, where I try not to look up from my screen.

We agree to extend our section on control to a renewed look at improving our writing environments.

But before we do that, we tolerate an aside, some thirty minutes before coming to closure about hypomania. Here is the dilemma that many of us still struggle with: At first, it seemed that hypomania was all bad. If given any headway, apparently, it would take over the writer and the writing, leaving both the worse for wear. Now we aim for a kind of controlled, moderated hypomania. While some of the devices for making this moderation work are in practice, writers still ask, "What is to keep so powerful a force as hypomania from displacing our simple controls of mild happiness, and pacing?" The answer demands a slightly more thorough understanding of how depression and anxiety relate to hypomania. In everyday experience, it turns out, the three phenomena are closely interrelated. To truly bring hypomania under the control of mild emotions and positive thinking, we must also moderate depression and its accompanying anxiety.

Consider how the three interact: Depression may well be the base state that makes writers vulnerable to excesses of hypomania. Because negative self-focus brings anxious discomfort, it inclines us to escape into alternatives such as bingeing. Apparently, over 70 percent of the binges evidenced by writers in the study group of fifty-two participants were immediately preceded by mild or moderate depressions. Why? Again, a main cause of depression is chronically self-focused negative thinking [45]. This negativity does more than make writing difficult for as long as we remain in a depressed state; depression based on negative self-focus also makes us overreactive to positive events. When we sense opportunities to supplant the passivity and pain of anxiety-provoking automatic thinking with something distracting or enjoyable, we may take the leap. But because hypomania works, at best, only until we finish a task or succumb to distractions, we soon resume our vulnerability to depression; one overreaction engenders another. Distractions that would not disrupt the writing of moderately emotional people trigger overreactions and irrationalities in depressives.

Two things come from this depression-induced vulnerability. One is a pattern of mood swings that seems difficult to change; the same writers who rely on binges to induce momentum and to escape negative self-consciousness may, as we saw earlier, rely on subsequent depressions to edit or reject the imprecise work conjured under mania. Writers caught in this vicious cycle of mania and depression may know no other way to write. The second result is often less obvious. Hypomanias that emerge from depressions are necessarily overreactions. Their reliance on uninterrupted and intense marathons of writing before momentum and imagination are ensured means that these hypomanias customarily move beyond self-control. The hypomanic writer is least well-suited to pause before projects are completed; with a cessation comes an occasion to note imperfections in the writing, to recall past failures and criticisms, and to grow anxious, negatively self-focused, distressed, and once again, depressed.

What, again, distinguishes the kind of hypomania that grows from the mild euphoria of translating prewriting into prose, easily but without hurrying? It is paced and planful; it proceeds patiently and subsides before fatigue and narrowing set in. It is moderate and helps maintain motivation without a distortion of imagination or a neglect of plans. And it is largely self-controlled and pleasant, during and after writing sessions. It does not, in my studies, incline writers to depression. And it does not, in opposition to traditional beliefs, diminish the creativity of writers compared to peers writing with the spontaneity of binges [46].

Appreciation of the link between hypomania and depression comes slowly but enthusiastically, in my experience; at first, writers may fail to recognize the emotions that accompany writing, especially in long sessions [47]. To make most of the points just overviewed, I revert to my professorial style; I lecture and explain while trying to engage writers in discussion and questions. As a rule, I repeat the most essential points and I distribute summaries in written form. No one, as far as I can tell, has trouble seeing the implications. This is how many writers react (including you?):

I think I know what it means. I know, full well, that I tend to be, as we say here, dysphoric, sort of depressed, and that my writing hasn't helped with my moodiness. I think that explains why I often want to give up writing. It explains why I want to get writing over in a hurry. It explains why I am chronically behind in my writing.

What it means for me is a commitment to giving up my old pattern of moving back and forth from periods of sadness about writing to binges of writing. I've had enough roller coaster experiences and mood swings as a writer . . . even though I hadn't quite realized why before now. I thought it somehow was necessary to creative madness or something like that. . . . Knowing this thing about the interdependence of depression and mania convinces me, once and for all, to try to give up bingeing. It doesn't work and it isn't efficient. I don't want the moodiness. It doesn't even allow me the most important thing, feeling in control.

What will it mean for me? Well, it will mean a far greater conviction that I must get rid of my negativism; I am becoming a devoted spotter of negative thoughts, like the sky watchers on Pacific islands who watched for enemy planes during World War II. It's going to mean a lot more focus on my moods and more insistence on being paced and pleased as a writer. I'm going to take better care of myself and I'm going to pay more care to my conditions for writing. I have already gone out and ordered a new notebook [word processor] that I have been wanting for some time. . . . I'm looking at ways to clean up and redecorate my study.

By this point, then, we are becoming involved in some new and exciting ways of building self-control as writers. We know, with some confidence, how to quiet the negative self-talk that discourages motivation, encourages anxiety, and heightens vulnerability to overreaction. And we know, albeit imperfectly, how to generate mild hypomania under mindful control, without the press of depression and impatience. The greatest satisfaction from these realizations lies in understanding the ubiquitous cycle that had undermined our writing: first, the mild, barely perceptible depression about the imagined prospects of not being able to write cleverly and without criticism; then, the plunge, with deadlines nearing, into bingeing that pushes aside passivity and its negative self-focus; later, the hurried, insufficient writing done under hypomania; and, finally, with the circle coming full, the return to passivity and a depression with overreactiveness to both failure and success. With that tendency to overreaction comes a perpetuation of exaggerated responses--periods of passive waiting interrupted by episodes of manicky rushing. Predictably, this density of information produces a rule to help make sense of things:

RULE #20: Hypomania works best in moderation, when spontaneity is constrained by a planful reliance on prewriting and when euphoria is tempered by a mild pace of working.

With this summary comes a period of restating other things we are just coming to appreciate. In one case, we reconsider the short-term escapes that underlie self-defeating acts. The point: When we follow a roller coaster pattern of depressions and manias, we limit ourselves to a steady diet of short-term solutions. Another reconsideration draws out the key role of depression in hypomania. Although not all depressions are solely the result of negative thinking [48], most dysphorias result from negative self-focus that can be controlled with strategies like RET. When we can temper the passivity and depression, we will be less vulnerable to the overreaction of strong hypomania. The third reexamination of depression prepares us for other ventures: Not only can we manage better conditions for writing through self-control, but we can also do more to manage our writing environments. As we practice self-control, we generally extend our concerns to our writing environments.

ENVIRONMENTAL CONTROLS

Some two decades ago, early in my routine of visiting the writing sites of patients, I was struck by how little attention most writers pay to their working conditions. Many worked in uncomfortable, unkempt rooms; few made concessions to pleasantness of view, sound, or smell. But, over time, I realized that I hadn't quite gotten it right. In fact, it seems, most writers exhibit a logic of sorts about where they write, however unspoken and unmindful. Many writers simply opt for a familiar location, much as they unfailingly sat in the same classroom chairs throughout semesters as students, perhaps for the comfort of familiarity. And many have chosen, when they thought about settings at all, to imagine that more pleasant surrounds would distract them from the fierce concentration they believe they need for good writing ("That's why I put my file cabinets in front of that window").

Still other writers have a reason that relates back to cycles of binges and immobility: time that could be spent writing is always in danger of displacement by other binges; office cleaning or redecoration can dislodge writing as much as any alternative activity imaginable (it can take on a fascinatingly obsessive focus when writers spend hours on acts like polishing door hardware). And once a writing binge is completed, writers may be too tired for redecoration and too far behind schedule on other important tasks to arrange better conditions.

Something else about writing sites came to mind in my early visits. The customary setting in which a writers works says a lot about his or her control of writing. Some surroundings are rigidly neat and controlled and allow no distractions. Others are wholly disorganized and unmindful--uncomfortable, overly distracting, and unpleasant. Neither extreme, of neatness or disarray, seems to be associated with optimal fluency and comfort in writing. But these were only impressions. I wanted more systematic facts.

A Study of Environmental Factors

So I looked first at my notes on the writing sites of my study group, then to writers' own journals and recollections. Over time, I added the results of an ever growing sample of participants until the now familiar study group of fifty-two writers produced a wealth of demographic information about conditions and habits. I use these data to help make decisions on what needs more emphasis in my programs. Because many of the writers in my groups have entrenched distastes for the sorts of graphs and tables that social scientists love to display,

I draw out only the most useful of distinctions and leave the more esoteric suggestions for private discussions.

Main factors. The first two practices analyzed, (1) writing with comfortable seating and seating postures and with (2) the regular practice of distance focusing (usually, but not always, through a window) are more characteristic of the most fluent writers. So too, minimizing the (3) presence of tempting and irrelevant reading materials at the writing site (e.g., magazines, journals, correspondence, newspapers), having (4) social supports on hand (e.g., people who prod us to write at writing times; writing partners who join us for regular sessions), and (5) arranging external cues as reminders about pacing (e.g., periodic signals for stretch breaks).

Secondary factors. Other conditions and practices, in contrast, show less connection to fluency at this point: Having one's office decorated with personally relevant objects only mildly differentiates the two groups of writers, more so for men. Tolerance of loud noises does not distinguish the two groups, perhaps because almost of all these fifty-two writers already wrote in settings without many disruptive sounds. Background music was also an uncommon and, apparently, unimportant factor in fluency [49]; while it did indicate a tolerance for moderate disruptions that carried a relaxing note, other writers arranged equivalently pleasant background noises by working near fountains, bird feeders, chimes, even whirligigs.

Reactions to this information. Overall, these data prove reassuring to most writers. The kinds of things we have supposed important, such as comfort, pacing, and distance focusing, are already especially helpful for writers most immersed in them. And, these same things have been practiced by almost everyone in the program, even if in less thorough-going form by some writers. We are all, we agree, making impressive progress, some more slowly than others. We are even, someone noted, following the prescription of one researcher on productivity for "doing less worrying and more doing" [50].

A few more minutes are devoted to related findings: there is, for example, satisfaction in discovering that the same patterns seen in these data hold for outcomes besides fluency. In other findings, not represented above, the same individuals who tended to be most fluent were also most likely to report the highest self-ratings of comfort, enjoyment, and confidence with their writing. These exemplars were also least likely to evidence the negative self-talk that had accompanied their writing earlier in the program. So, the same things that accompany fluency (e.g., pacing and comfortable seating) also couple with the pleasure and self-control experienced in writing.

Something else goes on at this point. I listen most attentively to the responses of writers who know, at least privately, that they are members of the less successful group depicted in the analyses. I wonder, to myself: Do they agree that these data reinforce the need to be more compliant? Or do they see themselves as exceptions to the principles under discussion? Most of these writers include themselves in, but not all:

I'm tempted to say, as a film mogul once did, you can include me out. But I'm in, I think. You know, this just convinces me all the more that I need to do the things that I know can work. Pacing is the hardest but I know I can do it because I am doing it now, from time to time. I don't know, really, why I'm not doing more RET; I like it and it works. Any suggestions? Can anyone help me?

No, I don't see myself operating under a separate set of rules. I need to do these same things. I'm really serious about restructuring my study and my writing times but I have just been putting it off until I'm not busy. At least that is what I use as an excuse. I believe that it is time, for me, for more regular practice of RET, preferably by resuming phone meetings with _____, to get at the real reasons why I procrastinate these critical things.

I may be in, I may be out. I'm not one of the chosen at this point, not one of fluents. Still, I'm doing all right. I'm modestly, adequately fluent. I've gotten an important review and prospectus done in the last few months. I just want to take the stuff I like from this program and leave some of the discipline behind. I hope that's all right. [The group and I readily agree that it is.]

The strongest consensus in these discussions is that the things we have learned about self-control and environmental control can be capsulized as another memorable rule:

RULE #21: For writers already accomplished at initiating fluency, the acts that help maintain and optimize it include comfort (e.g., attention to eye strain), personally pleasant decorations, mild happiness, minimizing temptations to read or socialize in disruptive ways, thoroughgoing prewriting, pacing, and RET.

Strategies for Building Environmental Controls

In the end, as we have just done in the twenty-first rule, we push for a few simple strategies to practice. This time we look again to the conditions associated with the ten most successful writers from the study group in each of these categories:

Seating comfort. This factor can be stated simply. The most comfortable writers (those with highest self-ratings of comfort; those with fewest self-reported aches, strains, and fatigues during and after sessions) tend to work in padded or plush chairs that provide back and arm support. Many, but not all, writers in this category work in recliner/plush chairs, with their writing pads or keyboards on their laps or lapboards, and with support for their shoulders and necks. Recliner chair writers, it figures, report the lowest incidence of neck and head aches during and after sessions. One other subgroup equals the comfort of recliner writers, individuals who move around from one plush site (e.g., a padded window seat) to another (e.g., a bed with great propping pillows).

Our assignment, and yours, is to systematically and patiently try seating arrangements and postures that may improve our comfort during writing. We contract to have one group member visit our writing site while we are working, to offer an outsider's expert opinion on our success in maximizing comfort. And we plan to present brief reports about our experiments in improving our writing sites and habits.

Distance focus. We all need to take better care of our eyes as writers. The only question is how best to do so when the habit is unfamiliar and when, in some cases, working in sites without windows. Exemplars provide helpful suggestions: They often ensure a habit of distance focusing by doing it as the first act of pausing for stretching and checking for comfort and pace. And when they lean back to stretch, they shift their eyes away from the writing and onto something more distant. They also, evidently, held that relaxed gaze for the few moments of their pauses.

For other answers, we can look beyond exemplars. What can be done to replace a window? Some writers gaze upon a bookcase, a pleasant picture or painting; some even tack up a mandala or a poster that mimics a window that draws their eyes away from writing. When distance focusing and related habits (wrist relaxation) do not become regular habits quickly, we can use mechanical cues such as electronic beepers or sand clocks to remind us to practice. Another thing helps, making a habit of distance focus and muscular relaxation throughout whole days so that both become more and more automatic. A final aid to adding this and other good habits is monitoring and recording each instance of practice. One writing group settled on using a toy on which disks could be inserted over a pole for each act of distance focusing. This colorful device was hard not to notice sitting next to a writer's view and its daily counts could be recorded for mention at the next group meeting.

Aesthetics. Here, we decided to skip the lessons of exemplars. Instead, we began by sharing Polaroid photographs of our sites that showed desks and walls of writing sites. These interactions produced some hearty laughter and quick decisions about what kinds of decorations, pleasantness, and memorabilia could be added. A second round of photographs (and, where necessary, a third) evidenced remarkable improvements of most writing sites (including more comfortable chairs). There was also a common theme in remarks about why most of us had previously done so little to provide satisfying aesthetics to writing sites: "It beats me. I can't think of any good reasons."

Elimination of temptations to read off-target materials. Here too, photographs revealed a plethora of nonoptimal conditions. Writing sites included surprising amounts of reading materials (newspapers, correspondence, etc.) that could and did deflect writers' attention for more than a moment. A modicum of struggle was reported in ridding sites of such material ("I like to take breaks and read something relaxing and I hate to get rid of it . . . although I would be better off without most of it"). Slightly more trouble was reported in keeping these materials from reentering. A few writers actually posted signs prohibiting themselves and others from bringing nonrelevent reading into the room or area. In the longer run, most writers made a habit of scanning for and automatically removing such items upon entering the writing site.

Social support. There was nothing surprising in the finding that exemplars worked with the help of more prodders or partners than did other writers. Many of us were, though, mildly surprised to be doing as well as we were. We were already accustomed to group activities of sharing ideas, struggles, criticisms, and supports. And most of us were practicing some form of social support for working in bds, for carrying out RET, and for critiquing each other's prewritten plans. Now, with the evidence showing that these practices coincided with fluency and comfort, we felt even more disposed to take a closer look at social supports in writing. Lone readers might feel a similarly sociable urge. I hope so.

The next chapter, the fifth, extends notions of control to the social side of an ordinarily private enterprise. As the trip continues, we put more value on companionship and support.

SUMMARY

This fourth chapter, on control, extends usual interventions for writing problems. Traditional interventions, for the most part, simply initiate fluency while doing little or nothing to maintain it. That is, the first three chapters (motivation, inspiration, and regimen) helped *initiate* fluency and comfort. Here, in contrast, we worked to *maintain* the new habits first acquired as initiating techniques. The acts designed to foster maintenance made up what I called control in Chapter 4.

We quickly found a focus for maintenance efforts. Two common deficiencies in self-control demand the most recognition and work--hypomania and depression. Rule #16 made part of the case for moderating hypomania: its chaos and spontaneity, when the mood is excessive, rob us of knowledge necessary to creativity, of stability that permits flexibility, and of the discipline that fosters freedom.

Rule #17 offered a practical place to begin to interrupt the usual cycle of depressions and manias in writing--noticing and disputing the irrational thinking that undergirds depression. It summarizes the insights and interventions borrowed from Rational-Emotive Theory (RET) and its founder, Albert Ellis: What commonly inhibits writers is little more than chronic, unquestioned irrational thinking. Common irrationalities are self-talk that is self-downing or that encourages low frustration tolerance; both can be spotted operating in the backs of our minds by way of noticing key words (shoulds, oughts, and musts). These and other irrational thinking can be disputed with rational questions and replaced with more objective and efficient thoughts and actions.

Ready success with RET led writing groups to collect and practice useful maxims that encourage rational thinking. Rule #18 summarized a collection of aphorisms we found most useful in Harry Browne's prescriptions for maintaining freedom: for example, the reminder that we cannot control dislikes and personalities (those of other people or our own), but that we can choose to associate mostly with people predisposed to like us and what we have to say.

Even with usual, mild depressions under control, writers need also to attend to the hypomanias that can institute dysphorias and immobility. To do so requires a giant, unfamiliar step for writers accustomed to focusing on nothing but their cognitions during writing. But writers can profit in learning to notice and control their emotions, especially those that signal depression, anxiety, and mania. Rule #19 makes the point in slightly different fashion: The worse the writer, the greater the inattention to emotions while writing.

Not all the conversations about the importance of serenity in writing found their way into the condensed version depicted in Chapter 4. We often, for example, shared quotes from famous writers that helped make sense of things. For example:

. . . you need to be calm to write well. Be detached--detachment is very important. It's not indifference, far from it! . . . He often talked about writing, the pleasures and pains. . . . "keep writing. Style doesn't matter--it's the vision that's important, and writing from a position of strength." He was right. I began to notice an improvement, a greater certainty in my writing.
   Paul Theroux, V.S. Naipaul, 1972

Our strategies for observing and restraining hypomania also relied on old methods from the program: pausing to ensure comfort, relaxation, and moderate pacing. And to an extent, interventions for managing impatience and overreaction overlapped with other daily activities; relaxation and pacing, for instance, begin with awakening and sitting calmly on the bedside to plan and slow down. But the most crucial change in establishing control over hypomania was the directive to make its occurrence the product of prewriting. Rule #20 abstracts the strategy: Hypomania works best in controlled moderation, as the planful outcome of working from prewriting that generates easy and enthusiastic prose (all, of course, while writers heed safeguards for pacing and session length).

As we closed out this fourth phase of the program, my writers and I began to notice the kinds of control important beyond the self-management of cognitions and emotions we had been practicing. Some of the stimulus for a wider view came from an update of outcome data: The most fluent and comfortable writers in the program demonstrate the importance of self-control practices such as immersion in RET and pacing. They also showed tendencies to work more at controlling their writing environments. They were, for example, more likely to ensure regular comfort in seating, in resting their eyes, in working amid personally valued decorations, and in removing temptations to read things that would distract them from writing for more than a moment (these principles were condensed in Rule #21). With this brief venture beyond self-control we set the stage for the next program phase, on social management (Chapter 5).

In the end, we come back to the beginning, Wordsworth's insight: writing takes its pattern from emotion recollected in tranquillity. It was also Wordsworth, you may recall, who inspired another theme common in this book, a wise passiveness. We proceed ever slowly, always with a goal in mind.

If a person asked my advice, before undertaking a long voyage, my answer would depend on his possessing a decided taste for some branch of knowledge, which by this means could be advanced. . . . It is necessary to look forward to a harvest, however distant that may be, when some fruit will be reaped, some good effected.

Charles Darwin, *The Voyage of the H.M.S. Beagle*, 1890

REFERENCES

1. Wordsworth, W. & Coleridge, S.T. (1969). *Lyrical Ballads*. London: Oxford University Press, appendix, p. 173.

2. Durant, W. & Durant, A. (1975). *The age of Napoleon*. New York: Simon & Schuster, p. 431.

3. Durant, W. & Durant, A. (1967). *Rousseau and revolution*. New York: Simon & Schuster, p. 171.

4. McCaul, K.D., Glasgow, R.E. & O'Neill, H.K. (1992). The problem of creating habits: Establishing health-protective dental behaviors. *Health Psychology*, 11, 101-110.

5. Ellis, A. & Knaus, W.J. (1977). *Overcoming procrastination*. New York: Institute for Rational Living.

6. Alloy, L.B. & Lipman, A.J. (1992). Attributional style as a vulnerability factor for depression: Validation by past history of mood disorders. *Cognitive Therapy and Research*, 16, 391-407.

7. Beck, A.T., Rush, J.A., Shaw, B.F. & Emery, G. (1979). *Cognitive therapy of depression*. New York: Guilford.

8. Meichenbaum, D. (1977). *Cognitive-behavior modification: An integrative approach*. New York: Plenum Press.

9. Salovey, P. & Haar, M.D. (1990). The efficacy of cognitive-behavior therapy and writing process training for alleviating writing anxiety. *Cognitive Therapy and Research*, 14, 515-528, at 517-518.

10. Boice, R. (1992). Combined treatments for writing blocks. *Behaviour Research and Therapy*, 30, 107-116.

11. Mavissakalian, M. & Barlow, D.H. (1981). *Phobia: Psychological and pharmacological treatment*. New York: Guilford Press.

12. Klinger, E. (1984). A conscious-sampling analysis of test anxiety and performance. *Journal of Personality and Social Psychology*, 47, 1376-1390.

13. Bandura, A. (1990). Conclusion: Reflections on nonability determinants of competence. In R.J. Sternberg & J. Kolligan (eds.), *Competence considered*, pp. 315-362. New Haven: Yale University Press.

14. Elbow, P. (1992). Freewriting and the problem of wheat and tares. In J.M. Moxley (ed.), *Writing and publishing for academic authors*, pp. 33-47. Lanham, NY: University Press of America.

15. Davidson, R.J. & Cacioppo, J.T. (1992). New developments in the scientific study of emotion. *Psychological Science*, 3, 21-22.

16. Oatley, K. & Jenkins, J.M. (1992). Human emotions: function and dysfunction. *Annual Review of Psychology*, 43, 55-85.

17. Oatley, K. (1992). *Best laid schemes: The psychology of emotions*. New York: Cambridge University Press.

18. Davidson, R.J. (1992). Emotion and affective style: Hemispheric substrates. *Psychological Science*, 3, 39-43.

19. Masters, J.C. (1991). Strategies and mechanisms for the personal and social control of emotion. In J. Garber & K.A. Dodge (eds.), *The development of emotion regulation and dysregulation*, 182-207. New York: Cambridge University Press.

20. Kohn, A. (1988). Madness of creativity. *Los Angeles Times*, December 12, Part II, p. 3.

21. DeAngelis, T. (1989). Mania, depression, and genius. *APA Monitor*, January, pp. 1&14.

22. Jamison, K.R., Gerner, R.H., Hammen, C. & Padesky, C. (1980). Clouds and silver linings: Positive experiences associated with primary affective disorders. *American Journal of Psychiatry*, 137, 198-202.

23. Eckblad, M. & Chapman, L.J. (1986). Development and validation of a scale for hypomania. *Journal of Abnormal Psychology*, 95, 214-222.

24. Jamison, K.R. (1989). Mood disorders and patterns of creativity in British writers and artists. *Psychiatry*, 52, 125-133.

25. Akiskal, H. & Weise, R.E. (1992). The clinical spectrum of so-called "minor" depressions. *American Journal of Psychotherapy*, 46, 9-22.

26. Thompson, M. & Bentall, R.P. (1990). Hypomanic personality and attributional style. *Personality and Individual Differences*, 11, 867-868.

27. Persinger, M.A. (1991). Canonical correlation of a temporal lobes scale with schizoid and hypomania scales in a normal population. *Perceptual and Motor Skills*, 73, 615-618.

28. Boice, R. (1982). Increasing the productivity of blocked academicians. *Behaviour Research and Therapy*, 20, 197-207.

29. Rothenberg, A. (1990). *Creativity and madness*. Baltimore: Johns Hopkins University Press.

30. Andreasen, N.C. (1987). Creativity and mental illness: Prevalence rates in writers and their first degree relatives. *American Journal of Psychiatry*, 144, 1288-1292.

31. Holden, C. (1987). Creativity and the troubled mind. *Psychology Today*, 21(4), 9-10.

32. Taylor, R.L. (1967). *W.C. Fields: His follies and fortunes*. New York: Signet Books.

33. Schou, M. (1979). Artistic productivity and lithium prophylaxis in manic-depressive illness. *British Journal of Psychiatry*, 135, 97-103.

34. Barron, F. (1963). *Creativity and psychological health: Origins of personal vitality and creative freedom*. Princeton, NJ: Van Nostrand.

35. Barron, F. (1986). This week's citation classic. *Current Contents*, No. 14 (April 7), 18.

36. Institute for Rational Living, 45 East 65th Street, New York, NY 10021

37. Boice, R. (1985). Cognitive components of blocking. *Written Communication*, 2, 91-104.

38. Browne, H. (1973). *How I found freedom in an unfree world*. New York: Avon.

39. Elledge, S. (1984). *E.B. White*. New York: Norton.

40. Broyard, A. (1976). Keep your compassion, give me your madness. *New York Times Book Review*, June 21, p.12.

41. Perkins, D.N. (1981). *The mind's best work*. Cambridge, MA: Harvard University Press.

42. Eisenberger, R. (1992). Learned industriousness. *Psychological Review*, 99, 248-267.

43. North, S. (1987). *The making of knowledge in composition*. Upper Montclair, NJ: Boynton/Cook.

44. Downey, J.E. (1918). A program for a psychology of literature. Journal of *Applied Psychology*, 2, 366-377.

45. Ingram, R.E., Johnson, B.R., Bernet, C.Z. & Dombeck, M. (1992). Vulnerability to stress: Cognitive and emotional reactivity in chronically self-focused individuals. *Cognitive Therapy and Research*, 16, 451-472.

46. Boice, R. (1983). Contingency management in writing and the appearance of creative ideas. *Behaviour Research and Therapy*, 21, 537-544.

47. Brand, A.G. & Leckie, P.A. (1988). The emotions of professional writers. The *Journal of Psychology*, 122, 421-439.

48. Shea, M.T., Widiger, T.A. & Klein, M.H. (1992). Comorbidity of personality disorders and depression: Implications for treatment. *Journal of Consulting and Clinical Psychology*, 60, 857-868.

49. Hartley, J. & Knapper, C.K. (1984). Academics and their writing. *Studies in Higher Education*, 9, 151-167.

50. Hartley, J. & Branthwaite, A. (1989). The psychologist as wordsmith: A questionnaire study of the writing strategies of productive British psychologists. *Higher Education*, 18, 264-271.

5

Audience

I never want to see anyone, and I never want to go anywhere
or do anything. I just want to write.

P.G. Wodehouse [1]

Most of us can sympathize with Wodehouse's misanthropic mood. We too may
feel the temptation to withdraw to do our best work. And, once doing it, we
might believe that we can continue only so long as there are no other
obligations.

But we know, even those of us who crave reclusion, that writing is
ultimately a social act. Writing reflects the communications we have heard,
read, or imagined; it takes form as we externalize our inner talk in public [2].
These two steps, of internalizing conversations and then externalizing them as
writing, hint at the dilemma for writers. At times we need to listen to our inner
voices. At other times we need to test our formulations on audiences. The
problem is that the first activity may seem more appealing than the second: in
the reclusive phase we can luxuriate in discovery and production; in the social
stage we risk criticism and rejection.

There are other reasons why reclusion may be favored over exhibition.
Solitude offers the chance to concentrate; when we do anything intricate
including photography, model building, or needlepoint, we want to work with
quiet emotions and close attention. Seclusion also promises unusually valuable
freedoms for bookish sorts like many of us. Writing in private frees us from
everyday pressures to conform and to conduct mundane tasks. It provides the
indulgence of individualistic, introspective work for which we can claim much
of the credit. And, it offers that special sort of single-mindedness that suggests
further action [3]. America is so convinced of the value of isolation that it
cossets its writers, at least its favorite prospects, in colonies of rustic cabins to

encourage productivity and genius. [4]

As I relate this picture, you might sense the imbalance in usual scenarios of writers at work. It could be an unanticipated scene in our journey together.

The Pathological Side of Excessive Solitude

We suspect many of the costs of immoderate seclusion for writers. In its extreme form, of necessity, isolation brings silence. In its usual form, secluded writing risks bingeing and depression, both of which encourage overreactivity and overreliance on praise.   With this comes shyness [5], because temperamentality, irritability, and inhibition work in league [6].   And with these, as we have seen, appear two other problems: one is suspiciousness, a readiness to suppose that "those who disagree with me dislike me" [7]; the other is an ever-growing reluctance to make one's work public [8], at least until it seems polished enough to deserve unambiguous appreciation [9, 10].

The point in all this comes back to balance: The same reclusion that works adaptively in moderation loses its value with excessiveness. Or, it can be said this way:

RULE #22:   Social isolation, carried to excess, risks misdirection, overreactivity, misunderstanding, and deprivation of ideas and encouragements.

But this rule raises initial doubts because many successful writers appear to defy it.   Consider three examples of exceptions that come up: Ernest Hemingway liked to say that good writers had to be social outlyers [11]. Isaac Asimov claimed that only the trial and error of working alone--not lectures, conferences, and books--could make writers of us [12]. And Paul Theroux maintained that he needed the lucidity of loneliness to capture the vision that seems special and worthy [13].

Under closer examination, each of these writers shows balance (despite their proud claims for antisocial tendencies). Hemingway apprenticed with avant-garde writers in Paris and remained, throughout his most productive years, sociable with prominent people.   Asimov read for inspiration, solicited mentoring as a writer from his editor, John W. Campbell, and often discussed ideas with other writers:

Campbell promised to read my story that night and to send a letter. . . . He didn't like the slow beginning, the suicide at the end. Campbell also didn't like the first-person narration and the stiff dialog. . . . By that time, though, I was off and running. The joy of having spent an hour or more with Campbell, the thrill of talking face to face with an idol, filled me with ambition. . . . It was Fred Pohl, once again, who came to my rescue. I visited him on November 2. (We visited back and forth constantly, as a matter of course.) We walked across Brooklyn Bridge, I remember, and while leaning against the rail and looking down at the river, I told him of my troubles with "Bridle and Saddle." His suggestions were excellent ones [14].

And Theroux, finally, gathers most of his material for travel writing while interacting with, spying on, and provoking people. While he may clarify his conclusions in private, he forms them in public. Often, then, we have to look beyond writers; superficial comments to understand the true role of seclusion.

When my groups and I reflect on the appeal of isolation, we find some telling reasons of our own. For instance, reclusion seems easier; we write more readily for ourselves. The literature on the development of writing skill suggests two explanations for this ease: Only with difficulty do writers learn to coordinate their ideas with the perspectives of others [15]. And, only rarely do we see writing modelled [16]; instead we are left to struggle in private with few clues about what successful writers do, about their habits of mind and work [17].

Why Is it Important to Strengthen the Social Side of Writing?

With a bit of discussion, the answer to this question may seem obvious. Writing is, first and foremost, communicating. Our main obligation as writers is to be coherent and to be read [18]. Without regular, public exposure, we learn slowly if at all about how to communicate.

We can find a wealth of confirmations of this first point, one a famous quote from Goethe: "Talent forms itself in quiet, character takes form in the stream of the world" [19]. Another citation is even more striking: When we are not heard, we stop listening [20]. We are also reminded, in slightly new ways, of how reclusion inhibits communication. Shyness is an irrational act intended to present a favorable public image. But even when it helps manage that, it also incurs self-defeating tendencies including (a) procrastination, (b) the fatal errors that encourage editorial rejection (e.g., the lack of confidence necessary to set a clear course and offer a clear organizing idea), and (c) problems in learning from criticism [21, 22, 23].

We already know many of the benefits of joining a conversation of writers, including social immersion that induces discovery and motivation [24]. You may detect something related: With social experience comes sagacity about arranging support networks [25], about finding ever-growing sources of new ideas [26], and about anticipating criticisms. G.W.F. Hegel put it this way: "Opposition absorbed is the crux of wisdom" [27].

How to Enhance the Social Side of Writing

As we design exercises for building audience, my groups and I alight on a few more things that catch our attention. One is about pacing, that key element in finding moderation and balance. Just as we have learned patience in the private side of writing, we can master it for audience. Consider that we have, more or less, already learned to cultivate social feedback in our prewriting. Now we want to work at involving ourselves in feedback at a steady, continuous rate, not just in occasional bursts of inquiring or sharing. But as the topic of pacing comes up, so does a widespread reluctance to rely so much on help and collaboration:

I couldn't do that, I think. It's my work and I wouldn't feel right about not first solving the problems myself. . . . Besides, I hate to impose on other, busy people.

Fortunately, the mere exposure of this sort of thinking soon reveals its irrationalities:

All right, all right. It's true that I could work more efficiently if I got criticism and input from the outset, from the time I draft my earliest plans. But I don't really like criticism (even though I know full well that by getting it sooner and on a steady diet I could prevent it coming in big doses later, when it counts most). And I don't like having other people see my work when it is unfinished and might still come across as stupid.

While discussing this crucial move in making writing more socially skilled, we draw up a rule to help guide us:

RULE #23: Social skill in writing includes the generosity of letting other people do some of the work.

Even having helped formulate it, we remain, many of us, uncomfortable with this rule. It looks somehow immoral, irresponsible, and manipulative. It seems to take advantage of others who might rather spend their time doing better things than helping us figure out what we want to say. But this worry, too, evaporates under public scrutiny; all of us, we come to see, welcome modest requests for our advice and expertise from other writers in our genre; all of us enjoy the chance to make inputs into unfinished manuscripts--especially at a point where change may still be welcome. Indeed, writers finally agree, we often read finished things by kindred writers and wish that we had been consulted at some early, formative point. The irony here is this: Even though we want to be asked for advice and help, we only reluctantly make the same request of others. Why?

Oh, one thing is pride, I suppose. I want to do it all on my own, without anyone's help.

Why? Because I'm the sort of person who always worries that I might be rejected in my request. Or, worse yet, that I will expose some horrible oversight that, given another week or two on my own, I would have discovered by myself. . . . More than anything, I guess, I cannot stand to be rejected or embarrassed.

Why? Under this examination, I guess I have no good reason. I'll have to say that it is just plain foolish to expect that something summoned up in total privacy will be best-suited for the audience I hope to reach. It is probably even stupider to refuse to tolerate any risk of criticism early. Why not find out about misunderstandings and so on as early as possible?

These same conversations produce other emerging senses of what we want to accomplish. We will, for one thing, need to moderate the cycles of shyness, irrationality, and overreactivity that can emerge from excessive reclusion. One of our biggest struggles may lie in tempering the overattachment to writing that comes with social isolation. Here, at last, we make an oft-stated notion [28] into a rule:

RULE #24: The worse the writer, the greater the attachment to the writing.

What has this to do with finding audience? It relates to something recalled from our earlier forays into the literature: The more creative and successful the individual, the readier the receptiveness to modifications of his or her creative work [29]. Put in terms of audience, this means that our creativity is, to an extent, dependent on openness to audience reaction. When we sustain our private attachment to writing beyond a reasonable point, we limit what we can learn and how well we can communicate.

To begin to detach ourselves from excessive privacy will require an unusual amount of sharing and modeling of how we work as writers. This seems an ideal time to rely heavily on thinking-aloud protocols. Here is the usual plan: We will work though four gradual steps of finding audience, each less private than the one before. And throughout, we will self-disclose, share, and model-- in the groups and elsewhere--in what may be our biggest, boldest step yet. From this final discussion of readiness, comes another working rule:

RULE #25: A sense of audience relies most crucially on exteriorization, at first of what we have to say to ourselves, then of what we have to say to the public.

The discussions that follow help make sense of this seemingly odd rule.

FIRST SENSE OF AUDIENCE: PERSONAL

Audience begins with skill at listening to ourselves [30]. Still, few successful writers tell us much about self-listening. John Gardner, for instance, teases us with suggestions that skillful novelists become interested in the secrets and rhythms that words carry, in finding their own metaphors, in looking over what they have written to see if it says what they meant to say [31]. But how? Gardner never quite says. Other heroes are equally inscrutable.

Only Joanna Field, a recent acquaintance (Chapters 3 and 4), provides helpful clues [32]. She remains nearly unique among writers for having: (a) systematically noted how she thought, felt, and worked, and, then (b) shared her private discoveries with the public. In the end, we recall, she found that a steady reliance on social contacts kept her healthiest because it pried her away from an excessive self-focus and a mean, chattering mind. By pausing to look again at Field, we are reminded of the value of self-study that puts action ahead of self-focus. Here are some consensus possibilities for finding the usually elusive sense of self-audience:

1. Self-audience will probably work best by fostering moderate self-consciousness (in contrast to the excessive self-focus that casts doubts, prematurely admits internal editors, and mircomanages writing a word and a sentence at a time). An adaptive sense of self-audience may depend on moderate pacing of work and monitoring for negative feelings and thoughts.

2. We learned exteriorization, most of us, by way of free writing; as we exteriorize our thinking on paper or screen, we discover what we can say [20].

3. As we practice exteriorization or "outing," by writing and rereading what we have to say, we can work more systematically at imagining our readers' situation [33]--what they could learn from us, how they may react to our writing. As we look outward, we are more likely to imagine what readers will value.

4. And in practicing ways to become better self-audiences, we can plan to attend more and more to what helps motivate this hard work: discovering something worth saying, feeling the need to witness it, and anticipating its acceptance [34].

As we generate and discuss these preliminary notions in groups, we model and practice the act of outing; that is, we remain unsure of what we have to say until we make it public and publicly clear. Stimulated by this brisk conversation and by our pleasant discoveries, we typically add more ideas like these:

5. We could truly profit in becoming better self-audiences [20]. Writers who can manage this skill, of listening to and appreciating themselves, see potentials for new discoveries and find ways of getting started.

6. And, finally, we want self-audience to be more than self-indulgence. Not only will we aim for discovery of what we have to say, but we will schedule regular checks, as we work alone, to reflect on how our ongoing work will be received by our probable audience. This is the sort of regimen we will need to build the "socio-cognitive ability" in our planning and writing that comes with anticipating the thoughts and feelings of readers [35].

As you consider these informal goals for improving our self-audience, you may discern something else. Personal audience, when practiced diligently, naturally grows more outwardly expansive. Why? Again, even our most private writing relies on what we have heard and read; to be effective, self-audience needs to remain grounded in social reality. When we excessively dissociate ourselves from our external audience we tend to lose our sense of direction or else set it too rigidly [36]. Another familiar caution comes up: when we work without the excitement of knowing whether our writing will find an eager audience, we deprive ourselves of vital motivation.

Exercises in Building a Personal Sense of Audience

The strategies we settle on are unusual for a writing program. They consist largely of learning, through self-exposure, about how well we work alone. To manage this, we think-aloud in retrospect and then we coach each other to listen carefully to how we ordinarily work as writers on our own. It is a challenging, initially unnerving, process.

First step. We begin by taking turns at thinking (and feeling) aloud, with old notes as cues, about how we worked at prewriting for a current project. As we read aloud from our prewriting, we recall how we functioned as a self-audience. The first reports reflect the confusion that often accompanies the initial formulation of this task:

I don't think I know what I'm supposed to do. It still doesn't seem completely clear what self-audience is. . . . Is this what we are doing here--listening now to see if we were listening well then? It is, I guess, [a matter of] looking back to see if we were making good use of the materials and ideas we had gathered?

In an interesting way, we notice once more, we are modeling the very thing we are looking to do with our memories of prewriting: we are now paying attention to how well we exteriorize, attend, and clarify our thoughts and intentions for each other (much as we might do for ourselves, on our own):

So what we want to do is to look and see if we did as well on our own as we did as a group in terms of listening and learning from ourselves, right? No doubt, I guess, we should find that our group will do a better job than we had . . . until we get to be better at it on our own.

At last we are ready to reflect on how we typically work at prewriting. For example:

A problem comes back to mind; it may be what keeps me from wanting to do prewriting. It is as though "myself and I" don't get along well when we get ready to write. . . .

Here is what I was thinking at the time I did this [refers to a point in his conceptual outline]: "My god, I could think of a million things that go here, that could go on this page. How am I supposed to decide? I hate this. . . . I'd rather just plunge into the writing and let all this work itself out."

With each such self-disclosure we do two more things. First we share our responses to a report just given:

I've experienced the same thing, almost exactly, although I don't know that I had put it so well in words. For me the struggle is about having to decide and stay with my decision. At some point, if I continue to look at more and more new possibilities, I go off in all directions and I feel like I am spinning my wheels. When that happens, I'm not in the habit of listening carefully to anything, certainly not to any clear, confident voice about what I want to accomplish or about what would work best. . . . I'm learning to pause and look for points where I need to settle on a plan and then to continue to look to see if it is working. That's being a good audience for myself.

This is what I'm reminded of: In the samples of prewriting that I've been looking at, I recall my resentment about having to decide so far in advance. I would rather, I'm sure, leave decisions to later . . . or not to make them consciously at all. But of course when I do that, I have less chance to think about what I really want or intend to write. . . . I guess part of it is impatience, *again*.

Well, I've been through this too and it *is* all about an inner struggle. I've had to continue to combat the part of me that is impatient and irrational. It doesn't want to listen to what the rational part of me wants to do . . . it doesn't want to take the time or go to the trouble to plan. And then it doesn't want to stay with plans. It doesn't want to listen, that's for sure. What I'm beginning to figure out is that I do need to develop a better sense of personal audience, self-audience. I've been my own worst listener.

Second, we work together to coach each other in more adaptive habits of listening to our rational selves as we prewrite. As a rule, our conversations include these kinds of elaborate insights:

Here is what I think. When we don't listen carefully to our inner voices and plans, we know the likely culprit--impatience. When our reconstructions of events suggest impatience, we were probably rushing. Our first step toward self-audience, toward ensuring a moderate pace of looking and listening, is one essential for any sort of audience.

How about this as an idea that follows from that one? When we work impatiently, we stop attending to the things that may not seem immediately essential. All these recollections of prewriting experiences tell us what?--that the first planned step of prewriting that gets dropped is the sort of imaginative exercises we had prescribed for us by [C. Wright] Mills. Remember? When we stop putting information into categories and scheming to make sense of them, what happens? We find that we can take our writing in all sorts of directions. When we skip the preliminaries of figuring what we can say, it's like entering a social conversation with a kind of blind impulsivity. We haven't planned, we're not listening to ourselves, and we're not being listened to by anyone else.

Further steps. To a lesser extent, the writing groups practice the same retrospective-thinking-aloud exercises with the next steps in writing. The transition from prewriting to writing provides the usual good material for reflection. Why? Because difficulties in making this jump from planning to prose reside as much in audience problems as in any other. Consider this common reflection about self-audience elicited now from notes that a writer had taken earlier:

This is what I was thinking as I was scanning the pages I had just written, "This is not good writing. It doesn't come close to the quality I see published by leaders in the field. . . . My writing, this stuff I'm grinding out, is not up to par."

Here too, group members respond supportively with kindred experiences:

I always do that. I expect my first draft to be as good as the best things I've ever seen in print. . . . But I've gotten better at disputing the irrationality. I know that I'm not allowing myself the privilege of revisions before expecting my writing to be really finished and polished. I'm also coming to realize something related to that. When I'm already looking away to some perfectionistic ideals, I'm not being a good listener for myself. I'm not giving myself a fair chance to use the things I've prepared and I'm not allowing myself to proceed with any sort of fluency and appreciation so long as I'm listening to perfectionistic chatter.

The directives for dealing with these hang-ups occur readily. Impatience is once again part of the problem; it rushes us to compose perfect prose in a first draft. So is the temptation to underutilize planning. Our reconstructions of successful transitions suggest a better alternative: When we work amid calm listening as we expand our conceptual outlining into prose sentences, the task goes quickly and painlessly.

In the next set of recollections, about how we revised earlier text, we uncover some of the most fascinating self-disclosures about how well we listen to ourselves. Here, more clearly than before, we recognize the importance of listening to what we have written (i.e., to see if it means what we intend). Still, we have successes to share:

The best experiences are coming when I can really pay attention to what I have already said, when I looking to rewrite. This time I was saying something pretty close to this: "Read it aloud, take your time, *listen*, and then act." As I did this, perhaps really hearing myself as writer for the first time (maybe coming to see at last how my readers react to my stories), I felt a glow. I said something like: "At last I'm in a position to make my writing better."

We even, in this sharing of our experiences and advice, begin to look at a preliminary way at handling external criticism; it is a topic never far from our concerns. Two encouraging realizations emerge as we discuss criticism. First, in our own experiences, where we have taken the time to listen carefully to what we have written (especially to revise in response to rereading), criticisms from readers and reviewers seem less frequent, less surprising. Second, as we work with more clarity of purpose and more confidence in having said what we wanted to, we are better able to sort out which criticisms are legitimate and relevant:

I realized that my critiquer was actually saying he wanted me to write the book the way he would have. When I saw that I felt relieved immediately. If he had said things to help me say what I wanted to say better, fine. He didn't. . . . The outcome was a good one. I ended up not feeling devastated by this criticism and I didn't even waste the energy of feeling angry at him.

Additional insights about self-audience. These unusual exercises produce some of the richest, most exciting discussions of my programs. They prove so reinforcing that some writers join small groups of their own for similar conversations. When we combine what we are learning in our groups with my summaries of what prior groups did, several themes suggest themselves, many with welcome redundancy:

The key to self-audience is exteriorizing (outing) our thoughts onto paper or screens.

To cultivate a patient sense of listening in ourselves, we need to learn to trust our own inner voices and feelings (once we are settled into a calm, rational state). To do this we may need to mimic the acts of hypnotically susceptible writers who unhesitatingly write as though taking inner dictation [37, 38]; in so doing, we practice trust and we delay closure, both essential acts of finding audience.

Assuming an effective sense of self-audience means looking out for irrationalities and anticipating the times they are most likely. Our shared experiences suggest that periods without calm, without planfulness, and without some attention to external audiences, occasion the least helpful self-talk [3, 32].

Effective self-audience is reinforcing because it offers more chance of self-control in terms of "steering," understanding, and happiness [3].

When we listen, note, and plan carefully from the outset, we make better decisions about which projects deserve our precious time. Most creativity is, as David Perkins notes, judgment-limited (because of irrational decisions made early on [39]).

At least one more advantage grows with self-audience--greater patience and skill in proofreading and editing our own writing. One of the most common reasons for editorial rejection is a failure of writers to practice the simple routines of proofing (e.g., looking for mistakes to cluster; checking for excessive strings of prepositional phrases; reading one's writing aloud [40]).

Even as we continue our shared exercises in building self-audience, we begin to construct a few simple prompts to help sustain our habits beyond these discussions. A useful version is a checklist to be posted at writing sites:

1. Exteriorize your ideas, plans, concerns about audience in writing, as part of your prewriting (as per Peter Elbow).
2. Listen to and note your inner thoughts about what you want to say and do.
3. Keep your self-talk calm and rational by outing it and by pacing the outing.
4. Encourage the self-talk and feelings that fit best into your plan for writing.
5. Pay attention to how you organize and write and realize that your habits are not inevitable; if you don't like your style, reinvent it.
6. Be more than a passive self-audience by asking yourself good questions (e.g., is this the sort of high-quality work that I want to be known for; am I staying on track and solving the right problem?).
7. Spend time each day, after writing, carefully reading what you entered to see if you are saying what you want to. Look and listen patiently.

When groups discuss these guidelines, another sense emerges. We remark that at last we have been listening to each other with great care; we have, someone invariably mentions, journeyed to the point where old resistances have largely vanished:

Maybe you [nodding toward me] have finally worn us down to where we all agree. Maybe, like EST where everyone sits on the floor until they "get it," you have kept us here until we got it. Seriously, I think I am getting it. The surprising thing is its simplicity: I needed to pay better attention to myself and to the input of a few people I can trust in order to grow, get better.

SECOND SENSE OF AUDIENCE: CONVERSATIONAL

This second phase of building audience extends the act of self-audience to hearing the reactions of others. This is a riskier step than when we imagined reader responses. But we do have an advantage that we didn't have at the outset. We are already familiar with notions of joining a conversation as writers

(Chapter 1); we need only a moment to review lessons about how best to join a conversation. For one thing, we need to observe the tone and content of the conversation [41]. And, while we notice the commonplaces of thought and the etiquette of action, we need to look for themes. Then, we need to see some prospect of being able to join and find appreciation.

Most of us, though, remain somewhat unclear about what a collaborative sense of audience truly means. Some writers do have a rough notion, one that they share readily:

This is my guess about what we're getting at. I can see that I counted on my brilliance, such as it is, to carry me. I've done almost all my writing from start to finish in private . . . with secrecy befitting military intelligence. I haven't really taken the trouble to figure out what readers, especially those I value most, want. Instead of that, I have imagined that I couldn't join the conversation until I had ready the best contribution they would ever hear. . . . In my old muddled thinking I wanted to join in a blitz, ambushing them with my masterpiece. They were supposed to, I guess, drop what they were doing to marvel at me, this sudden captor.

Soon after this sort of interaction, though, all the groups settle into a practical approach to understanding what a conversational audience requires. We work together to sort the process of joining into its basic steps.

Step 1: Joining as a Reader

This wouldn't necessarily be the beginning step, we agree. We might first have gotten interested by way of spoken conversation. But as a rule, we decide, we will want to do some systematic reading early in the process; most of us feel the need to be scholars of sorts. Moreover, we enjoy recalling admonitions from famous writers about reading.

Sharing readings. I often initiate the recounting. Paul Theroux may be the most succinct: "You have to read everything" [42]. More specifically, there are reasons to anticipate benefits in "writerly" reading [3]. By taking notes as we read and carrying out a dialog of sorts with the writer we are reading, we not only build our involvement in an ongoing conversation. We also get a sense of what *we* will want to say. Group members bring in favorite excerpts to confirm what we have been saying, as in this quote from John Gardner:

Hemingway once remarked that "the best way to become a writer was to go off and write." But his own way of doing it was to go to Paris, where many of the great writers were, and to study with the greatest theorist of the time, and one of the shrewdest writers, Gertrude Stein. [43]

The point, once again: Even writers who join the conversation may be reluctant to admit their reliance on it later.

And some excerpts seem, at first hearing, tangential. Consider the case of Lynn Bloom, who writes compellingly about joining the dance of writing:

The dancer, the dance, and the place of performance are inextricably interrelated; they cannot be understood in isolation. Teachers, dissertation advisors, researchers, counselors, friends, or others working with anxious writers need to understand the writer's problems in the appropriate contexts in order to provide specific, workable solutions adapted to the writer's temperament and to the performance of multiple roles in multiple contexts. [44]

The message we came to agree on is that we too must find helpers who have joined our own personal conversation.

Someone else who usually comes up is Rita Mae Brown. She seems to mix useful advice (e.g, the value of learning Latin for improved writing in English) with obfuscation:

I would like to close this chapter with something I think every writer should engrave on his/her wrist. Somerset Maugham said, "There are three rules for writing a novel. Unfortunately, no one knows what they are." [45]

The problem with her advice (and of Maugham's) in our view: Some successful authors reinforce traditional notions that "the conversation" we hope to join will reveal nothing but mystery. But we easily manage to find and share more useful excerpts from our reading about writing. A favorite comes from the best-known of books about writing blocks, by Karin Mack and Eric Skjei:

The notes you take while reading another's work will lay the foundation for your own, as words, phrases, concepts, organizational possibilities begin to stir your own creative juices. [46]

One point comes up: We already know this advice, chiefly by way of C. Wright Mills and finding imagination (Chapter 2), but we find comfort in seeing it confirmed. A more extended point: Joining the conversation demands some experimentation in mimicking the writing of other members.

Perhaps the most reassuring excerpt comes from a writer who offers an unusually high level of immediacy and openness to other writers, Mike Rose:

Because writing can be such a private act, we tend to forget that it is also, paradoxically, a social act. Writing is learned. . . . And as it is learned, learned as well are the myriad explanations, opinions, and biases of the immediate societies of institutions and communities that teach and receive writing. [47]

The implication: Our usual audiences and conversations, whether we have noticed them or not, have powerful effects on our expectations and styles as writers. Thus, as per the advice from Harry Browne (rule #18), we might do well to seek out more supportive, accepting conversations. After all, even the best-selling of authors need only attract a small percentage of the populace as readers.

A more recent rule (#23) comes to mind as we share and learn in our groups, the one about the value of letting other writers do some of the work.

Step 2: Joining as Self-Presenter

It is one thing to listen to a conversation, another to take the risk of presenting our ideas to the public. As one writer put it, "the hardest part of writing is standing up and saying, more or less, this is who I am." You probably know why. Public statements, especially those made in print, invite comparisons, criticism, misunderstanding, and rejection. They can even, in the rarest and worst of scenarios, expose us as the frauds we sometimes suspect ourselves of being. The mere prospect of being read and reviewed can be painful, especially when reviewers seem to intend hurtfulness. My groups and I have an all-too-ready store of anecdotes in mind, some by way of reading, some via personal experience.

To lighten the mood we conduct a brief contest to see who can restate the most cutting criticism seen or experienced. One winner: "His height [referring to a writer who was a short person] is his only concession to brevity." With this gallows humor comes a reminder about the value of sorting out only the most helpful parts of a criticism (i.e., the problem of brevity was the only potentially worthwhile message in the example above). Then, forearmed, we focus on our own recent experiences with acceptances and rejections. Invariably, the first shared memories deal with audiences who did not seem to listen carefully:

When I sent my ms. around to friends and acquaintances to read, I was surprised that all but a few didn't find or make the time to even peruse it closely. And those who did were disappointing. They seemed more concerned with finding fault than in looking to enjoy the story. In one case, while looking over a critique, this is what I thought: "I don't think that she read this carefully enough to understand what I was trying to do. Yes, she may be right that I could be more like her favorite writer (or, more to the point, like her). OK. But I wish she had made more effort to appreciate me as a writer with something to say."

I could tell, instantly, that the reviewers didn't even read my paper carefully enough to understand it. They completely missed the point.

In response, fittingly, other group members talk about instances where better listening was ensured.

Yeah, that's true. I had to realize, however, that I'm often guilty of the same thing [when I do reviews]. Unless I'm careful, I tend to critique rather superficially, looking only for glaring omissions, or else I glibly suggest a better style to emulate. It wasn't until I paid more attention to what I wanted readers to do for me that I saw the light. . . . Now I'm working harder to see the things written by other people more from their perspective. I'm also working at asking my readers, specifically, to do what I want. I say to them, "See if you think I'm saying what I want to say, if I make it clear what I have to offer that is unique to me but that other people might find interesting. Please look at the parts I have marked and at the questions I'm wondering about."

Then we are ready to move to recountings of what else has helped writers. Some accounts seem oblique at first:

Patience is helping me as much as anything. I've just been rereading the autobiography of a writer who is especially inspiring to me. I've decided to slow down and take a hard look at the most like-minded souls I can find, so I'm taking an unusual amount of time and attention in this rereading. This is what occurred to me last evening: "I not only need to write more slowly but I need to read, at least for important things, more slowly. My usual style in reading is rushed. Even with fascinating stuff I'm skipping parts and worrying about getting finished." But that isn't what I'm really getting at. It made me reinterpret something else. I stopped to reevaluate two critiques of my writing I've gotten in the last week. I said (to myself): "You know, you expected too much of a pair of casual readers. What makes you think they will submerge themselves in it to the extent you have? You know you would do better to find readers who are more like you."

And some reports are immediately uplifting:

Well, I've had just the right kind of experience recently. I found two people, kindred souls as we call them here, who resonate with what I'm writing. When I looked over their comments the other day, I was thinking: "This is nice. This is something I need to work harder at getting more often. Isn't it nice that they both said they loved the plot line, with its penultimate twist and my backstreet characterizations of Chicago. . . . This makes me feel motivated to do more good work."

Inevitably, conversations refocus on finding better ways to deal with criticism. All of us can provide examples of being recipients, few can say that we have managed it well. In this case, I act more directively, suggesting proven strategies for handling criticism.

Coping with criticism by agreeing (more or less) *with critics*. The most effective guidelines I know for coping with criticism come from social skills therapists [48]. These practitioners use a simple approach to determine which skills contribute most to social success: They begin by observing what the most popular and admired people do. In the case of criticism, exemplars do this: they listen to the criticism calmly and patiently; they find something in the criticism with which to agree (and in so doing, moderate most of the emotion that might otherwise pervade the interaction); they ask the critic for clarification of the criticism and for suggestions of what she or he wants done differently; and then they decide which parts, if any, of the criticism to do something about.

In my two decades of offering programs for writers, this social skills approach has worked with surprising ease and effectiveness. It generally takes us through the following exercises (in each of which I state the principle and sample writers' responses):

1. *Listen calmly and patiently.* Make yourself read or hear what is being said with as much dispassion as you can manage (e.g., imagine yourself in the role of a cultural anthropologist making an objective observation). If the criticism is written and you suppose that you cannot read it calmly, have someone else summarize and edit its content for you in a kind but informative way. If you cannot face a verbal criticism, inform the critic that you want the comments in writing. With any form of criticism, help ensure your detachment, objectivity, and attentiveness by taking notes as you listen or read.

How do writers react to this directive? Offhand responses are somewhat optimistic, despite the uncertainty that this can work for normal people:

All right, I might be able to manage that. But I honestly don't imagine myself remaining calm. . . . Maybe I can to a degree, though, if I'm attending more to the content by taking thorough notes.

As we rehearse this script for managing first reactions to criticism, we see the need for practice. This, for instance, is the response of a writer whose manuscript sample her group had just criticized for over two minutes (in role-play fashion), restating criticisms she had gotten from real-life reviewers. (The essential message was that her writing could have been done differently; e.g., ". . . here, in the second paragraph, I would have said it this way"):

I hate this, even if it is practice. And no, I didn't really want to listen because it made me mad, almost as mad as when I first got these reviews a month ago. I was thinking more about revenge or leaving the group and not about trying to learn from the critiques. . . . [When asked how she felt 10 minutes after the critiques?] I'm still upset. I'm embarrassed that I, ah, overreacted.

What helps writers respond more calmly, attentively? In my experience two things help the most: One is repeated experience and the other is planful rehearsal (where we imagine ourselves in the situation, working and listening for useful information). Both take practice.

2. *Listen for something in the criticism with which you can honestly agree.*
When we do this, we listen more attentively and we stay calmer. I usually begin by demonstrating effective responses to the most potentially hurtful criticisms that I have experienced from reviewers (e.g., in response to "I don't think that Boice, for all his admonitions to writers, writes very well"): "You could be right, in a way" or "I guess I can understand how you might feel that way."

I then list the crucial acts in finding something with which to agree: (a) keep your responses entirely honest, no matter how ambiguous; (b) but do make your response a carefully considered reaction to what the critic actually said (e.g., In reaction to the criticism that my own writing is flawed: "I really can imagine how some of my own critics might expect me to write perfectly if I'm so bold as to presume that I can give them advice"); (c) resist temptations to hurt the critic in return (because revenge only heightens your own intrusive emotions and inclines the critic to hurt you more); (d) put your critic and yourself at further ease by adding a statement that indicates your willingness to think further about what the critic has said that might be helpful (e.g., "I'm going to try to learn from this so I'll think some more about it later"); (e) or, in the face of a patently unfair criticism, talk about what you might have done, however unintentionally, to elicit such misunderstanding (e.g., "Maybe I need to look again at the first few pages to see where I turn some readers completely off and ask myself if my off-putting words can be tempered"); but also (f) where the critic is unfair give him or her a calm appraisal of what kinds of changes in the criticism would have been helpful to you (after, of course, beginning with at least a partial agreement with the criticism). For example:

You know what would have helped me, I think, is if you could have soft-pedaled the remarks about my personality. That made it harder for me, I think, to benefit from your expertise in the other things you had to say. Does that sound reasonable?

This makes for a difficult exercise. At first, even in our role plays, writers tend to fight back in their responses to criticisms:

Well, I disagree. I think you're not only wrong but you're not really qualified to say that.

That's not fair. I've worked hard on this. . . .

With practice over several weeks, progress becomes evident:

OK, right off I can agree with at least some of what you said. It's probably true that the lead character isn't always consistent. I've sort of felt that myself.

I'll say "ouch" with a smile and I'll also say that I think I can agree in a way. I suppose I can appreciate why you might not like my analysis and how you might suppose that I'm in error. Maybe what I need to think about doing is looking again to see if I make my rationale clear at the beginning.

With this progress comes invariable reporting of more comfort in dealing with criticism:

For sure it hurts me less when I'm looking hard for something that can help my writing. I think it's easier on the critic too because I am listening with an open mind and I'm not so inclined to think that she is out to get me.

    3. *Calmly ask critics for clarification.* Most criticisms are vague in some ways (e.g., "your writing is poorly organized"). So, to truly benefit from feedback, writers usually need to ask for clarifications. This request can add useful information, and it can disarm the critic. It may even incline him or her to say something more considerate and constructive. At best it elicits more specific information about what you might do in response to the criticism. For example: "All right, I'll try to see it your way. But please give me some specifics about how I could make the manuscript better organized. I mean, will you show me an instance where I might start?" This is an especially effective way to learn from editorial rejections, many of which tend to be terse.

    When I periodically survey editors, they tell me that only rarely do writers call or write and calmly ask for more specific, useful criticisms from reviewers. The same editors tell me that they reserve singular respect for the few writers who do so, perhaps to the point of giving them the benefit of the doubt in future transactions ("Although," said one, "it may be that they do better because they learn more about how to improve than do other writers"). This too is difficult at first:

Hey, this is like egging your critics on. You're saying, "hit me again, give some more." It sounds a little masochistic.

Here too practice helps:

[in response to a role play where group members prompted a preliminary version of a letter to be sent to an editor and reviewer] How about this? "I think you might be right about my plot being too busy and improbable. I know that I've seen it happen to other mystery writers so I can imagine it could happen to me. But you could help me by putting your comments in a slightly different way. For one thing, could you give me an example or two of which of the threats to the detective seem most improbable and why? I would really appreciate your taking the time to transmit this helpful information to me."

4. *Restate the essential and helpful criticisms in your own words to check for understanding.* Summarizing helps you, as the recipient of a criticism, make better sense of what has been said or written (and is often an ideal occasion for free writing to help clarify what you can agree with, as you take notes). Summarizing provides a chance to compare your interpretation with that of the critic (e.g., "Let me see, is this what you mean?"). Summarizing even begins to suggest remedies:

Now that I'm accustomed to listening better, I can quickly restate the constructive parts in my own words. I'm definitely past some old hang-ups. I'm not paying so much attention to being hurt or rejected, to looking for personal motives. I'm listening for what I can learn and use. I'm keying in on what I could do better such as, in my case, providing more of a preview of where I'm headed in my research papers. I'm pretty sure that this helps, don't you agree?

In the end, writers see especial value in forcing themselves to listen and restate parts of what they hear or read from critics; with exteriorization comes more self-control. And writers can see a related benefit in the practice of planfulness. Without rehearsal, strategies for coping with criticism work awkwardly and unreliably. Anticipation of where we are likely to meet criticism offers the best means of coping with criticism--avoiding it or preparing for it.

Another old point seems all the more apropos now. With this experience we learn to set goals as writers that will affect readers, even to solve problems that would otherwise ensure conflict with audiences [49]. To all that, finally, we add a seemingly new point. Ideal training for writers may include experience as a reviewer, editor, teacher, and even collaborator. Collaborating, after all, is a mere extension of reviewing, editing, and teaching--even of reading.

THIRD SENSE OF AUDIENCE: COLLABORATING

What does collaborating have to do with building a sense of audience? It brings synergy and a chance to learn what partners know. It offers increased productivity and publishability, perhaps because multiple authors help keep each other on schedule and foresee more potential objections in an audience [50, 51]. As with any social venture in writing, it also carries risks. Coauthors sometimes disagree on what to say and how to say it, they may argue over credit for ideas and orders of authorship, their intellectual and personality differences may translate into different work habits and disparate contributions to the work, and they may pessimistically disengage [52]. Collaboration, then, amplifies every aspect of the pluses and minuses of writing in public.

Collaboration also raises another familiar theme; it works best with balance and moderation. Even a modicum of social contracting (e.g., collaborating to assist one another in staying on a schedule) helps patients in health maintenance programs find long-term compliance [53]. Even an hour a week of teamwork with a more experienced colleague can make the difference between new faculty members who thrive and those who fail on their campuses [54]. In the long run, writers manage more productive writing by doing nothing more than committing to common writing times with other writers working on their own [55].

But because collaboration often takes writers into the realm of coauthoring, of intense cooperation, it may seem the most daunting of all the kinds of audience. Writing is, after all, something most of us learned to do alone. Where we have collaborated, the experience may have been all too memorably associated with projects in which we did most of the work for our partners. Still, having seen the power of other kinds of audience, writers in the program are willing to give collaboration a new look. "Perhaps," as a novelist put it, "having learned to be better listeners of criticism, we are becoming more likely to think and explore before criticizing and rejecting."

Writers usually agree about benefits for the simplest form of collaborating, making social contracts to write together but on separate projects. Experience in the program has taught us why social contracting works so well:

What else [besides staying on schedule]? Feeling like a writer among writers. Having a few people to discuss my writing with when we finish our session. Picking up a tip or a habit here and there just sitting by sometimes and watching them work and write.

There is good reason why writers find profit in regular occasions to talk about their ongoing writing. Some of what writers have learned in finding their own successes can be elicited in informal, spontaneous interactions with each other. Even more is revealed when we learn to make tacit information more explicit by asking the right questions [56]. (For example, "When do you revise and share?")

What are some other productive questions for successful writers? One kind asks about the true nature of the task (e.g., daily work is generally required). A second asks about tricks of the trade in dealing with editors (e.g., knowing when and how to ask for a second, fairer set of reviews from an editor [25, 57]). Yet another inquires about the most valuable of habits learned (e.g., waiting before committing to set plans or prose while looking to collaborators to suggest alternatives). Again, the more open we remain to change and the more we expose ourselves to multiple perspectives, the more creative our writing [58].

Other benefits accrue to this simple sort of collaboration. For one thing, it inclines us to follow the rule (#23) about letting other people do some of the work. For another, it sets the stage for the modeling, openness, and social support that promote self-efficacy, that quality of resilience that helps us believe we can succeed at a difficult task [59]. Finally, social contact during writing may help break us out of a most dangerous assumption, the belief that we come to tasks like teaching or writing as experts with little to learn [60]. As we enhance our interpersonal perceptiveness we get a better feeling for what we know and don't know, all with a growing awareness of where we can make up deficits--usually by way of more social contacts [61].

What else comes from this strangely reassuring realization (that with maturity as writers we gain a better sense of what we do not know)? We acknowledge that we will profit in moving beyond the simple level of social contracting to more demanding, mutually shared writing sessions. One part of this shift seems familiar, beginning by reading and sharing our notes about collaborating in writing projects. The other part of the shift is the actual jump into collaboration as coauthoring.

Advice for Collaborators

Groups feel guilty about setting up still another exercise in reading and discussing. We have just done one. "No matter," someone says, more-or-less, "we still enjoy it and profit in it." To reinforce this point we find some richly informative readings to share, and we put the matter into a slightly new perspective. Our purview takes us all the way to a new literature, on cooperative learning. From it, we depict the sort of interaction where small groups or pairs work together, often by thinking aloud, to solve problems [62]. This is the format we hope to make work as writers.

Still, writers at this point display an unmistakable mood of minimalization; they want to pick out only the most useful information about coauthoring and to "go with it." Specifically, they want suggestions about methods that might minimize the problems of collaboration experienced in the past. The following summary of a single good source, from the writing authority Joe Moxley [40], is typical:

1. Ask, do I like this person well enough to spend considerable time with her/him?;
2. will we work equitably in finding mutually convenient schedules and in sharing responsibilities?;
3. are there social differences (e.g., social status; gender or age differences) that may interfere?;
4. do we have compatible styles of pacing and of finishing the work on schedule?;

5. are we similarly inclined to attend to details and correctness?;

6. do we agree on who has priority in authorship and deciding on final versions?; and,

7. will the ultimate value of the collaboration (i.e., getting to know another writer) and of the jointly produced work merit the effort?

Not surprisingly, many writers see limitations in sets of rules like these. "We won't," one science fiction writer said, "really get to know most of these things until we work together." But, just as quickly, groups generate a sense of why looking beforehand for answers to questions such as these can only help:

I think it is because, obvious as they may seem, we can all too easily jump into a collaboration without actually having considered their prospects carefully. I have. What can it hurt to take the time to discuss these questions?

To test this notion each of us commits to a brief coauthored project to be carried out in the near future.

Experiences in Coauthoring

First reactions to this assignment recall the reservations of writers who supposed their genre exempt from the exercises at hand (e.g., the reluctance of a science fiction writer to see the value in joining the conversation in his area-- Chapter 2). Here the reservation lies in wondering if coauthorship is practical in genres that commonly rely on the imagination and experience of a single writer. We can easily think of successful collaborations amongst researchers (e.g., the many references to findings by the composition experts Linda Flower and John Hayes in this program) and scholars (e.g., the historians Will and Ariel Durant). But only with some struggle do we find information about novels, mysteries, short stories, and the like that benefitted from coauthoring [63, 64, 65, 66].

Even so, we see a short-run solution for learning to work productively with another writer. Each of us agrees to take on occasional brief projects to bring more novelty to our writing lives; all but of few of us agree to find opportunities to write book reviews or short essays in collaboration. That way, we argue, the investment is small if there are incompatibilities. And that way, cowriters can keep the complexities of cooperation at a reasonable level. Oddly, only 7 of the 26 nonacademic writers in the study sample had attempted such a collaboration beyond school (except, perhaps, for committee reports in the work place). And only 9 of the 26 academic writers had done real, shared authoring where they felt they had made significant contributions to the organization and prose of the final manuscript. (A larger percentage had been collaborators with graduate students and with colleagues who added their names to lists of coauthors as a professional courtesy.) Even academics who had coauthored as true peers had only rarely shared the process (e.g., prewriting) of that writing with collaborators.

The initial assignment, then, was this: everyone would work for a minimum of a few joint sessions of writing. At the least we agreed to collaborate at prewriting a brief review or essay. The usual plan was to contract with a coauthor for a meeting or two of discussion and planning, then a few mutual writing sessions. Follow-up interactions were typically conducted in writing or by phone. My role in these interactions was to monitor how pairs worked together and, while making occasional calls to collect information about progress and compatibility, to prod writers to stay on schedule. I had learned this pushy role in my efforts to arrange mentoring for new faculty on large campuses; unless pair members knew I would be calling to check on progress, they tended to stop meeting when they felt busy [67].

In this structured framework, all but a handful of the writers finished at least one jointly written review, essay, or letter that appeared in print. Only twelve had to restart with new collaborators and only three started over with new topics. In this sense, the assignment proved surprisingly easy and enjoyable:

It was nice making a friend. We had a good time and, I believe, wrote a better, broader, fairer book review than either of us would have on our own.

Still, most writers reported initial strains:

Well in the first place I'm not used to explaining what I plan to do and why I choose the expressions I do. . . . I imagine what I had to learn was another form of exteriorization. So did _____ and I don't think it was any easier for her. But as we got to be better at it, the writing went well, very well. I learned something from doing this.

My problem came in trying to work with someone who hasn't been in our [writing] program. He just isn't used to prewriting the way we do and he isn't accustomed to following plans once they are made. . . . At first we had a real fight in quiet way. He liked to work spontaneously and for me to make only small changes in what he had written. I had to show him some benefits in having an agreed-upon plan and then staying with it. . . . By our third meeting it worked and we were both fairly pleased.

I didn't expect it but she treated me as her assistant. She admitted it when I pointed it out and then we proceeded in all-right fashion.

We hit it off from the beginning and we had fun and we wrote a nice essay. And we're going to do something else. What more need I say?

When we had finished our assignments there was a gradually emerging sense of what can be gleaned in working closely with another writer:

It depends on the writer, of course. But there are interesting things to be learned, I would argue. . . . Only in our group exercises on sharing our prewriting moments and so on did I feel something like it. I realized that I have a lot to assimilate about the various ways in which writers can work together. For instance I had never thought about stopping to read what I had written--aloud. My partner did and she was taken aback that I didn't do something similar. And she liked to look in her thesaurus and dictionary and software for various ways of saying things. Now I know that may sound obvious but I hadn't done it since college.

What I learned is mainly about finding clarity. When I had to explain to someone sitting next to me what I planned to say and why, you know, I had to be a whole lot clearer and to the point. Patiently. When I asked him questions to get more clarity I could see how I need to ask myself similar questions.

Yes all those things are true. But what I liked most was the security of having another imagination on hand to make the review better and to make the project more fun.

I learned something by doing my own thinking-aloud-exercises about the coauthoring. I got in touch with my irrational reactions such as feeling that her disagreement had to mean personal disapproval of me. I even got her to practice some of it [thinking aloud] as we worked together. It helped us become more candid and it shortcut the process of coming to agreement and comfort.

What I liked most was that when we became comfortable with each other, we established a pleasant pace of working and writing. . . . We had to listen and wait as the other person talked or wrote aloud and that, I think, slowed us down and made us both more patient. That's what we thought at the time and I still agree.

It's still dawning on me how effective social writing is when you give it a chance.

With these comments, one realization becomes dominant, then another. First, if we could learn more about how others react to our writing as we write, we might do a far better job of communication; conceivably, we could ward off many of the criticisms and rejections we would ordinarily face. Second, there seems to be a whole sphere of social intelligence to be learned about making writing public and publicly acceptable. This moment, of appreciating how little we know, impels us to see what can be learned in our journey.

FOURTH SENSE OF AUDIENCE: BECOMING SOCIALLY SKILLED

Here too the knowledge tends to be tacit. It is taught, if at all, in old-boy networks, largely by way of modeling and imitation. While the prospect of uncovering this tacit knowledge once seemed daunting to my writing groups, it is no longer. We are, by this point, making rapid strides as more public, sociable, and collaborative writers. While we are readying ourselves for some regular exercises in building social skills as writers, I interject one more idea. In the related field of mentoring, there is the sense that apprentices can find especial advantages in modeling after experts. Apprentices benefit by learning how masters decide which tasks are worth attempting (much as in recognizing which comments are worth making in a conversation). And, in watching and interacting with experts, apprentices see how they can ideally behave, talk [68], and spend their time (e.g., successful authors may spend as much time socializing about their writing as in doing it [69]).

But the aspect of expertise that becomes the focus is this: learning more about the social skills of dealing with reviewers and editors. To do this, we attempt something new. Each of us, working with a partner, calls an expert writer to ask for advice about coping with editors and reviewers. To these notes each of us adds the comments of at least one successful writer who has made such tacit advice explicit, by putting it in writing. From our collections we make still more lists and rules.

What Successful Writers Tell Us

The first thing we share is our surprise in discovering that most writers, no matter how successful, are not accustomed to verbalizing their tactics. They need to be pushed to specify what they have learned about getting past gatekeepers. Still, all but a few of our contacts proved enthusiastic sharers of information once talking on the topic. What follows is one group's brief list of how socially skilled writers act around gatekeepers:

Balance. The most important lesson is, at first, the most difficult to grasp; only with continued probing do we appreciate how much time and effort successful writers spend on building and maintaining social networks. They get to know other writers in their genre and make regular time to write, visit, or call them. They are patient about settling for little more than small talk in many such contacts. But they are persistent in seeking out interesting writers and editors whose work they have seen or heard about. Most tellingly, we suspect, they get to know editors and maintain ongoing conversations with them, even before gaining their first acceptances from them. The message behind this finding merits summarization as a rule.

RULE #26: Successful authors spend as much time socializing around writing as writing (and they spend only moderate amounts of time at each).

Information. The second lesson is about how best to utilize social networks. Successful writers use them in part for small talk and friendship. They also employ them for conversations about how problems of writing and publishing might be solved; with social skill comes a cognizance that most writers like to be asked for advice (in moderation). As they respond with solutions, these sociable writers gradually reveal how they have learned to cope with editors. One example stands out for us, the habit of sending a preliminary conceptual outline to an editor to check for interest. So does the reason why it works. Evidently, most editors would rather tell a writer that a planned project has or does not have a ready audience (or, equally important, a compelling theme) before, not after, the manuscript is written. Moreover, sociable writers tell us, they listen carefully to apprehend an editor's well-practiced sense of what will work in a plan and what may not; when editors sense that writers listen, they become collaborators of sorts in their projects. Editors in this role are, again, more inclined to accept the manuscripts they herd from the time of their inception. This strikes groups as ruleworthy.

RULE #27: The earlier the feedback and the closer its source to gatekeepers (e.g., editors, reviewers, leaders), the more useful to the writer.

Self-management of negativity. Here too successful writers often model a social skill that they can only vaguely specify when first asked. With a modicum of listening and questioning, the principle becomes clear and familiar. These are writers, we conclude, who self-manage their negativity, especially when dealing with gatekeepers. This is what exemplary writers commonly tell us they have learned about editors: Like the participants in any conversation, editors shy away from whiners and guilt-inducers. They are even warier of people who react to criticism with anger.

What exemplars model, then, is a tendency to stay away from the role of the victimized writer [70]. How do they do this? We already know part of the answer. Whether they have gotten to know Albert Ellis or not (Chapter 4), these writers commonly rely on self-help strategies of spotting and ridding themselves of irrational thoughts. These same writers exhibit something else familiar and worth emulating in most specifics. They work hard, often with the help of early and informal feedback from colleagues, to anticipate criticisms and objections. They learn what editors want (i.e., that gatekeepers often want clearly compelling questions or ideas and dominating theories or plots [71]). Here too there is a rule worth remembering.

RULE # 28: The best way to handle criticism is to anticipate it, to acknowledge it, and to learn from it.

Then, feeling good about our conversations, we spend a few moments on summarizations. Notable among our conclusions is the realization that writing cultures and conversations can only be understood with great patience. Here too the key word is WAIT. By the following week someone in the group usually brings a thought or quote like this one from the anthropologist E. T. Hall:

The Navajo were not amenable to what movie directors call a "fast cut"--quick or sudden changes. . . . Once I had turned off the motor of my pickup, Sam and I would sit motionless in the cab, not saying a word, letting the dust settle and allowing the feel of the place to penetrate the very pores of skin. Once the crew, which was already there, had mentally adjusted to the fact that we had arrived, we could then quietly descend from the cab of the pickup as though we were guests. The foreman would approach in his ambling gait, greeting us with a smile, a "*Yatekei*," and a handshake, all to make us feel welcome the proper Navajo way. [72]

Exercises in Socially Skilled Writing

"We all know the drill by now," one writer said, referring to how we would turn the messages just listed into exercises. Here again the strategies would have to be brief and, in the main, fit unobtrusively into the few moments available during breaks for planning and rest.

Balance. Every writer I have known, even by this stage, has seen special difficulty in implementing this seemingly simple act (rule #26). To spend as much time socializing about writing as writing not only seems unrealistic in terms of rewarding opportunities. It also begs the question of where already busy writers will find the time for this sort of balance. Yet, we almost always manage.

We begin by agreeing to work toward increasing scheduled times for socialization in gradual fashion. Initially, most writers make a single phone call or visit about writing per week, or even write one letter per week to a kindred writer. This schedule, for most writers, represents a significant increase over customary levels of socializing. At first, if necessary, we take the time for a call or letter from a scheduled writing time. This ensures the opportunity for socializing and, because writers don't like giving up their writing time, it magically opens other brief windows in workdays for calls and letters. I have yet to see a writer unable, eventually, to find at least an hour a week for this activity. Discussions about finding time for writerly socializing flow with unusual vigor in the groups:

In the first place, I couldn't believe I had time for this. But I did. In the second place, I didn't think I would enjoy writing letters to writers, particularly to some I don't know. I did. And in the third place, I didn't expect to get much from it. I did. Just writing to say what I like in someone else's writing and to ask for some advice about my plans is an exercise in getting my ideas straightened out (and, maybe, someone else's).

This has to be one of the hardest things I have done in the program because I am hesitant to impose on other people. I actually worried that when I called _____, she would say she had never heard of me and hang up. . . . She may not have (and I did have to call back a few times to catch her at a good time), but we ended up having a pleasant and reassuring conversation. And do you know what she said? She said that she generally felt isolated from other writers and wished she could do the same thing. So I said, in a nice way, "What's keeping you?"

Some of our most interesting conversations dealt with questions about where we would find the time for this sort of balance:

From giving up activities that were superfluous. Like taking the time for reading every inch of the newspaper including all the obituaries and watching mindless TV or talking on the phone for hours with people like my sister-in-law who are not nearly as interesting as other writers.

I guess not all of it, but some of it, comes from writing times. I think now that I was writing too much and not doing my best writing. . . . I'm back to an hour per day for writing and up to thirty minutes for calling and writing letters.

In these discussions a question comes up for me: How often do writers I've worked with actually spend as much time socializing as writing? My brief response is: only about a quarter to a third do it consistently, and even they manage true balance only gradually. I essentially agree with my critics in the groups: an approximate balance seems to work well enough, far better than our old habits of rarely socializing about writing.

Another question, asked again, helps settle these discussions for the moment. Writers just starting to establish social networks wonder what benefits will accrue to them, as shy people, from this kind of balance. A good sense of advantages can be relayed in just a few points drawn from the reflections of writers interviewed a year after completing the formal program. First, no matter how initially shy, they report feeling drawn into the community of writers, of being helped to feel like writers. Second, they value the support and compliments that come from sharing plans, prose, and problems with colleagues (more so for shy writers). Third, they seem to forget about shyness as they report that the strongest advantage may prove to be a broadening of perspective and of trust in sharing:

I had thought at first that I would be reluctant to share my good ideas for stories because someone might steal them. I even might have felt that when I learned how much other writers were getting done I would feel compelled to rush. Neither of those proved important. If anything, I've gotten more good ideas in my chats with other mystery writers and I know now that we all, all of us working at it regularly, have far more ideas than we can ever use anyway. . . . You know the funny part was discovering that I was already getting much more done than the people I'm interacting with. And I'm spending less time at it. So I'm not feeling left behind or disadvantaged.

The fourth value enumerated by program graduates, putting a kind of balance into writerly socializing, is no small matter either. In their conversations with other writers, program graduates often take the time and establish the trust to share some truly crucial things--about the most effective literary agents, about editors who demand unexpected kinds of preparations, about publishers who push for contracts that take advantage of writers, and so on. The balance, then, lies in modest self-disclosiveness about knowledge and short comings--and in quiet encouragement of colleagues to do likewise.

Does this sort of balance work? No writer I've known concluded that the investment in trust and openness was not worthwhile after giving it a fair trial. Indeed, all but a few writers have listed this exercise as one of the most satisfying aspects of writing. There are, though, always a few writers who socialize only grudgingly; they continue to quote Wodehouse admiringly.

Early feedback. Soliciting early feedback is hardly a new exercise at this point in the program. We already practice it as part of routines in, for example, conceptual outlining (Chapter 2). Nonetheless, the prospect of this more extensive assignment proves discomforting for most writers. The reasons are even more familiar than with exercises in procuring criticism:

Ohhh. I just don't like sharing early drafts. We've been through all this before. Why show people your rough work if you want to make a good impression on them? Why not WAIT? Another thing: Asking editors to spend time on a half-baked idea burdens them and might be an invitation for poor treatment in return.

What helps counter this reserve are excerpts from my collection of testimonials; I can share an impressive stock of reports from writers who have prospered with early feedback from gatekeepers. For example:

I sent a neat, carefully rewritten two-page summary of my plan for a research paper, along with a separate sheet with a single paragraph of explanation of what I was planning, to the editor of a prestigious journal. Within two weeks I got a reply. My project wouldn't have done as I had put it to him. . . . He said that the premise didn't really fit the results (and I agreed). I had missed a crucial reference. Even so he was encouraging and complimentary and I resubmitted another, slightly longer conceptual outline about six weeks later. He liked the revision and recommended my proceeding with it and submitting it to him. I'm doing it. . . . The important thing is that I didn't spend a lot of time writing the wrong manuscript. . . . Incidentally, in a phone call, this editor said that he didn't mind giving advice about plans, that very few authors asked for it, that he wished more did (because the part of editing he dislikes most is rejecting), that he was impressed with my workman-like approach.

Never had I gotten to know editors beforehand. My agent took care of that, of lining up prospects and circulating my final draft. So I had her, my agent, do the same with my conceptual outline, my idea for a feminist romance. There was one more difference. I enclosed a note explaining what sorts of advice I was looking for (like "did the idea, the plot seem worth pursuing?") and asking the editor to call or write me, not her, with a response. Four out of six did and it was wonderful. We didn't just discuss my prospectus, but we talked about other things and I felt I made one or two friends and learned some things about the business. . . . Oddly, though no one fully liked my plan, I felt encouraged. I came out of it with a crystalline impression of what not to do: to not overload my story with characters and not to make it so preachy that I lose my audience. I came out with a new conviction that I am on the right track; two of the four thought I was generally on the right track, doing something new and exciting about _____. They've seen a revised plan. I'm working with renewed enthusiasm on sample chapters. We've been talking contract and I'm feeling better about the whole business of coping with gatekeepers.

I am still surprised at my experience. I sent the conceptual outline and explanation and, as per our plan, a friendly notification that I would arrange for a phone call in three weeks. When I called, we got right into a deep conversation about how I would develop some of the ideas. . . . I found myself having to think of my plans in whole new ways. It was an intense education in just fifteen minutes. . . . Talk about worthwhile experiences!

Self-management of negativism. Here too we have a set of strategies in place (Chapter 4). Their extension to social interactions including letters, calls, and direct conversations is simple. This is the usual agreed-upon strategy: Before each contact we would remind ourselves about the penalties of bringing depression and negativism to social interactions: Speakers who anticipate rejection and victimization behave self-consciously and anxiously; they tend to present their ideas too impatiently and narrowly. And they respond too defensively to criticism because they either maintain too great an attachment to their plans or else abandon them upon hearing a single criticism. A related reminder: the hallmark of negativity, as we saw in the preceding chapter, is overreaction and extremism. When we opt to display depression and victimization, other people avoid or withdraw.

Then, having kept these reminders about perils both brief and calm, we would move to considerations of constructive things to do. We could, first of all, ask specific questions of our colleagues (e.g., "do you think I should be worrying about having too many murder victims in the plot?"). And when we have requested alternative ways of solving our problems (e.g., "How do you think I could say this better?), we could listen carefully enough to be able to agree with and reflect the advice ("I think you may have a good idea there; please help me see if I understand how it would fit here.").

Combining the exercises. Specifically, my writers and I agree at this juncture to carry out three simple rules in each collegial interaction with writers and editors: (1) to suppress complaints and anxieties; (2) to ask at least once for advice or help; and, (3) to listen without interrupting (while acknowledging suggestions for change in a way that suggests your respect for the critic). Here too we have lively interactions in practicing role plays of our "reformed" conversational styles and in reporting the results of our early, imperfect attempts to carry out our assignment:

The hardest parts? All the parts! I always tend to talk too much and listen too little. I complain too much. I do...and I'm starting to do it here [laughs]. Where was I? This call to _____ was the perfect time to change my ways and I pretty much stuck to my plan. I could spot the points where I would usually butt in on what he was saying and I could tell that I was making myself listen much better.

The best part for me is coming to life slowly, just perceptibly. The more I get this early feedback, the more I can anticipate the criticisms I am likely to get. This is the sense of audience I will value. . . . I won't always want to submit to every suggestion, of course, but I won't be so surprised when I don't and I may be able to fend off some of the misunderstandings that have plagued my prior efforts.

In some groups we add exercises to the triad just overviewed (balance, early feedback, and delimited negativity):

One added exercise--pacing. With a bit of reformed experience at letter writing and conversing, we are reminded of an old problem. Most of us report drifting into impatience and/or hypomania as we draft correspondence or talk with mounting excitement. These are, too often, things for which we have allowed ourselves the barest of minimums in time and patience; we rush and we grow fatigued, even while making brief contacts. The experience presents a dilemma: none of us wants to mute our enthusiasm in communicating--or our efficiency in limiting the time we spend on it. Yet we want to pace it so as to avoid fatigue and the other problems of rushing.

Fortunately, familiar notions of pacing work nicely for social interaction, three especially well. The first is a matter of entering the contact in a relaxed state (cf. the temptation to write or call while already busy). The second is checking for tension as we write or talk and, where we spot it, slowing down or taking a break. The third is planning a limit on the length of the contact and sticking with it. If more can be said or written, we agree, we will save it for another day.

A second added exercise: calling or writing back. With this paced practice at socializing about writing, another need becomes painfully apparent. Many of us are derelict about responding to calls and letters from other writers; here we have an opportunity to observe procrastination in its most insidious guise. As the groups and I recognize this shortcoming of not returning calls or letters in timely fashion, we spend little time discussing the obvious; clearly, if we are to carry on conversations with colleagues, we must synchronize our turn-taking. So instead of lamenting our foibles, we move to a summary of what we know about procrastination:

1. It typically occurs when we have made the reinforcements for a task negative (e.g., when we finally do it to avoid the consequences of not doing it [73]).
2. It often occurs in concert with patterns of fast pace and bingeing.
3. It subsides when we manage tasks in brief, patient, and regular bits of work.

The following strategy then seems practical: We will begin with some sort of response to each communication on the day it arrives (for example, by taking five minutes from time scheduled for socializing to make a decision about actions such as: (a) no response; (b) form letter; (c) notes toward an eventual response; or (d), a brief call to make an appointment for a later call). Then, on the next day or days, we will stay with the contact, usually in brief bits, until it is completed. And, in the spirit of writerly conversation, we will keep our notes about contacts in files that can be consulted when we contact the same writer again.

The expected result invariably occurs, in my experience. As writers respond patiently and without fatigue, they report enjoying the task. And, as they meet this social responsibility in timely fashion, they talk about their relief in no longer having to worry about annoyed communicants waiting for a reply (and about discomfiting things piling up on desks). Said one writer, about his newly cleared desk top: "I can't tell you how much calmer it makes me feel."

Afterthoughts About Social Skills and Writing

In the end, as groups reflect on the simple strategies for enhancing social skills, there is a sense of real accomplishment underway. Where have we made progress? We have become better at exteriorizing. As we share more of what we are doing as writers, and we get kindred writers to do the same, we learn more about how to write clearly--for ourselves and others. We have also learned to place more value on social supports. To enjoy writing and prosper at it we need the ongoing appreciation of readers we respect and the advice of writers who have learned to succeed with gatekeepers, reviewers, and other things usually kept mysterious.

Something else often resumes the foreground in our conversations. We note that even though we have covered a nearly overwhelming amount of material, we have only begun to master the social skills of writing. Learning a personal, conversational, collaborative, and publicly acceptable sense of audience will take practice, perhaps a lifetime's worth. At this point I ask, "Is this prospect disheartening?" The replies are reassuring:

No. If the learning experience remains as pleasant as this one--of getting to know other writers and their secrets of success and of figuring ways to deaden the blows of criticism--if this is it, I can push on. In fact, I think that the experience of continuing to learn about writing will sustain me, keep me at it.

No. I don't mind working at progress. I just need to know where and how to find it. . . . I think I'll like it.

To help remind us of the directions we have taken with success, we finish in our usual fashion. We sum up with a restatement of crucial points and rules that we can keep at hand for ready reference.

SUMMARY

We began this chapter with an example of reclusion in the extreme, P. G. Wodehouse's memorable wish to be left alone to do nothing but writing. From that we moved to consider reasons why the private side of writing often dominates the public side (e.g., we rarely see the process modeled; we are schooled to suppose that it is best done in seclusion and revealed to the public when finished). And we looked at the costs of overdoing social isolation. Rule #22 put it this way: Social isolation, carried to excess, risks misdirection, overreactivity, and deprivation of social supports.

Then we considered an especially strong reason for preferring to work alone: Most of us want all the credit for our accomplishments as writers. The counter to this maladaptive attitude was condensed into rule #23: Socially skilled, successful writers let other writers do some of the work (and take some of the credit). There is also, my groups and I discovered, a particularly frightening penalty for excessive isolation. The more we work alone, the less receptive we become to opportunities for creative change and public acceptance. We turned an already familiar notion into a rule (#24) to reinforce this point: The worse the writer, the greater the attachment to the writing.

What helps writers make the move toward a more reasonable involvement in the public side of writing? Perhaps the single most important element was one we had already practiced in some comfort--exteriorizing (outing). Our initial exercises in outing assumed the form of free writing, but here we took the next step, one captured in rule #25: Audience relies most clearly on exteriorization, at first of putting what we have to say to ourselves in writing, then of outing our writing to the public to see what we have to say to them. As we moved away from an emphasis on ourselves as the most important audience (through conversational and collaborative senses of audience), another accustomed notion reemerged. To effectively utilize public feedback and support for writing, we share what we plan and write from the outset. Rule # 27 says it this way: The earlier the feedback and the closer its source to gatekeepers, the more useful to the writer.

The surprise in discovering what works in becoming more sociable as writers did not lie in discovering the rich values of procuring support and knowledge. It did not even come in ascertaining if our work was on track. Rather, it lay in learning the rule about the extent of socialization required for optimal results in productivity, publishability, and popularity (rule #26): The most successful authors spend as much time socializing about writing as writing (and they spend moderate amounts of time at each).

What participants found most useful from this segment of the program was practice and coaching at handling and anticipating criticism. This, in their opinion, was the hardest exercise in the whole project: learning to listen to and agree with (at least in part) criticism about one's writing, even to ask for more. Rule (#28) makes it sound easier than it is: The best way to handle criticism is anticipate it, acknowledge it, and learn from it.

This fifth chapter of the program, on audience, brings the formal part of my writing programs to its final leg. Our long journey together is nearly finished, except for some lingering conversations. In the next chapter, on resilience, I describe what happens when my writers and I "fade" the program structures including regular groups meetings with me. As we prepare for that inevitability we look for a final conclusion about what we have learned in this excursion into making writing more sociable. The consensus in my groups so far is this: As we make writing more public, we may have taken the crucial step in ensuring its long-term persistence. Why? Because in making it conversational and collaborative, we make it more enjoyable and less frightening. And in making it more socially skilled, we feel more like real writers and we experience more of the acceptance due to writers who listen, learn, and work regularly. Said another way, we are coming to see ourselves as veterans who have learned how to travel well.

REFERENCES

1. Jasen, D.A. (1981). *P.G. Wodehouse*, p. 247. New York: Continuum.

2. Bruffee, K.A. (1984). Collaborative learning and the "conversation of mankind." *College English*, 46(7), 635-652.

3. Oatley, K. (1992). *Best laid schemes*. New York: Cambridge University Press.

4. Lear, M.W. (1988). Ping-pong, box lunch boxes, and the muse: A colonist at MacDowell. *New York Times Book Review*, March 3, 1988.

5. Baum, A., Grunberg, N.E. & Singer, J.E. (1992). Biochemical measurements in the study of emotion. *Psychological Science*, 3, 56-60.

6. Garber, J.A. & Dodge, K.A. (1991). *The development of emotion regulation and dysregulation*. New York: Cambridge University Press.

7. Kuiper, N.A., Olinger, L.J. & Martin, R.A. (1988). Dysfunctional attitudes, stress, and negative emotions. *Cognitive Therapy and Research*, 12, 533-547.

8. Holden, (1987). Creativity and the troubled mind. *Psychology Today*, 21(4), 9-10.

9. Ferrari, J.R. (1992). Procrastinators and perfect behavior: An exploratory analysis of self-presentation, self-awareness, and self-handicapping components. *Journal of Research in Personality*, 26, 75-84.

10. Hewitt, P.L. (1991). Dimensions of perfectionism in unipolar depression. *Journal of Abnormal Psychology*, 100, 98-101.

11. Baker, C. (1968). *Ernest Hemingway: A life story*. New York: Charles Scribner's Sons.

12. Asimov, I. (1981). *Asimov on science fiction*. Garden City, NY: Doubleday.

13. Theroux, P. (1980). *The old Patagonian express*. New York: Pocket Books.

14. Asimov, I. (1979). *In memory yet green*. New York: Avon Books, pp. 197 and 319.

15. Scardamalia, M. (1981). How children cope with the demands of writing. In C.F. Frederiksen & J.F. Dominic (eds.), *Writing: Process, development, and communication*, pp. 81-103. Hillsdale, NJ: Erlbaum.

16. Zoellner, R. (1969). Talk-write: A behavioral pedagogy for composition. *College English*, 30, 267-320.

17. Tremmel, R. (1989). Investigating productivity and other factors in the writer's practice. *Freshman English News*, 17(2), 19-25.

18. Johnson, W. (1954). You can't write writing. In S.I. Hiakawa (ed.), *Language, meaning, and maturity*, pp. 100-111. New York: Harper & Row.

19. Durant, W. & Durant, A. (1967). *Rousseau and revolution*. New York: Simon & Schuster, p. 585.

20. Wason, P. (1980). Conformity and commitment in writing. *Visible Language*, 14, 351-363.

21. Baumeister, R.F. & Scher, S.J. (1988). Self-defeating behavior patterns among normal individuals: Review and analysis of common self-destructive tendencies. *Psychological Review*, 104, 3-22.

22. Bartol, K.M. (1988). Manuscript faults and review board recommendations. In G.P. Keita (ed.), *Understanding the manuscript review process: Increasing the*

participation of women, pp. 15-21. Washington, D.C.: American Psychological Association.

23. Fleming, T. (1985). The war between writers and reviewers. *New York Times Book Review*, January 6, pp. 3 and 37.

24. Olsen, G. (1992). Publishing scholarship in humanistic disciplines: Joining the conversation. In J.M. Moxley (ed.), *Writing and publishing for academic authors*, pp. 49-69. New York: University Press of America.

25. Sternberg, R.J. (1988). *The triarchic mind*. New York: Penguin.

26. Epstein, R. (1991). Skinner, creativity, and the problem of spontaneous behavior. *Psychological Science*, 2, 362-370.

27. Durant, W. & Durant, A. (1975). *The age of Napoleon*. New York: Simon and Schuster, p. 649.

28. North, S.M. (1987). *The making of knowledge in composition*. Upper Montclair, NJ: Boynton/Cook.

29. Csikszentmihalyi, M. (1990). *Flow: The psychology of optimal experience*. New York: Harper & Row.

30. Lehr, F. & Lange, B. (1981). Writing for audiences and occasions. *English Journal*, November, 71-74.

31. Gardner, J. (1983). *On becoming a novelist*. New York: Harper Colophon.

32. Field, J. (1981). *A life of one's own*. Los Angeles: J.P. Tarcher.

33. Elbow, P. (1992). Freewriting and the problem of the wheat and tares. In J.M. Moxley (ed.), *Writing and publishing for academic authors*, pp. 33-47.

34. Bloom, L.Z. (1992). Writing as witnessing. In J.M. Moxley (ed.), *Writing and publishing for academic authors*, pp.89-109.

35. Kroll, B.M. (1985). Socio-cognitive ability and writing performance. *Written Communication*, 2, 293-305.

36. Goodman, P. (1952). On writer's block. *Complex*, 7, 42-50.

37. Boice, R. & Myers, P. (1986). Two parallel traditions: Automatic writing and free writing. *Written Communication*, 3, 471-490.

38. Bowers, P. (1979). Hypnosis and creativity: The search for the missing link. *Journal of Abnormal Psychology*, 88, 564-572.

39. Perkins, D.N. (1981). *The mind's best work*. Cambridge, MA: Harvard University Press.

40. Moxley, J.M. (1992). *Publish, don't perish*. Westport, CT: Praeger.

41. Bartholomae, D. (1985). Inventing the university. In M. Rose (ed.), *When a writer can't write*, p.134-165. New York: Guilford.

42. Theroux, P. (1985). *Sunrise with sea monsters*. Boston: Houghton Mifflin, p. 228.

43. Gardner, J. (1983), *On becoming a novelist*, p. 77.

44. Bloom, L.Z. (1985). Anxious writers in context: Graduate school and beyond. In M. Rose (ed.), *When a writer can't write*, p. 132.

45. Brown, R.M. (1988). *Starting from scratch*. New York: Bantam Books, pp. 20-21.

46. Mack, K. & Skjei, E. (1979). *Overcoming writing blocks*. Los Angeles: J.P. Tarcher, p. 81.

47. Rose, M. (1985). Complexity, rigor, evolving method, and the puzzle of writer's block: Thoughts on composing-process research. In M. Rose (ed.), *When a writer can't write*, pp. 227-260. New York: Guilford, p. 232.

48. Monti, P. & Curran, J. (1985). *Social skills*. New York: New York University Press.

49. Flower, L. (1990). The role of task representation in reading-to-write. In L. Flower, V. Stein, J. Ackerman, M.J. Kantz, K. McCormick & W.C. Peck (eds.), *Reading-to-write*, pp. 35-75. New York: Oxford University Press.

50. Fox, M.F. & Favor, C.A. (1982). The process of collaboration in scholarly research. *Scholarly Publishing*, 13, 327-329.

51. Matkin, R.E. & Riggar, T.F. (1991). *Persist and publish: Helpful hints for academic writing and publishing*. Niwot: University Press of Colorado.

52. Schrier, M. & Carver, S.C. (1992). Effects of optimism on psychological and physical being: Theoretical overview and empirical update. *Cognitive Therapy and Research*, 16, 201-228.

53. McCaul, K.D., Glasgow, R.E. & O'Neill, H.K. (1992). The problem of creating habits: Establishing health-protective dental behaviors. *Health Psychology*, 11, 101-110.

54. Boice, R. (1992). *The new faculty member*. San Francisco: Jossey-Bass.

55. Boice, R. (1991). Combined treatments for writing blocks. *Behaviour Research and Therapy*, 30, 107-116.

56. Boice, R. (1993). Writing blocks and tacit knowledge. *Journal of Higher Education*, 64, 19-54.

57. Boice, R. (1990). *Professors as writers*. Stillwater, OK: New Forums Press.

58. Getzels, J.W. & Csikszentmihalyi, M. (1976). *The creative vision: A longitudinal study of problem finding in art*. New York: Wiley.

59. Bandura, A. (1987). Self-efficacy: Toward a unifying theory of behavioral change. *Psychological Review*, 84, 191-215.

60. Bullough, R.V., Knowles, J.G. & Crow, N.A. (1991). *Emerging as a teacher*. New York: Routledge.

61. London, M. (1993). Interpersonal insight. Manuscript submitted for publication.

62. Cooper, J. (1990). What is cooperative learning? *Cooperative Learning and College Learning*, 1(1), 2.

63. Ede, L. & Lunsford, A. (1992). *Singular texts/plural authors*. Carbondale: Southern Illinois University Press.

64. Stillinger, J. (1991). *Multiple authorship and myth of the solitary genius*. New York: Oxford University Press.

65. Foreman, J. (1992). *New visions of collaborative writing*. Portsmouth, NH: Boynton/Cook.

66. Parker, J. (1969). Naked truth on stranger: A hoax. *New York Times*, August 3, 32.

67. Boice, R. (1990). Mentoring new faculty: A program for implementation. *Journal of Staff, Program, and Organization Development*, 8, 143-160.

68. Brown, J.S., Collins, A. & Duguid, P. (1989). Situated cognition and the culture of learning. *Educational Researcher*, January-February, 32-42.

69. Creswell, J.W. (1985). *Faculty research performance*. Washington, D.C.: Association for the Study of Higher Education.

70. Scarr, S. (1982). An editor looks for the perfect manuscript. In G.P. Keita (ed.), *Understanding the manuscript review process*, pp. 81-103. Washington, D.C.: American Psychological Association.

71. Tavris, C.B. (1988). Publishing strategies for women and minorities: Starting with basics. In G.P. Keita (ed.), *Understanding the manuscript review process*, p. 23-26. Washington, D.C.: American Psychological Association. [check]

72. Hall, E.T. (1992). *An anthropology of everyday life: An autobiography*. New York: Doubleday, p.105.

73. Skinner, B.F. (1983). *A matter of consequences*. New York: Alfred A. Knopf.

6

Resilience

> . . . the man who works so moderately as to be able to work
> constantly, not only preserves his health the longest, but in the
> course of the year, executes the greatest quantity of work.
>
> Adam Smith [1]

Adam Smith, writing with the advantage of two centuries of foresight, anticipated the central theme of this book: Calm and persistent writing affords both health and productivity. He might just as well, in mentioning persistent well-being and accumulated output, have used the word "resilience."

At the end of our long journey together, writers want resilience. So, in response, I do some specific things. Instead of ending the program abruptly, for instance, I gradually "fade" program supports and stretch the times between meetings. And, not surprisingly, I encourage talk about resilience. We wonder: "Which of us will make it over the long run and which will fail?" Then we begin, in our now biweekly meetings, to look for clues in our own experiences.

Three possibilities for strengthening resilience generally come to mind. One reflects Adam Smith's observation about the value of calm pacing and brief, daily sessions in promoting persistence. Working without fatigue and with easy accumulation of output creates a base for durability. The second hint is nearly as obvious and comes from our recent exercises on audience. There we saw the potential of social networks of support and direction to keep us on track as writers. With time growing short (and the book nearing a close), I add a third source of information, about what makes for durable habits; it reflects my background in psychology.

The interventions that make learning easy and enduring are priming, prompting, and fading [2]. We already know variants of the first two. Joining the conversation of writers exemplifies *priming* (as in the excitement of to act and inclined to make the right general responses. *Prompting* reminds us of what we already know. When we write with a conceptual outline at hand, we are prompted to say and do the appropriate things; prompts maintain momentum by providing the small reminders that minimize mistakes and failures. And finally there is *fading*, that gradual removal of formal primes and prompts as learners rely more and more on internalized cues to carry out routines. Many writers recollect this strategy from grade school where a poem was written on the board and then faded word by word, until they could continue to recite it with the board completely erased. Fading dominates the experience of participants in this last section of the program; in the end, as you will see, writers are reminded of some old ideas in new ways but left largely on their own to make use of them.

Here is what I have observed while implementing this sequence (of priming, prompting, and fading) in the closing stanza: First, it prompts writers to recognize the resilience that comes of well-entrenched habits. Lasting success at writing depends on regular practice (and, writers notice, on the well-timed use of primes such as the action readiness of mild enthusiasm). But this sequence also profits from the habit of noticing (i.e., prompting ourselves to see) what we are doing differently and better as writers. For instance, we commonly pause here to consider the contrast to the way most of us learned to write. Previously, most of us worked largely in private with few primes (often waiting, instead, for inspiration or deadlines). Our prompts too often came as harsh criticisms and magical admonitions (not as social supports or well-prepared prewriting). And fading, the gradual removal of scaffolding once the structure is in place, had no ready parallel to how we learned; traditional instruction in writing provided few models of how writers work that could be withdrawn as we learned. No wonder so few of us reached adulthood equipped with resilience as writers.

Then, as we look over resilience, we turn to a familiar habit. We peruse the literature and share the work of summarizing and reporting information about counterparts of resilience.

OUR CUSTOMARY OVERVIEW OF THE LITERATURE

As often happens, we demur over this assignment. Just as quickly, we concede that this variety of collecting and organizing our ideas not only reinforces what we learned earlier (Chapter 2), but that it is also enjoyable:

Most of us writers like a bit of bookishness now and then. We have fun with this. . . . Besides, we almost always learn practical things in these surveys. . . . We have learned, I'd say, to make quick work of them, don't you agree?

No, I like this. I even like to do it by myself; I constantly take a break from the office and go to the library and check out things and make notes. For the first time since college I feel like a learner and this time I'm doing it for myself. . . . I think this is just the kind of thing that will help with resilience.

Here is a sampling of what we share: First, we see that resilience, our central topic, looks much like the concepts being developed by stress researchers; "hardiness," for instance, has roots in personal and internal control over one's work and in reacting to life changes as challenges rather than as threats [3]. There is a link here to our earlier discussions, about responding to rejections as calm listeners and learners, not as victims. A second discovery: resilience resembles the autonomy and self-direction that seem to grow as writers manage more tolerance of ambiguity and of abstraction [4]. And a third: resilience probably coincides with the self-confidence of being able to take risks in a safe, collegial career setting [5]. Studies of life stages make similar points, as in Daniel Levinson's *The Seasons of a Man's Life*:

A man at around 40 is not simply reacting to an external situation. He is reappraising his life. . . . Mid-life individuation enables us to reduce the tyranny of both the demands society places on us . . . and [to make the person at midlife] more interested in using his own inner resources. [6]

Resilience, we agree in this fleeting discussion, may come by way of dissociating our writing from the strong excitements or external provocations that had once been necessary inciters to action [7].

This first glance at expertise on resilience leaves most writers with mixed feelings. Is it too highly concerned with autonomy and too generally vague about how writers achieve resilience? And what, we wonder, do we really want at this juncture? The answer usually comes as a request: Most writers ask for more information about my own observations and analyses of writers who have completed the program. "What," several writers inquire in one way or another, "is the difference between writers who prove to be resilient and those who do not?"

WHAT CAUSES RELAPSES

I start with summaries of what I have learned about the obverse of resilience, susceptibility to relapse. (As a source of my conclusions, I rely mainly on thinking-aloud protocols from my follow-up sessions conducted at bimonthly intervals for the year after "graduation" and at six-month intervals for the year or two after that.) In particular, I dwell on my attempts to reconstruct the experiences during seemingly crucial turning points where planned writing projects were abandoned for at least a week. (In the subsection just ahead, I rely mainly on data from repeated follow-ups with sixteen of the twenty-three graduates who experienced the most frequent and serious relapses--the individuals I designate as least resilient. Only six of that total, incidentally remained blocked for more than half a year.)

Four components of susceptibility appear reliably and somewhat independently in my analyses. Each is a condition of writers that corresponds with (and seems to invite) a relapse:

Distractibility and Overreactiveness

Most obviously, relapses occur as slips in attentiveness and momentum. Plans fall prey to distractions and writing becomes erratic. This is a typical answer from a writer who has proven distractible, when I ask, "Can you recall recent instances of significant distraction and interruption while writing?"

[Laughs] No problem. The phone rings. I answer it. I may or may not get back to writing. The door bell rings and, of course, I answer it. Do I go back to my writing? Maybe, maybe not. . . . Lately, it doesn't take much, even the slightest discomfort or twinge of sadness.

Then, as we turn to retrospective-thinking-aloud protocols to reconstruct these experiences of derailing, something else becomes apparent. The problem isn't so much the distraction, it is more the overreaction:

So what am I thinking when I have hung up the phone? [pauses, shifts posture markedly, looks away, and recites rapidly] "I'm not in the mood anymore. I'm too worked up. I'm too tense. I'll do some cleaning, some, what?, dish washing until I calm down."

You know, I even understand the greater principle here, no matter that I can't put it to good use. Pat Riley says it as "It isn't what happens to you, but what you do about it." Albert Ellis, I guess, says much the same thing. So do I. (You see what fine company I keep.)

To help writers accept the reality and commonness of overreaction, I remind them of parallels amongst some of our heroes. P. G. Wodehouse, the recluse we met earlier in our journey, sometimes wanted complete seclusion because social interruptions could keep him from writing (Chapter 5). Ayn Rand's example is even more germane: "when there was someone I had to see, the emotional and intellectual switch would cost me two or three days work" [8]. Most dramatic are accounts of Dickens as distressed and distractible:

. . . there nonetheless emerges the portrait of a man who was mentally agonized, sleepless, depressed, who broke down in paroxysms of grief at the death of friends, and who was terrified for his life during train journeys. [9]

When we share these examples of overreaction, there is visible relief for each of us in reminders that our overreactions are neither idiosyncratic nor as bad as some. And with that instant of comfort, writers start to notice links between these accounts of overreactiveness and other things:

Wait a minute. Wasn't Ayn Rand a binge writer of the highest rank? Didn't you tell us that she worked in great marathons, until she was sick, exhausted, and depressed? Yes, you did. . . . So that must somehow tie in with her emotional reaction to disruptions, right? Too attached to her work!

Dickens fits all too well, doesn't he? He binged with such intensity that he often took walks of twenty to thirty miles to calm down, sometimes all through the night!

To spot overreactions to what, for most people, would be mild disruptions, we moved to some more thinking-aloud exercises. Recollected thoughts and feelings like those of the following writers (each of whom appended some conclusions) helped identify three common, overlapping moods associated with overreaction:

   1. *Mood/style = Narrowed.*

When I relive, uhm [pauses], revisit the moment, I feel a surprising, frightening intensity where I'm holding my breath and struggling. I was totally focused in on my writing, possessed by it, so much that I can hardly recall any ongoing thoughts except for jerky outpourings of content and the pauses to correct or change a few things. Then what? Then what? Only when the generator noise suddenly started up outside my window did I stop. That moment I can remember. Suddenly, I had put my notes down and I got up, saying this: "Well, that's that. I've lost a good train of thought. . . . I can't work under these circumstances." I turned off the computer, still feeling totally out of the mood to write, and left my office in a daze.
[Conclusions] No doubt you expect me to see a moral in this. And I guess I do, good "student" that I am. I was too narrowly focused, too invested, too ready to be distracted. Yes, I was acting like a monomaniac. I was not practicing the message of one of our cardinal rules, the one that says that writers handicap themselves by being overattached to their writing. . . . Pretty good analysis, eh?

   2. *Mood/style = Impatient.*

I could tell you the same exact story about any one of my big "derailments." Every one of them would do Ayn Rand or any derelict writer proud, I think. Here's the one where I quit again after finally making a good start and finishing three good pages. I had my writing set up; I was going and I kept at it. This is what I thought soon after I sat down. I suddenly realized, sitting there and staring at the screen, that my head was full of thoughts. I stopped myself and asked our prescribed question: "How is my posture, what am I thinking, and how is my pace?" Then, my response: "What I am thinking, mostly, is about the disagreement we, I, just had before lunch. I'm still reliving that and I, I'm still as rushed as I was when I drove, speeding all the while, back here after lunch." I then sat there, stiff and silent and defeated, thinking, "I can't do anything while I'm feeling like this." You know, I didn't.

[Conclusion] What do I think now? I let a tiny, truly insignificant little argument and my own habit of rushing around all day get in the way of something I really wanted to do, something I would have enjoyed if I hadn't been so tense and rushed. When I couldn't settle down immediately, I gave up. . . . Impatience, always impatience.

3. *Mood/style* = *Intolerant.*

This is it, my special instant: I was already distracted, trying to get focused. As the student opened the door without knocking, I didn't even think. I reacted. I whirled around in my chair, like the mummified mother in *Psycho*, and shrieked, "You've got a nerve, coming in here like this, when I'm trying to work." Of course, she left. What else? When I tried to write again, immediately I was thinking of all the annoyances that had come my way: "I didn't sleep well. I don't feel good; I think I am coming down with something. Someone put a big scratch on my car the other day and I'd like to figure out who. I'm tired of whining students. . . ." That wasn't the whole of it. I sat there feeling guilty about my explosiveness.

[Conclusion] What do I make of it, given the wonderful wisdom of hindsight? It was one of those moments for me, I think, where I was too oversensitive to concentrate on my writing and too uncharitable to put up with interruptions. At that instant (can you imagine?) I felt with all my heart that no one else's problems were a match for mine...no one needed peace and quiet more than I. . . . I get like that. But do I have to? This is the sort of thing, I'm coming to see, that keeps me from making it as a writer.

Resistance to exteriorization. With these careful revisits to crucial moments, a still deeper kind of realization emerges. The insight begins with an awareness that most of our distractible moods take hold with an insidious shift in focus. Where the spotlight had been on generating prose it moved inward, to a morass of thinking that could quickly sidetrack writing:

Now I see it a little more clearly. I was feeling sorry for myself at the same time I was trying to get back to writing. . . . I was trying to do the right thing when I thought, "I'm not going to let this insult [from a colleague] interfere. I'm going to look at the screen and my notes and continue with the chapter. I need to concentrate." But there were two conversations going on, the one about the page in front of me and the other one about my "friend's" criticisms of me. When I let it dominate, that louder, more insistent one, I stopped keyboarding and I sat and carried on more of this upsetting conversation with myself. It was, I think now, easier to move inward, to my self-pity, than outward, to putting ideas on the screen.

In reconstructions like this one lay a clue about what may be the pivotal act in becoming distractable. When writers focus more on thinking than doing (i.e., on self-focusing versus getting thoughts on paper), when they turn inward, they risk negative rumination and abandonment of the external act of writing. Self-focus hazards distraction, depression, and immobilization.

The discussion of this tendency to self-focus proves fascinating. We have, I remind groups at this point, already seen studies that made a similar point: When writers converse with themselves while writing (as opposed to thinking, reviewing, and planning during occasional pauses from writing), the quality of their writing decreases [10]. The predictable things occur for writers who spend less time thinking and more time doing: They feel less obliged to write, they produce more, and they experience less self-doubt [11].

I point out another clue that arises in a question common amongst writers feeling stuck in their projects. They ask me, "What should I think about when I write?" My response is this: "You may be asking the wrong question. You might better ask what you should be doing when you write. My answer, then, would be that you would do better to exteriorize--to put thoughts and images onto paper or screen."

What survives from this stream of comments and insights about writers suffering with distractibility? Overall, it leaves the curious suggestion that thinking can be a very limited way to control thinking. Writers often find this unanticipated notion attractive:

Do you know what happens with my customary, with my usual resolve to stop the blind, negative thinking? At best I accomplish a brief centering, but only for the moment before other thoughts pop back into mind. Do you know what happens when I try to think about what I want to write? Sometimes it works. Sometimes it goes off in all sorts of directions. . . . It is vulnerable, I think, to the slightest distractions; then the train of thought is gone in an instant. . . . I think I'm finally getting to understanding it, though. It's deceptively simple, isn't it? If I want to be writing, and not wasting my time and energy, I need to be doing more and ruminating less. . . . That realization alone has been worth the price of the journey.

I can see them now--some of the dangers of relying on thinking alone--for clarity and rationality. Unless I stop and ask myself (and often the asking and answering need to be spoken aloud, quite audibly) what I am thinking and what I want to be doing, I may lose my direction at any moment. . . . If I'm not doing something when I'm supposed to be writing (either putting things down, or else pausing and carrying on an action-oriented conversation with myself about whether I am doing what I want to do), I'm *not* being very productive or satisfied. . . . I'm astonished now, when we look back at some of my writing experiences, at the squandered time spent on reliving hurts and slights and on imagining revenge and what not. When I could have been writing. I could almost get embarrassed [pauses and smiles]. I would rather spend the energy doing more constructive things.

But things are never quite as simple as they first seem when we uncover the factors of susceptibility. There are, it turns out, problems in oversimplifying exteriorization of thought into action. When writers immoderately reduce this "outing" to its narrowest, most sterile function, of mere transcription of thinking, other problems arise:

No, it doesn't work so well when I exteriorize (what a lovely word) in a passive, detached way . . . when I just take dictation. I mean, it works to get things down on paper but it seems to leave me open to conversation about other things as I write. So I either find myself drifting off into other reveries or agonies and my writing taking odd turns with odd expressions. Or else, the inner conversation just stops the writing because it is proves more (what?) compelling. The (what do you call them?) stenographer just sits and listens.

Why do you think Gertrude Stein's writing is so odd? It's mostly automatic writing, taking inner dictation. She wrote in a self-hypnotic trance.

So, on the one hand, distractibility can come from a resistance to outing (when inner focus grows excessive). And, on the other hand, distractibility emerges from unthinking immoderation in putting thoughts out for external examination (when the output is unpaced, unplanned, unexamined automaticity). As usual, balance and moderation enter the equation. When writers are at their most distractible, it seems, they are at their most monomaniacal, doing only one thing at a time [12]; they are either self-focusing or writing automatically. More efficient, resilient writers manage to do more than one thing at a time: at some moments they are rewriting and clarifying; at some, reviewing and planning; at some, generating new prose and ideas to see what can be said; at some, stretching and relaxing. But, for the most part, they are planfully active and doing or redoing.

Depression. Self-focus and an overreliance on internalized thinking not only produce the well-known negativity and misery of depression. They also create conditions for overreaction because depressives overreact to both failure and success [13]. And depressives tend to overreact in a more subtle way. When the are not overreacting, they tend to be passive and inhibited [14]; they think rather than act, they consume time with fantasies of vengeance or reconciliation, and they remain distractable by making themselves all the more vulnerable to depression triggers [15]. Depression tends to breed more depression because it carries constant reminders of tasks and opportunities unfulfilled. (And, often, when it finally impels action, the result is bingeing and hypomania.) With this continuing discomfort comes the temptation to opt for short-term solutions, the sorts we labeled beforehand as self-defeating behaviors [16]. Most of these avoidance strategies, including procrastination and face-saving, help make writers susceptible to relapses.

How, specifically, does depression turn into distractibility? It turns self-focusers away from action, as we have just seen. Its pain and impatience incline writers to make "capture errors," irrational decisions to act in old, familiar, and unproductive ways that promise short-term relief [17]. When impatience and impulsivity dominate, writers often abandon carefully laid plans and prewriting for the hollow comfort of spontaneity:

When I'm deep in the doldrums, I can tolerate no discipline. If I can make myself write at all, it must be on my terms, my old magical terms (as you call them). This particular time, for example, I thought, as I recall, aah [pauses], "I don't feel like it. I don't feel like dealing with all that paperwork, all those notes and all that bureaucracy. I just want to be free and write. . . ." "The hell with Boice and all his goddam rules," I thought. But only moments later, I can see now, I wasn't writing at all, despite all my self-awarded freedom. I was back at my ruminations about what a victim I had been. I blamed everyone else for my lack of freedom as a writer. . . . All I wanted to do (all I did finally) was to write some more without a plan, where ever the writing took me. I liked the emancipation but I didn't like the writing when I stopped to look it over.

These accounts also help clarify how depression acts to disrupt by way of overreaction:

Some things (little things) made me cry if I stopped to think, if I didn't keep going. (I agree with you that my love of bingeing is as much a fear of stopping and letting my gremlins catch up with me as anything.) Anyway, this is what I was saying to myself: "Oh, that reminds me of [mentions a former lover], of what he said when we were at _____ together." I'm sad. I'm crying softly. I've stopped writing. . . . Within the next minutes, you know, some things made me irritated, the smallest and most insignificant things. . . . But I made myself stop and focus. I shifted, sort of abruptly, back to my unfinished sentence. I free-wrote it, I reworded it, and I reentered it. I was almost thinking of the sentences ahead, forming them, starting to write them out, if you know what I mean? But then my little girl yelled something . . . in another room. I was angry at the interruption, at the violation of a rule that everyone in the house understood. . . . I stopped for the day; I had never managed a solid beginning.

How big a factor is distractibility in relapses and silences? In its various forms, ranging from overnarrowing to overreaction, it is usual common culprit in writers I have tracked. Still, my analyses show other common correlates of susceptibility.

Unmet Expectations

The second category of underminers is more a matter of unrealistic expectations than of distractibility. It commonly shows ties to the kind of perfectionism that keeps writers from beginning, continuing, or finishing. And, it demonstrates a dimension of perfectionism not often appreciated: Perfectionists are remiss in setting clear, manageable goals. And they are reluctant to collect the feedback that would tell them how well they are meeting whatever goals they have. This combination is an invitation to relapses--goals fail without feedback, and feedback is useless until compared against progress toward goals [18].

We can readily spot perfectionism in many of its appearances. In its best-known form it sets standards that cannot be met and it demands error-free work in a way that substitutes obsessive worrying for doing [19]. For example:

The funny thing is that I get caught here every time and every time it surprises me. This time I was writing the first page of the first draft (and I had duly reminded myself that it did not need to be perfect). This is what I remember most clearly: all of a sudden I found myself looking at it and stopping and asking, "So how good is this going to be? Is this going to be excellent enough for publication in [names prestigious academic journal]? And just as quickly, I notice now, I'm scanning the sentences. I see a long, awkward sentence and I think: "You can't write. Almost anyone could do better. . . . This isn't what you want."
[Conclusion] How this strikes me now? Well, it seems silly, doesn't it? I had my usual unrealistic expectations. I didn't give myself even the slightest chance to revise and improve before passing my harsh judgment. I talked myself into quitting just as I was getting something going and I talked myself into feeling like a worm.

Perfectionism, as we just saw, can induce procrastination. As writers procrastinate, they often put on marvelous displays of busyness [20], of looking active but accomplishing little of note [21]. Many of the relapses I observe in progress are revealing; while writers often excuse their hiatus from writing by claiming it gave them time to do other things, the evidence says otherwise. Writers, seeing me watch them, reflect and then spontaneously admit the inefficiency of their busyness to me:

Do I really need to spend all this time answering these memos with my most carefully crafted writing? No, of course not. Why do I do it? I guess because I like to keep busy . . . maybe because this is easier than my real writing?

But, we soon notice, perfectionistic expectations do more than induce delays and distractions. They make the return to writing even more difficult. Procrastination undermines our confidence, our belief in our own self-efficacy, and, at the same time, heightens our fears of failure [22]. The longer we procrastinate, the less control we feel over the task we put off, and the less likely its resumption and completion. Procrastination with its roots in perfectionism is, in my analyses, second only to distractibility as a correlate of susceptibility to relapse.

Another common basis for procrastination, overreacting to the aversiveness of a task, is part of the next, third common pattern in susceptibility.

Mindlessness, Planlessness

Pessimists quickly settle into passivity, take fewer steps to avoid bad events, and do less to stop them once they are underway [23]. Could we ask for a better recipe for relapse and silence than this? Perhaps. Procrastinators, again, can compete with any diagnostic group. They do not, for one thing, realistically judge the time required for writing [21]; so it is that they fare poorly at writing, an assignment that requires the planful, patient use of time [24]. Nor do procrastinators realistically plan the content or aims of their writing. They remain so self-focused or busily distracted that they are unable to predict the gains and costs of their actions, especially those with long-term gains. Vague planning, of course, risks still more disappointments [6]. This is a common story to accompany the theme:

My problem is that I can't tell how much time my writing will take and I always run out of time. I don't think I will, but I almost always do. Always. There are always deadlines for my pieces and I often miss them. . . . Sure, it *is* costly. I lose work, good assignments, because editors lose faith in me as a finisher. I stay disillusioned with myself, this person who just can't quite figure things out.

The form of procrastination that most affects relapses in this category is related to task aversion. Writers who have not learned to associate their writing with pleasantness and accomplishment are most likely, in my observations, to experience surprise at the difficulty of a writing project:

OK, I admit it once more, I have never liked writing. Almost every time I find it an enormous struggle (although I guess this program has helped at times). Where was I? Oh, I know. I don't expect it to be so awfully difficult. . . . For instance: I'm stopped to look over what I have written, maybe three or four pages so far. "My god," I'm thinking, "there are a lot of things to take into account here. A lot to keep in mind while I write. It isn't so easy and fun as I hoped. This is difficult and I don't like it. . . . Yes, I know that Albert Ellis would tell me it's illogical to suppose that it should be easy, but I don't care. This is just too hard right now and I don't feel like doing it right now." So I put it aside and went out to run some errands.
[In response to my question, "How could a more planful approach have helped reduce the aversiveness of writing?"] Well, I think I know what you would say: More prewriting, I'll bet. If I had better plans, better scaffolding that I could use and fade away, my chore wouldn't seem so difficult and so unmanageable.

Fatigue and Irrationality

This fourth common cause of relapse is the most telling in the end. When writers constantly struggle with wasted energy of distractibility, with the disappointments of unmet expectations, and with the on-and-off rushing of planlessness, they understandably grow weary. Arguments and occasions can be found to dispel the best of intentions.

There was, I like to tell burned-out writers, a fascinating era of study about fatigue, much of it old, forgotten, but still illuminating [25]. Time-and-motion researchers determined optimum expenditures of energy, even for writers. Their studies inspired Marx and other productivists to hope they could eliminate useless labor (and its contribution to class struggle). Time-and-motion experts also influenced psychotherapists who worried about patients suffering constant exhaustion.

The keenest of these productivists noticed something telling about tasks like writing: Attentiveness as usually practiced is abnormal, transient, exhausting; but attentiveness exercised with more moderate rhythms including rest is less taxing, more productive. Then, just in time, I control my bent for windy lectures and bring the topic back to more interaction with my writers.

Instead, I ask a few interrelated questions to provoke a focused discussion: What causes some people to become more exhausted than others? Is it their tendency to work under negative controls (e.g., where writing continues because the cost of not writing would be even worse [2])? Is it their pacing, their tendency to work at a hurried rate and over prolonged durations, both of which induce unnecessary fatigue? Is it the monomania, the single-minded attentiveness, that works so fast to exhaust? The answers come as quickly and as definitely as did this one:

All right, I get the point. No doubt they all do, right? [In response to my gentle question, "What were the causes again?"] OK, you've primed me, right? (And you may have to prompt.) The three causes of unusual tiredness in writing are, first, I can't remember that one, but I know numbers two and three: pacing, of course, and imbalance, of course, where we are too intensely focused. And the first was [pauses, then responds to my reminder, "what about someone writing only to avoid a worse fate?"]. Oh, yes, working under negative motivation, a sin of which I am often guilty. So it is pacing, imbalanced attention, and bad motivation.

Irrationality. There is, I add, a telling kind of mindlessness about working in fatiguing ways. We see it when we trace interruptive tiredness back to its roots. How can we, I ask, begin to look productively for ways to combat fatigue? Whose techniques can we use? The answer often resembles this combination:

I think I would do as Joanne Field did. Sure. If I am constantly stopping and asking myself the usual, "How's my posture, how's my pacing, how's my thinking?," I might notice early that I'm getting tired and down. For sure, I'll notice that I'm no longer relaxed and enjoying a sort of mild happiness. . . . In fact, I have done it, just not as often as I should.

Come on, I know what to do. To catch the fatigue early, during my stretch breaks. . . by watching for impatience and rushing and discomfort, the things that I know full well lead to tiring. . . . Why do I need to do a better job of this? Because, dummy (no I don't want to be too hard on myself, at least not in front of you), when you get tired, you don't do your best work.

And, when primes and prompts like these elicit reflections and recollections about what leads to fatigue, we move more squarely to the costs of fatigue. Writers by now can recite several expenses from ready memory: Fatigue makes writing, now and later, less desirable; it can trigger impatience as productivity lags and as the temptation grows to pick up the pace; it can bring anxiety and its pernicious narrowing; and it heightens susceptibility to irrationality.

Thinking-aloud exercises reinforce the point. This is what we decide happens first while we reconstruct moments of memorable fatigue: Our attention wanders and we fight back, much like a sleepy driver trying to stay awake and on the road. Next, commonly, we come to sudden doubts about what we are doing; we begin to question the purpose and worth of the writing [26]. Then, with equal impulsivity, dysphoria takes hold and with it intrusive thoughts and an inability to suppress them [27]. With that comes a reinstatement of mindlessness in moving to quick, relieving solutions such as putting off writing until a "more propitious time." What happens at worst? Writers settle into the interiorization of self-focus and into reclusion.

What Writers Say, in Retrospect, Undermines Their Resilience

When I have shared my summaries of these experiences with all the program graduates, a reaction like this is common:

What bothers me about this is that I, like the others, know what to do, but I don't remember to do it. Why is that?

Some writers are primed to say even more:

My complaint is very much like Joanne Field's in *A Life of One's own*, isn't it? But I can't, for the life of me, remember what she did to overcome it . . . [My prompt: "Remember what she did on a regular basis?"] Wasn't it her habit of stopping and asking herself what she was thinking? Yes. And didn't she also find it valuable to spend more time doing things, especially in groups? ["Yes."]

"If," someone in the conversation usually continues, "I am going to do better at remembering, I'll need more prompts, better habits." Even at six months or a year out of the formal program, writers have not lost touch with the custom of capsulizing and listing reminders. With each writer I reformulate the next rule:

RULE #29: Four common, interlocking conditions for relapsing from comfort and fluency in writing are (1) distractibility due mainly to insufficient exteriorization of thinking, (2) unmet expectations of perfectionism, (3) unanticipated but avoidable problems such as mindless surprise about the difficulty of a project, and (4) fatigue and irrationality owing mostly to inefficient pacing.

With this rule in place, the next step seems inevitable. Writers ask about what makes the most resilient writers different:

Is it just the opposite of the things in the rule, doing better at externalizing and pacing and so on? It had better be something like that. I don't want to hear that they do better than I do because they're more stoic or smarter or born that way.

CORRELATES OF RESILIENCE

When we get to the point of discussing what I have learned about the distinctive qualities of resilient writers, my writers and I are meeting only monthly at most. I present my analyses simply and quickly, much as in the list below of common correlates of resilience. But even while traveling along at a rather brisk gait, we take time for noticing. At first glance, resilience seems to consist of a handful of positive acts, of about six focal points.

Resilience Seen Broadly

What is a usefully broad definition of resilience? I define it, usually, as consisting of reasonable consistency, productivity, and happiness in writing-- through obstacles. The acts of resilient writers that seem most correlated are mostly familiar; for each act I add some notes, just for fun, from my recollections of historical luminaries who anticipated the point:

1. *Brief, daily sessions.* Bds contribute, as we have seen, to constant, regular, and moderate outputs that, in the long run, far outstrip other patterns of writing.

Buffon: "make haste slowly" (or as John Wooden put it, "Be quick but don't hurry").

Herbert Simon: "It is not enough to know what the principles are; you must acquire deeply ingrained habits of carrying them out, in the face of all kinds of strong urges to stray" (or as William James put it, "Habit is the great flywheel of society")

2. *Prewriting, planfulness, and shared early plans and output.* By this point in the program (with habits of productivity more or less in place), the part of planning and sharing that matters most is setting clear, realistic goals and arranging ongoing feedback toward those goals. Current discoveries about what makes for ideal work motivation and satisfaction lead to a similar inference [17]: Performance that is judged successful leads to satisfaction and to more commitment to the task; as writers find success, they build self-efficacy, and with it even more daring and skill in setting higher standards and the plans to achieve them [28].

John Locke: "habits work more constantly and with greater facility than reason, which, when we have most need of it, is seldom fairly consulted, and more rarely obeyed."

Buffon: "those who write as they speak, however well they speak, write badly; and those who abandon themselves to the first fire of their imagination take a tone which they cannot sustain. . . . It is for lack of plan, for not having sufficiently reflected on his purpose, that even a man of thought finds himself confused."

Rousseau: "education should be a happy process of natural unfolding, of learning from nature and experience, of freely developing one's capacities into full and zestful living"

3. *Anticipating blocking points.* Resilient writers are uncommonly good about noticing what is going on when they block or experience otherwise self-defeating acts (e.g., setting unrealistic goals; sinking to face work; failing by choking under pressure) and at noting possibilities for repeated problems in their plans. They not only anticipate, they prepare themselves to prevent or moderate usual pitfalls (e.g., by putting more detail into prewriting so as to avoid the confusion and aversiveness of discovering that there is too much or too little to say at crucial points in the manuscript).

Napoleon: "If I seem equal to the occasion, and ready to face it when it comes, it is because I have thought the matter over a long time before undertaking it. . . . I have anticipated whatever might happen. It is no genie which suddenly reveals to me what I ought to do or say."

Graham Greene: "Writing is a form of therapy; sometimes I wonder how all those who do not write, compose or paint can manage to escape the madness, the melancholia, the panic fear which is inherent in a human situation."

4. *Inventing new behaviors.* Resilient writers have a fourth, somewhat surprising quality; they invent new behaviors, insights, and skills to suit their

changing perceptions of themselves and their writing. The most common examples: Writers who change their entire daily schedules to accommodate writing while allotting even more time to more valued activities such as teaching, social life, reading, or exercising. Writers who arrange whole new social supports for their writing. Writers who adopt greatly heightened goals. Or writers who learn to write amid comfort, with feet propped up, necks and backs supported in a recliner chair. Some writers feel they reinvent themselves as newly calm, mildly happy, unrushed, and sociable crafters of prose (and quite often, poetry).

Alfred Kazin: "In a very real sense, the writer writes in order to teach himself, to understand himself, to satisfy himself; the publishing of his ideas, though it brings gratifications, is a curious anticlimax."

5. *Seeing new links to new habits*. Resilient writers surprise and delight themselves by noticing that strategies they have just learned apply to other, broader things. Some professorial writers, for example, see that the writerly principles they have been practicing apply as well or better to activities such as grant writing [29]. But special benefit await noticing of generalities that excite writers and change their outlooks on how they work. Consider the discovery of links to what is nowadays called reflective practice [30]. It is a Zen-like stance where writers work in the moment, with an open mind that focuses processes of thought and action in the present, that keeps the mind from being pulled to and fro by distractions. It is a detachment from ego, a leap of faith back from the familiar, that helps writers understand things as they are and to discover how to say them. What happens when other group members point out that insights like this one are little more than restatements of what we have been thinking and doing in the program? The response is a reminder of the value in reseeing and restating what we already know in new, personally valued terms. These responses also prompt writers to mention that the making of these links brings more sense of ownership. Finally, these exhilarating discussions usually include a mention of the legitimacy that builds when we can see that writerly rules work in general ways.

Robert Pace: Good things go together.

6. *Moderation and balance*. This sixth quality is most pervasive among the correlates of resilience. Moderation shows itself in obvious ways, notably in pacing (working in calm, nonfatiguing, reflective fashion) and in limit setting (sticking, as a rule, to planned session lengths; picking a point where a manuscript no longer profits in more polishing before being sent out for preliminary review).

Dr. Johnson: "do not convey any day's journey into fatigue."

But balance, for the twenty-two writers in the study group with the most resilience, took on more curious qualities. Some aspects of balance followed old prescriptions. Resilient writers indeed spent nearly as much time prewriting as at writing overall. And they nearly balanced time spent writing with time for socializing about writing. What made their practice of balance most strikingly different from that of less resilient writers, though, was flexibility. While the most resilient writers did stick more reliably than did their peers to the programs, they also showed the most planful exceptions to them. Two instances stand out. One was their response to noticing the need to stretch the rule about brief, daily sessions on occasion. When, for instance, writers were revising or proofing entire manuscripts, they often wanted an integrated sense of how it read as a whole. So for these occasions they set aside long sessions, sometimes entire days, for concentrated immersion. (Still, they managed those long sessions with careful pacing and frequent breaks.) The second instance of flexibility was less anticipated. Resilient writers in my analyses tended to do more than one thing at a time. They managed, for example, to take phone calls and visits in stride as they wrote (as with the sort of tolerance of distraction that we have already seen). But the majority of resilient writers also reported moving to a preference for integrating writing with other relaxing activities. Once they had the confidence of being able to return to writing at will, they liked to mix it with leisurely things (e.g., gardening, strolling, reading the paper), even with what had once been strenuous endeavors (exercising; preparing parts of lectures). Or, more commonly, they managed to do some preliminary parts of writing such as note-taking while watching television.

Why? For one thing, because this "polychronicity" reportedly made working more fun and freed writers from the enslavement to punctuality and rigidity that had bothered them about the program [12]. And, for another thing, because managing this kind of flexibility demanded a new, rewarding level of self-education. A common example occurred when readers or writers could manage to attend lightly where superficial attention sufficed, but concentrate where necessary. This selective use of attention and action may be the ultimate skill of time management [31].

These points about flexibility, more than any in the program, are met with quiet appreciation. All writers, resilient or not, tell me they feel especial hope in the promise of finding flexibility and inventiveness. All writers, it seems, would like to operate with more options and more free time. And almost everyone speaks with hopefulness about combining pacing with flexibility. "That's a nice mixture," one writer said. "I want my habits to work, but I want some occasional relief now that I have more confidence and wherewithal." Here too, with the list considered and discussed, each of my writers and I move to compress what we have discussed into a rule that we can post as a prompt:

RULE #30: The six distinctive acts of resilient writers are (1) regular, constant practice of adaptive habits, (2) clear, realistic plans and repeated feedback about progress toward goals, (3) anticipation of blocking points through noticing, tracing, and planning, (4) inventions of new behaviors, (5) generalizations writerly habits and insights to broader ways of working, and (6) movement toward planful flexibility in practicing moderation.

Perhaps because there are six principles of resilience, many writers want the formula made simpler. Or at least they want another, more succinct way of appreciating resilience. "I sense there must be another, a shorter way of saying this, and you must too," one writer said to me over a decade ago. I suspected she was right. "It wouldn't necessarily have to replace the six points," someone else added, "it would just be a different perspective." As more and more participants primed me with similar observations, I looked harder for a simplified version. With a prompt here and there from my writers, a more succinct version became apparent.

Resilience Seen Simply, as Two Factors

When the answer came to me, I realized it had been in front of me all along. The same pair of factors has wended its way through my writing programs for over twenty years--the duo of moderation and balance. One way or the other, it seems, lasting fluency and comfort in writing rely on moderation and balance. The problem with those labels, though, is that they only vaguely specify the essential acts involved.

Two equivalent labels that provide better specificity are *pacing* (as in moderation) and *exteriorization* (as in balance). We know pacing from our exercises in moderating impatience and avoiding passivity. The second transformation of concepts, of balance into outward acts, requires some explanation. Consider the role of balance (exteriorization) in prewriting. Effective prewriting demands coordination of two alternating acts: one act is thinking and noticing; the other is putting our thoughts on paper or screen for discovery and clarification. Balance enters the scene in another accustomed way. It equalizes the advantages of solitary concentration with the profits of making early formulations public. In each case, balance works only with exteriorizing.

We first saw exteriorization in the earliest program segment (Chapter 1), as a standing away from the accelerating thought that otherwise becomes impatience or self-conscious negativity. With that move away from inner focus, we moved our spotlight outward to actions like relaxation and limit setting. We next saw exteriorization with the scheme of C. Wright Mills; instead of merely reading and thinking before writing, for example, we balanced reading and writing in what we called writerly reading (taking notes as we read and entering notes about our dialogue with the author and with our notes). We then performed a basic act of outing in outlining. Later, we used Joanna Field's argument for exteriorization: writers fare better when they relocate their thoughts onto paper and into group interactions for objective scrutiny of what works and what does not.

Outing also applies to anticipating writing blocks. When we mindfully notice our usual sticking points and plan for the possibility of their reemergence, we transport thoughts about blocking from their usual stance of ambiguity and mystery to clearer, more external statements. And as we exteriorize these anticipations, we help put them to the test. Exteriorization, finally, applies to finding more autonomy and flexibility in balance. How? By way of action-oriented mindfulness that clarifies ideas, suggests plans, and notices alternatives. A common instance occurred when resilient writers looked beyond their usually private modes of writing and modeled after writers whose habits suggested different ways of doing writing.

RULE #31: Resilience, like comfort and fluency in writing, depends mostly on two tendencies, moderation and balance. Or, stated in terms of actions, resilience builds on pacing and exteriorization.

How do writers react to this condensed model (of pacing and exteriorization) and to the sudden rush of seemingly new ideas? With delight, with readiness, and with a sense of closure:

I like it. I really do. It makes sense; it brings a lot of things together for me. It's not new, really; it's just a new way of seeing. It has me doing a lot of thinking and noticing. . . . You know what, I wouldn't have been ready to make sense of this at the beginning, I wouldn't have been able to put it to such good use. Timing is everything. ["And so," I added, " is balance."]

There must be a hole in it. I mean, how can pacing and outing account for everything? So far, though, I can't find a resilience factor that doesn't fit in. I think it will help.

Moderation and balance. We knew that "dynamic duo" worked from the beginning, didn't we? But maybe not why. Pacing and exteriorization, they do seem to be what matter in the long run. That, I think is the most important thing I learned in the program. The best for last.

Don't you agree that it's the best way to finish this journey together, with a discovery that puts the whole thing into one memorable picture?

So here, as we go our separate ways, we take with us a simple theory that ties the writing program together. It proves provocative enough, writers tell me, to induce reunions of some group members. Some are professional writers who, at long last, buy the reasons for slowing down for better work, even to reach out for more sense of support and audience. Some are professors who extrapolate pacing and exteriorization to teaching (e.g., at their simplest, the two factors may be pausing and listening while teaching--uncommon acts in the classroom). And a few are therapists who try out pacing and exteriorization with depressed patients (e.g., steering patients away from negative self-focus and from excessive pacing of everyday living).

From these brief reunions comes the last formal act of our long journeys together. We christen the theory and, with some coaching from each other, we make it a rule, a final rule that reflects the foreword for this chapter on resilience:

RULE #32:   Adam Smith's rule, restated, is that writers who work with a moderate constancy and a shared rationality of their thoughts not only preserve their well-being but produce the most satisfying prose.

REFERENCES

1. Smith, A. (1863). *Wealth of nations*. Edinburgh; Adam and Charles Black (Originally published in 1776 and edited in 1863 by J. McCullough), pp. 37-38.

2. Skinner, B.F. (1983). *A matter of consequences*. New York: Alfred A. Knopf, p. 96.

3. Nowack, K.H. (1988). Coping style, cognitive hardiness, and health status. *Journal of Behavioral Medicine*, 12, 145-158.

4. Fox, M.F. (1985). Publication, performance, and reward in science and scholarship. In J.C. Smart (ed.), *Higher Education: Handbook of Theory and Research*. Vol.1, pp. 255-282. New York: Agathon Press.

5. London, M. (1985). *Developing managers*. San Francisco: Jossey-Bass.

6. Levinson, D.J. (1978). *The seasons of a man's life*. New York: Alfred A. Knopf, pp. 32, 33, 36.

7. James, W. (1911). The energies of men. In *Memories and studies*, pp. 229-264. New York: Longmans Green & Co.

8. Brandon, B. (1986). *The passion of Ayn Rand*. Garden City, NY: Doubleday, p. 255.

9. Ackroyd, P. (1991) *Dickens*. New York: HarperCollins, p. 1035.

10. Williams, J.D. (1983).   Covert language behavior during writing. *Research in the Teaching of English*, 17, 301-312.

11. Hartley, J. & Branthwaite, A. (1989). The psychologist as wordsmith: A questionnaire study of the writing strategies of productive British psychologists. *Higher Education*, 18, 264-271.

12. Bluedorn, A.C., Kaufman, C.F. & Lane, P.M. (1992). How many things do you like to do at once?   An introduction to monochronic and polychronic time. *Academy of Management Executive*, 6, 17-26.

13. Ingram, R.E., Johnson, B.R., Bernet, C.Z. & Dombeck, M. (1992). Vulnerability to distress: Cognitive and emotional reactivity in chronically self-focused individuals. *Cognitive Therapy and Research*, 16, 451-472.

14. Garber, J. & Dodge, K.A., eds. (1991). *The development of emotion regulation and dysregulation*. New York: Cambridge University Press.

15. Newberger, H. & Lee, M. (1974). *Winners and losers: The art of self-image modification*. New York: Signet.

16. Baumeister, R.F. & Sher, S.J. (1988). Self-defeating behavior patterns among normal individuals: Review and analysis of common self-destructive tendencies. *Psychological Bulletin*, 104, 3-22.

17. Oatley, K. (1992). *Best laid schemes: The psychology of emotions*. New York: Cambridge University Press.

18. Locke, E.A. & Latham, G.P. (1990). Work motivation and satisfaction: Light at the end of the tunnel. *Psychological Science*, 1, 240-246.

19. Frost, R.O., Marten, P., Lahart, C. & Rosenblate, R. (1990). The dimensions of perfectionism. *Cognitive Therapy and Research*, 14, 449-468.

20. Boice, R. (1989).   Procrastination, busyness, and procrastination. *Behaviour Research and Therapy*, 27, 605-611.

21. Burka, J.B. & Yuen, L.M. (1982). Mind games procrastinators play. *Psychology Today*, January, 32-44.

22. Rothblum, E.D., Solomon, L.J. & Murakami, J. (1986). Affective, cognitive, and behavioral differences between high and low procrastinators. *Journal of Counseling Psychology*, 33, 387-394.

23. Seligman, M.E.P. (1991). *Learned optimism*. New York: Alfred A. Knopf.

24. Hull, G. & Bartholomae, D. (1986). Teaching writing. *Educational Leadership*, 43(7), 44-53.

25. Rabinbach, A. (1990). *The human motor*. New York: Basic Books.

26. Daly, J.A. (1985). Writing apprehension. In M. Rose (ed.), *When a writer can't write*, pp. 43-82. New York: Guilford.

27. Conway, M., Howell, A. & Gainnopoulos, C. (1991). Dysphoria and thought suppression. *Cognitive Therapy and Research*, 15, 153-156.

28. Bandura, A. (1988). Self-regulation of motivation and action through goals systems. In V. Hamilton, G.H. Bower & N.H. Frijda (eds.), *Cognitive*

perspectives on emotion and motivation, pp. 37-61.   Dordrecht: Kluver Academic.

29. Lucas, R. (1992). *The grants world inside out.*   Champaign, IL: University of Illinois Press.

30. Tremmel, R. (1993). Zen and the art of reflective practice in teacher education. *Harvard Educational Review*, 63, 434-458

31. Sternberg, R.J. (1988).   *The triarchic mind: A new theory of intelligence.* New York: Penguin.

Conclusion: Rules for Comfort and Fluency

I suppose there may be finer rides in the world. There are said to be some at least as fine in Porto Rico itself. But to my mind that flight from Ponce to Arecibo in the freshness of the morning has advantage over any ride that it has been my fortune to take--and I've had some fine ones first and last, over the Amalfi Road, over the Grande Cornice, over divers and sundry Swiss passes, and over the Greek mountains from Andrit saena to Olympia; but none of them offered anything much more splendid than that gorgeous tropic highland, as it wound in spiral curves up the mountain ridges of Porto Rico. . . . The banks were aglow with flowers. Water dripped down the sides of shadowy cliffs, and broad-bladed banana trees arched the road.

Philip S. Marden, *Sailing South*, 1921

Travel has its rewarding moments. So too these long journeys with writers. At times we suffer and wish we were elsewhere, back with the familiar. But the moments of enjoyment and discovery make the trip worthwhile.

In these programs for writers, many of the most memorable and useful experiences and lessons were expressed as the rules we saw dispersed like milestones throughout the book. These, rather like photographs from a trip, are what writers tell me they are most likely to look at from time to time, afterward. The rules refresh and admonish. So it is that this concluding chapter consists of little more than a restatement of those rules. Little more is needed, so I have been told, by writers who have made the trip.

None of the rules fits successful travel better than the first. And none is more useful as a starting principle to combat the usual impatience that gets in the way of calm, fluent writing.

Rule #1: Wait.

This does not mean passive waiting, for Muses or deadlines or binges. It does mean putting off prose as long as possible while noticing, collecting, conversing, and readying oneself for the actual writing. It means putting off submission for publication while rewriting and proof editing.

The second rule bespeaks another quality of optimal travel experience, a moderate level of immersion (and, at the same time, of detachment) that we call involvement here:

Rule #2: Writers fare best when they begin before feeling fully ready. Motivation comes most reliably in the wake of regular involvement.

Initially, this second rule seems to contradict the first. It, after all, counsels writers to launch projects somewhat impulsively, without full confidence of feeling inspired or knowing what will be said. But, in practice, beginning early means beginning with immersion in the kinds of prewriting exertions that make active waiting productive and reassuring. When we begin by involving ourselves in the conversions of writers and by collecting things we can add, we build a calm, enduring motivation for writing. As a rule, motivation comes in the wake of (not in advance of) regular involvement.

Rule # 1 is easier said than done. In travel, and in the program, impatience keeps emerging as a problem. Thus impatience demands its own, specific reminder:

Rule #3: Impatience blocks writers by associating writing with rushed, incomplete work.

This rule reminds voyagers that impatience does more than keep us from doing our best work. It has the particularly bad quality of connecting the experience of writing with fatigue and unpleasantness, both great deterrents to lasting motivation.

With writing, far more than with other travels, we have the luxury of breaking the monotony of constant experience. We can change our activities and perspectives. We are not so bound to the scenery as, say, a passenger on a river steamer in the fifty thousand navigable miles of the Amazon:

. . . there is absolutely no relief from the dense walls of forest which stretch interminably, except the infinitesimal spots where man has left his work in the shape of a town, a clearing, or a hut. One lives eternally between two green masses. No hill rises in the distance, no rack hampers the myriad trees, no barren spot is there to break the endless chain of tropical verdure which entwines itself around the very soul of poor helpless man, and holds him a prey to an overpowering weariness.

F.W. Up De Graff, *Head Hunters of the Amazon*, 1923

Still, varied travels can teach us something about dealing with impatience. We do better when we live for the moment and accept the reality that good work and good travel often take time and patience.

Some things about writing are less like travel and more like athletics, at least at first glance. Writing, as with golf or any other sport that requires finely tuned skills and endurance, demands habitual practice. It must be done almost daily and kept in mind even more often:

Rule #4: An essential part of instilling an enduring motivation is a regular habit of writing.

Like golfers who play only occasionally, sporadic writers can expect to struggle and think of giving up the game. One of the great fallacies that many novice writers bring to their work is the sense that they are already expert, that they need only the proper inspiration and conditions to quickly show the brilliance that lies untapped within them.

Experienced travellers and writers would make the argument that only with continued practice did they notice the most important details and appreciate meanings, even in the most languid of scenes:

And all the while the breeze blows softly but steadily from the water, through arbors, through ropes, through flowering vines. A fountain plashes pleasantly in the garden toward the north. . . . Why do anything?

Philip S. Marden, *Sailing South*, 1921

Wise practice at writing, as at travel, brings out another surprising lesson. While motivating ourselves to get started may seem to be the essential struggle, it turns out to be no more important than knowing when to break off:

Rule #5: Learning to stop is as important as managing to start writing.

Why? Because when we continue onto fatigue we do superficial work. And because, when we go too long, we tend, sooner or later, to impatience and rushing. While great marathon sessions of writing have the appeal of euphoria and quick completion, they carry risks of nonreflective work and depressive aftereffects. In fact, writers who work in moderation, in brief daily sessions, accomplish more in the long haul than do binge writers. And when writers stop in the middle of things (sentences, paragraphs, manuscripts), they have less trouble returning to writing than do writers who stop at ends. Wise practice amounts to wise passiveness.

The sixth rule expands on the first, second, and the fifth. As writers learn to wait, to begin before feeling ready to start, and to pause before feeling ready to stop, they become more patient about writing. With patience comes more attention to the things that prepare us for painless, creative prose:

Rule #6: The most fluent, efficient, comfortable, and imaginative writers spend as much time at prewriting as at writing.

The sixth rule also highlights the importance of balance in finding motivation and imagination for writing. When we prewrite (i.e., systematically notice, collect, organize, plan, and share), we take away needless pressures to think and write at the same time once we get to prose. And according to the evidence, this act of patience and waiting saves time and fosters better writing.

There is, in these rules for finding imagination, a parallel with travel. Often, we have to revisit and resee things to appreciate them:

Rule #7: Imagination, or new vision, comes most reliably from revision.

Imagination, too, is an exercise in patience. Writing, in all its stages from prewriting to final drafts, profits in the exciting discovery of redoing. But like any other habit, revision profits from balance and moderation. Editing and rewriting work best in small amounts, distributed across the process of preparing and completing a manuscript. When we edit too early, too demandingly, we risk blocking. When we edit too late, we risk rejection.

The eighth rule respecifies one of the crucial points of the sixth rule, by reminding writers how to navigate the customarily difficult rapids between planning and writing:

Rule #8: Prewriting distributes the usual suddenness of having to generate our best imagining and wording as we start writing. Instead, it demands little more of prose writing than rewriting.

Other things also help moderate the abruptness that comes with a cold start in writing. One, again, is not stopping at ends--of chapters, paragraphs, sentences--for the day. Another is the constant habit of noticing and noting things that can be added while writing later, things that can help bring a bit of surprise to the task ("I wonder how this might fit in?"). When writers collect and prepare in advance, they write before they realize they are writing. When they write before writing, they reduce the pain of writing.

The next rule is one of the most surprising. It counters usual advice to make writing a high priority, one that would subordinate other activities until it is done, one that would help make writing painful:

Rule #9: Writing, in usual practice, need be nothing more than a modest daily priority, one that ranks well below more important priorities like social life and exercising. Unrealistic priorities and goals, like most New Year's resolutions, typically fail and torment.

Why? Because, putting writing ahead of more meaningful things like our health and social life makes it aversive, something to be delayed or rushed, something to be done perfectly but quickly, something that should seem more desirable than it really is. Even traveling, with all its prospects of escape and discovery, demands the balance and moderation of returning home from time to time to do other things:

> But there was no denying that it was nice to be back. As we followed our
> porter through the crowd . . . we felt an absurd impulse to congratulate everyone who
> was wearing a bowler hat or reading the *Daily Express*, or talking about the weather.
> . . . "Well, anyhow," said Roger, "we're all right now. We've had all that is coming
> to us on this journey." . . . Reality is a commodity hard to come by: and, when found,
> not always easily recognizable.
>
> Peter Fleming, *Brazilian Adventure*, 1934

One thing that the most comfortable and perceptive travelers and writers learn about reality is the need for a regular discipline. Routines help make things we might otherwise put off, like writing, habitual. They help instill a habit of noticing and collecting. And, because, they help prescribe how much is enough for a day, regimens help us move on to other things:

Rule #10. Learn to adopt brief, daily sessions of writing as all the writing you need or want to do for the day; being able to enjoy evenings, weekends, and vacations without feeling pressures for writing is an essential pleasure (and opportunity for unplanned discovery).

After our long journey, incidentally, this tenth rule is the admonition that writers most often cite for its lasting memorability and usefulness. Brief daily sessions, the "bds" so often mentioned throughout, may have been the most practical discovery of the trip.

The significance of the tenth rule led to its elaboration into two more prompts about the advantages of writing in bds, Rules 11 and 12:

Rule #11: Avoid writing during times when you would better be getting rest or recreation; working in large, undisrupted blocks of time invites bingeing and procrastination.

Why? With bingeing comes hypomania, the near-mania of euphoria and rushing. With bingeing comes busyness--because each binged task is followed by the need to complete other, overdue tasks while emitting all the busy signs of not wanting to be disturbed. And with bingeing comes a failing to find the times for rest and renewal that could provide energy and ideas for writing. One other thing happens with bingeing: great spacings between writing episodes demand large investments in warm-up before writing can be resumed:

Rule #12: At a minimum, stay in touch with your writing projects on a daily basis; at the least, peruse what you have been doing, contemplate, and make notes on what lies ahead so that each project remains fresh in mind.

But routines and practice are not enough. Comfort may be just as important as skill. Seasoned travelers are not reluctant to note discomforts:

A creaking board counter, barely five feet long, was the only available sleeping space. The only means of avoiding asphyxiation was to leave the door open to any passing sneak-thief or congenital hater of gringos. . . .
               Harry A. Franck, *Vagabonding Down the Andes*, 1917

Writers, curiously enough, often work in almost complete indifference to discomfort. And oddly, they customarily try to maintain the habit of writing amid distractions that cannot be ignored. Thus a rule about tempering discomfort and distraction:

Rule #13: Make a habit of writing amid comfortable, moderately uninterrupted conditions where almost all you do is writing (or things supportive of it).

Stated another way, writers do well to arrange comfortable surrounds where they will feel like writing and where there is little else to do but writing (while, nonetheless, tolerating occasional and moderate interruptions).
     At difficult points, writers often need short-term prods to more or less make them write, regardless of mood. Common but maladaptive varieties of such spurs to write are deadlines and binges. More planful substitutes work better (especially if used temporarily):

Rule #14: Use external pressures to instill (or reinstall) a regular habit of writing, at least until the habit begins to self-sustain. Employ minimally effective forcing (e.g., finishing a bds before doing something more tempting, like reading a newspaper or watching a news telecast) but plan to replace it with internally generated motivations such as the force of habit and enjoyment.

Even with all fourteen preceding rules in practice, writers reencounter difficulties. It helps, evidently, to put these hindrances into realistic perspective. Traditional notions of writing blocks tend to obscure the real reasons why we don't write:

Rule #15: The dysfluencies we ordinarily call blocking might better be labelled self-defeating behaviors such as self-handicapping, face work, shyness, choking under pressure, learned helplessness, and ineffective bargaining strategies.

An advantage of re-seeing blocks in practical ways lies in being better able to moderate and change them. When we make writing less mystical and magical, we can more easily imagine that its obstacles need not be passively accepted.

One temptation in magical thinking about writing is to suppose that it is best and most creatively done with spontaneity. Romantics have long and mistakenly concluded that discipline and planfulness work at cross purposes with quality and creativity. But it was one of the romantic pioneers of research on creativity who began the push for a more realistic perception:

Rule #16: Frank Barron's conclusion reminds us why the chaos of spontaneity works in self-defeating ways: "Without knowledge, no creation; without stability, no flexibility; without discipline, no freedom."

Another failing of traditional thinking about writing lies in the belief that writers must await the proper mood before writing. A more constructive approach is proactive. It encourages writers to observe and improve their moods so that writing time and energy are not lost to dysphoria. One proven approach for writers is widely practiced:

Rule #17: Albert Ellis and Rational-Emotive Therapy point out the irrational thinking that commonly inhibits and depresses writers: the shoulds, oughts, and musts that cause self-downing and low frustration tolerance. Writers who spot such irrationalities and supplant them with rational self-talk can replace depression with more economical, productive thinking.

Another approach to rationality often favored by writers in the program is less well known:

Rule # 18: Harry Browne's maxims for finding freedom from depression remind us that while we cannot control dislikes and personalities, including our own, we can control our reactions to irrationalities by more carefully choosing our social interactions. In that way we can better please ourselves and the minority of people predisposed to like what we have to say (even if we are fortunate enough to write a best-seller).

The surprising thing about controlling our self-talk and reactions is that control does not mean strong suppression of emotions. Instead, self-controlled writers learn to pay attention to emotions, to use them as aids to writing, and, often, to moderate them to the state of mild happiness that optimizes problem-solving tasks including writing:

Rule #19: The worse the writer, the less the attention to emotions while writing.

What emotion most needs restraint while writing? It is the same one that we often use to generate euphoria and ideas--hypomania. When we completely unleash it, we risk excesses including those we have already seen (fatigue, superficial work, ensuing depression):

Rule #20: Hypomania works best in moderation, when constrained by reliance on plans and prewriting and when assisted by the ease and enthusiasm of mildly paced euphoria.

Self-control, managed well, moves away from self-focus. It includes active attention to usually unnoticed habits and environmental conditions that affect motivation and persistence:

Rule #21: For writers already accomplished in initiating fluency, the things that help maintain and optimize it include regular attention to comfort (e.g., minimizing eye strain), pleasant surrounds, happiness, prewriting, minimizing temptations to read or socialize in disruptive ways, self-talk, and pacing.

These small routines, more than any other, made the difference between writers who used program lessons to real benefit and those for whom fluency and satisfaction lagged. Travelers, at least the most renowned of them, often excel at the little things:

At sundown I made couscous and had it with beans and tuna, and a pot of tea. . . . As I ate I listened to the radio--and when darkness fell and night grew buggy I got into my tent and, by the light of my overbright flashlight, read *The Sexual Life of Savages*. After that I listened to the BBC World Service in the darkness: news of the other world, all of it sounding inconsequential.
                    Paul Theroux, *The Happy Isles of Oceania*, 1992

Self-control, as we master it, takes the center of its practice ever outward, away from self-focus and from its tendencies to mean-spirited thinking. It starts, as we have just seen, with attending to good habits and comfort. And it moves to include more deliberate management of social situations. Self-control ultimately incorporates social control (or perhaps it is the other way around). There is a real peril for writers who do not make this transition:

Rule #22: Social isolation, carried to excess, risks misdirection, overreactivity (to both failure and success), and deprivation of ideas and encouragements.

What constitutes excess? It depends one's culture and on how wide an audience a writer wants:

"He has no wife. No kids. That is terrible. What does he do all day?"
"He writes things."
"He is wasting time. He should come here. We will find him a wife."
I said, "A fourteen-year-old in a grass skirt with flowers in her hair?"
"Maybe fifteen," Leendon said.
Paul Theroux, The Happy Isles of Oceania, 1992

Isolation not only hurts writers in terms of loneliness and understimulation. It makes writers work harder than they need to:

Rule #23: Social skill at writing includes the generosity of letting others do some of the work.

What can others do? Inspire, model, critique, redirect, suggest new ideas and sources, collaborate, edit, and praise. What keeps most writers from following rule #23? Rule #24.

Rule #24: The worse the writer, the greater the attachment to the writing.

What disposes us to this overattachment? The answer is more disbeliefs about writing, among them the supposition that true genius must be exhibited by way of work done in private. And part of the inclination owes to self-defeating greed, the desire to take all the credit for what we write.

The exercise promoted in this program to help writers become more adaptively sociable uses the awkward but telling labels of exteriorization or outing as its pivotal concept. Lasting comfort and fluency at writing depend on consistent work at getting things out and away from our usual inclinations to self-focus. Thus, when writers ask me, "What should I be thinking when I get ready to write?" they might better wonder what they could be doing.

When we act to translate thinking and imaging to action, we exteriorize. And, when we put out our private notes and formative manuscripts for public comment, we do the same:

Rule #25:   An adaptive sense of *self* in writing relies most crucially on exteriorization, of what we can see or have to say to ourselves (clarified on paper or screen).   An adaptive sense of *audience* comes by way of putting our formative writing outward to see what we have to say to the public (augmented most when we write out and share our interpretations of constructive feedback).

Exteriorization is a matter of balance:

Rule #26:   The most successful authors spend as much time socializing about writing as writing (and they spend only moderate amounts of time at either).

As writers gain the confidence and experience to exteriorize, they learn where best to get practical directives about whether or not they are on the right track:

Rule #27:   The earlier the feedback and the closer its source to gatekeepers (e.g., editors, reviewers, and leaders in the field), the more useful to the writer.

Nothing during this long journey, or after, is harder than reaching out for critiques of plans and formative writing.   And nothing, ultimately, undermines writers' progress more than rejection (including faint praise).   Some of our most intense and demanding experiences as we traveled together revolved around coping with criticism.   The rule makes it sound easier than it is:

Rule #28:   The best way to handle criticism is to anticipate it, acknowledge it, and learn from it.

In other words, exteriorizing threatens because it elicits public evaluation.   To thrive in the public arena, writers need to learn from mistakes.   Coach Pat Riley puts it this way: "It isn't what happens to you, it's how you react to it that matters."   And, while learning from mistakes, writers need to find success, by working planfully and mindfully.

It may not be inept to liken the attainment of the North Pole to the winning of a game of chess, in which all the various moves leading to a favorable conclusion had been planned in advance. . . . Always, it is true, I had been beaten, but with every defeat came fresh knowledge of the game, its intricacies, its difficulties, its subtleties, and with every fresh attempt success came a trifle nearer; what had before appeared impossible, or, at the best, extremely dubious, began to take on an aspect of possibility, and, at last,

even of probability. Every defeat was analyzed as to its causes in all their bearings, until
it became possible to believe that those causes could in future be guarded against...
> Robert E. Peary, *The North Pole*, 1910

There was, not surprisingly, a lingering question after my writers and I
shared inspiring accounts of writers and explorers who persevered. We asked,
"What made them more persistent and resilient than the rest of us? From my
long-term studies of writers, I could suggest some commonalities in resilience.
My groups and I first put the information into a rule about what causes writers
to stumble:

Rule #29:   Four common, interlocking reasons why writers relapse from
comfort and fluency are: (1) distractibility due mainly to insufficient
exteriorization of thinking, (2) expectations of perfectionism to be met quickly,
(3) unanticipated but avoidable problems such as mindless surprise about the
difficulty of a project, and (4) fatigue and irrationality owing mostly to
inefficient pacing of the writing.

Then we translated the data into a rule that inventories the distinguishing
characteristics of the most resilient writers:

Rule #30: The six distinctive acts of resilient writers are: (1) regular, constant
practice of adaptive habits connected with writing; (2) clear and realistic plans
combined with repeated feedback about progress toward goals; (3) anticipation
of blocking points by way of noticing problems, tracing them back to origins;
(4) inventing new behaviors to prevent their recurrence; (5) seeing connections
for writerly rules to other, broader activities; and (6) occasional flexibility in
bending or breaking this and all other rules stated here.

When we put this information into everyday practice, we decided to add
another, simpler version of what we had learned about resilience:

Rule #31: Resilience, just like comfort and fluency in writing, depends mostly
on two tendencies--moderation and balance. Or, stated in terms of actions,
resilience requires care in pacing and in exteriorization.

With our journey together drawing to a close, we decided that the timing of the
two-part explanation of resilience was nigh perfect. We were, at that point,
ready to comprehend and to utilize a simple but deceptively complex rule. Our
last act together, in group after group of travelers, was to put the notion in
terms of ideas of someone who started a similar journey long before us:

Rule #32:   Adam Smith's rule, in the end, is that writers who work with a constancy and a shared rationality of their thoughts not only preserve their health but produce the most quality and quantity of prose.

When I have seen some of these writers later, when our paths recross briefly, they remember and cherish Adam Smith's rule.   They also mention what they often come to call Wordsworth's rule, on the wisdom of working at writing with a wise passiveness.

Selected Bibliography

Barrios, M.V. & Singer, J.L. (1981). The treatment of writing blocks. *Imagination, Cognition and Personality*, 1(1), 89-109.

Bloom, L.Z. (1992). Writing as witnessing. In J. Moxley (ed.), *Writing and publishing*, pp. 89-109.

Boice, R. (1992). Combining writing block treatments. *Behaviour Research and Therapy*, 30, 107-116.

Boice, R. (1993). Writing blocks and tacit knowledge. *Journal of Higher Education*, 64, 19-54.

Brande, A.G. (1989). *The psychology of writing*. Westport, CT: Greenwood.

Brande, D. (1934). *Becoming a writer*. New York: Harcourt, Brace.

Brown, R.M. (1988). *Starting from scratch*. New York: Bantam Books.

Browne, H. (1973). *How I found freedom in an unfree world*. New York: Avon.

Burka, J.B. & Yuen, L.M. (1983). *Procrastination*. Reading, MA: Addison-Wesley.

Creswell, J.W. (1985). *Faculty research performance*. Washington, D.C.: Association for the Study of Higher Education.

Csikszentmihalyi, M. (1990). *Flow: The psychology of optimal experience*. New York: Harper & Row.

Downey, J. (1918). A program for the psychology of literature. *Journal of Applied Psychology*, 2, 366-377.

Elbow, P. (1973). *Writing without teachers*. New York: Oxford University Press.

Elbow, P. (1992). Freewriting and the problem of wheat and tares. In J.M. Moxley (ed.), *Writing and Publishing for Academic Authors*, pp. 33-47. Lanham, NY: University Press of America.

Field, J. (1981). *A life of one's own*. Los Angeles: J.P. Tarcher. (Originally published 1936)

Flower, L., Stein, V., Ackerman, M.J., Kantz, K., McCormick & Peck, W.C. (1990). *Reading-to-write*. New York: Oxford University Press.

Flower, L. & Hayes, J.R. (1980). The cognition of discovery: Defining a rhetorical problem. *College Composition and Communication*, 31, 21-32.

Gardner, J. (1983). *On becoming a novelist*. New York: Harper Colophon.

Hoelkeboer, R. (1986). *Creative agony: Why writers suffer*. Bristol, IN: Wyndom Hall Press.

Jamison, K.R. (1993). *Touched with fire*. New York: Free Press.

Kellogg, R. (1994). *The Psychology of Writing*. New York: Oxford University Press.

Leader, Z. (1991). *Writer's Block*. Baltimore: Johns Hopkins University Press.

Lucas, R. (1992). *The grants world inside out*. Urbana, IL: University of Illinois Press.

Mack, K. & Skjei, E. (1979). *Overcoming writing blocks*. Los Angeles: J.P. Tarcher.

Minninger, J. (1980). *Free yourself to write*. San Francisco: Workshops for Innovative Teaching.

Moxley, J.M. (1992). *Publish, don't perish*. Westport, CT: Praeger.

Murray, D.M. (1978). Write before writing. *College Composition and Communication*, 29, 375-381.

Murray, D.M. (1991). *The craft of revision*. New York: Harcourt Brace Jovanivich.

Nixon, H.K. (1928). *Psychology for the writer*. New York: Harper.

Oatley, K. (1992). *Best laid schemes: The psychology of emotions*. New York: Cambridge University Press.

Olson, G.A. (1992). Publishing scholarship in humanistic disciplines: Joining the conversation. In J. Moxley (ed.), *Writing and publishing for academic authors*, pp. 49-69. Lanham, NY: University Press of America.

Perkins, D.N. (1981). *The mind's best work*. Cambridge, MA: Harvard University Press.

Rose, M. (1985). *When a writer can't write*. New York: Guilford.

Rothblum, E.D. (1990). Fear of failure. In H. Leitenberg (ed.), *Handbook of social and evaluation anxiety*, pp. 497-537. New York: Plenum Press.

Scarr, S. (1982). An editor looks for the perfect manuscript. In G.P. Keita (ed.), *Understanding the manuscript review process*, pp. 81-103. Washington, D.C.: American Psychological Association.

Seligman, M.E.P. (1991). *Learned optimism*. New York: Alfred A. Knopf.

Stewart, J.E. (1981). *Jack Woodford on writing*. Seattle, WA: Woodford Memorial Editions.

Tremmel, R. (1989). Investigating productivity and other factors in the writer's practice. *Freshman English News*, 17(2), 19-25.

Tremmel, R. (1993). Zen and the art of reflective practice in teacher education. *Harvard Educational Review*, 63, 434-458.

Wallace, I. (1968). *The writing of one novel*. New York: Simon and Schuster.

Woodford, J. (1980). *Trial and error*. Seattle, WA: Woodford Memorial Editions.

Index

About the Author

ROBERT BOICE is Professor of Psychology at the State University of New York at Stony Brook where he teaches the history of psychology and the psychology of writing. He has published over 180 scholarly articles, many about writing, in places like *Behaviour Research & Therapy* and *Journal of Higher Education*. His recent books include *Professors as Writers* (1991), *The New Faculty Member* (1992), and *Building a Diverse Faculty* (1993). He is a licensed psychotherapist with a private practice limited to writers.

ISBN 0-275-94907-9

HARDCOVER BAR CODE